Contents

Introduction

When I first compiled *Students' Money Matters* back in 1992 (this is its 12th edition), student loans were being introduced for the first time, and I felt there was a need for such a publication. I introduced the book then by saying: 'When it comes to money, there is no doubt that for most UK students going on to higher education things are tough and are likely to get tougher.' I was right. But I had no idea then just how tough the going was to get and how sweeping the changes would be over the next 14 years. If this book was needed then (and it certainly was popular), it is even more essential today with the introduction of top-up fees. Unless your family has a bottomless purse, or you have a private income, getting through university financially is going to tax your ingenuity to the full.

But don't let this put you off university. It is still the great experience it always was. Students will have fun. The social scene is as active as ever. Students are resourceful by nature, and most are managing to get by financially. Certainly they are leaving university with massive debts to pay off, and these will get worse – but remember, as a graduate with a good degree you are likely to earn considerably more during your lifetime than you otherwise would. Estimated starting salaries for graduates for 2006 range from around £15,500 to £36,000 with a median figure of £23,000 (source: AGR Graduate Recruitment Survey 2006), and graduates can expect to earn at least 62% more than non-graduates. But it's the financial hurdle of the next three to four years that you have to get over first, and this is where *Students' Money Matters* can help.

How *Students' Money Matters* can help you

In this new edition of *Students' Money Matters*, we investigate the means and methods by which students can support themselves while studying for a degree, HND or other HE qualification. It is aimed primarily at students starting their HE studies this year (2006–2007) and beyond.

The book does not set out to argue the rights and wrongs of the financial situation students find themselves in nor, in fact, to tell you what to do. The aim of *Students' Money Matters* is to give helpful information and advice, and to point out the pros and cons to be considered when seeking loans, overdrafts, work experience, jobs, a roof over your head etc. It is for you to weigh up the evidence and information and make your own decision – because what's right for you could be totally wrong for somebody else.

However, it does include comments from employers, university tutors, careers advisers and, above all, students. As you might expect, the undergraduates with whom we discussed students' financial situation were very forthright in their views. These have been included, uncensored. There is nothing more valuable or illuminating than a report from the battlefield.

Here's how the book is organised:

- ⊙ **Chapter 1**, entitled 'That's the way the money goes', looks in detail at how students spend their money. An important section gives information on how much it is likely to cost you to live as a student in different parts of the country, plus detailed budgets from several students so you can get a picture of your likely expenses. There is information on the cost of university accommodation and how banks will help you out. The information is bang up to date and comes from a new *Students' Money Matters* survey carried out among students across the country earlier this year.

- ⊙ **Chapter 2**: Once you know how much you are going to need, the second chapter looks in detail at where the money is likely to come from. Topics covered include: top-up fees, loans to cover fees, maintenance loans, grants, bursaries, means-testing, paying back your debts, additional hardship funds and why parents have never had it so good.

- ⊙ **Chapter 3** provides advice for students who fall into special categories (such as Scottish students, mature students, students from abroad), and the financial and social implications of studying for part or all of your degree abroad are discussed.

- ⊙ **Chapter 4** deals with working and earning money – before and after your course. A high proportion of students work during vacations, and a growing number work during term time.

- ⊙ **Chapter 5** covers possible sources of additional finance such as sponsorship, scholarships, trusts, charities and professional institutions.

- ⊙ **Chapter 6** has tips on how to approach different funding bodies.

- ⊙ **Chapter 7** looks at funding for postgraduates.

- ⊙ **Chapter 8**: 'Budget like a bastard' was the advice given by a first-year student at Northumbria University in our student research. With that in mind, the final chapter of *Students' Money Matters* gives you all the information you need to budget without it becoming a burden.

How to use this book

To produce *Students' Money Matters* we drew up a list of all the questions we thought you, as a student, would want to ask about financing your studies. We then set about finding the answers. As a result, the book is written largely in the form of a dialogue. The answers given have been kept as short, simple and direct as possible. We've cut through all the red tape and official jargon. Where we felt that you might want to dig deeper into a topic, alternative reference material has been suggested, along with appropriate organisations you can contact.

Occasionally you will find that information has been repeated. This is to help you, the reader, find the information you need quickly, rather than having to flick from one section to another.

Students' Money Matters has been written in a logical order. You will probably find the next question is the one you would want to ask. However, it is a reference book, and readers need to be able to dip into it, seeking answers to questions as they arise. To help you find the section you require quickly there is a contents list and an index. The contents list covers the main points addressed. In addition to the index, each chapter opens with a list of the main topics covered. If your exact question is not there, turn to the section covering that topic and you will probably find the answer. In the unlikely event you don't find the answer, do contact us (studentsmoneymatters@trotman.co.uk) – we are always interested in hearing of any omissions. Throughout the book you will also find useful nuggets of information such as thrift tips from current students.

Money, especially the lack of it, can be a depressing subject. We hope you'll find *Students' Money Matters* an illuminating, helpful and amusing read, and that the information given will make your time at university or college less worrying and a lot more fun.

In the last edition we asked for your comments, criticisms and suggestions for the next edition. These are included here along with the updated facts and figures, a new survey of the student scene and a new appraisal of the student situation. But nothing is static, least of all the pecuniary plight of students, so please keep those comments coming. It is only by being vigilant and keeping in touch with 'campus correspondents' that we can pass on the right information to those who follow. Our thanks in helping prepare this book must go to all those students who were an invaluable source for so much of the information – and also to the employers and financial and higher education institutions who have given vital assistance in the research of the material.

Gwenda Thomas

Major changes to the student funding system this year

- Top-up fees (see page 33)
- Fee loans (see page 37)
- Grants for lower-income families (see page 41)
- University bursaries (see page 42)

That's the way the money goes

How much is it going to cost you to be a student?

This chapter answers questions on:

- ⊙ What makes so many of you do it? (page 2)
- ⊙ Fees overview (page 2)
- ⊙ Your living expenses (page 3)
- ⊙ How students budget around the country (page 19)
- ⊙ Travel (page 19)
- ⊙ So how do so many students manage? (page 24)
- ⊙ Typical student budgets (page 26)

So how much will it cost you? As much as you have, and probably a lot more. Students have always been hard up, but never more so than now.

In the last year there have been numerous stories in the press about students having to give up their degree courses because they just couldn't make ends meet. Drop-out rates in some universities have increased. But we do have over a million first degree students in higher education in the UK at the moment, and that figure has been increasing. How are they managing?

Many factors can affect your financial situation. Some students are luckier – or perhaps more determined – than others in:

- ⊙ Raising additional finance
- ⊙ Managing to work as well as study
- ⊙ Choosing to study in cheaper parts of the country
- ⊙ Finding additional bursary funding
- ⊙ Living at home
- ⊙ Being excellent money managers.

While others ...

- ⊙ Find that money slips through their fingers like water
- ⊙ Are great socialisers and imbibers
- ⊙ Take courses for which they have to buy expensive equipment or books, or need to travel
- ⊙ Have expensive tastes and hanker after all the good things in life
- ⊙ Have a wide range of hobbies and interests
- ⊙ Study in expensive areas such as London.

Obviously you should not pick your course on the basis of where the living is cheapest, but it is as well to know what costs you are likely to face. This first chapter looks at what it is likely to cost you to get a degree, HND or any other higher qualification. But first ...

What makes so many of you do it?

Last year around 486,000 young people applied for a higher education course in the UK. What is the great attraction? Why did they want to forfeit the chance of having money in their pockets to become a near-penniless student and increasingly get into debt?

Here are some reasons given by students taking part in the *Students' Money Matters* research:

'I want to get a job I enjoy.'

'To improve my job prospects with the hope of getting a varied career. I'm not a 9 to 5 person.'

'I wanted to continue learning; university was the obvious path.'

If we asked everyone now studying in universities and colleges across Britain, we'd get thousands of different answers. Most would be positive, but not all:

'I don't rate uni at all. I wish the government would encourage people to do something they are good at and not waste money and time pushing people into a place they don't want.'
Law and Japanese student, Oxford Brookes

Many, however, would say money – or the potential for earning it. And there is no doubt a degree can help increase your earning power. Young graduates can expect to be earning £7000 pa more than their non-graduate counterparts in their 20s and the differential just keeps climbing. In fact, on average, during their lifetime graduates earn 62% more than non-graduates, and around £120,000 more than those with A levels.

But whatever your reason for studying, it's going to be hard going financially for the next few years. How are you going to manage?

Fees overview

(See Chapter 2 for more details.)

Will I have to pay them?

Yes – but not the whole fee and not if you're a Scottish student studying in Scotland (more of that later). Most students who started their course in or after 1998 have had to pay something towards the cost of it – this year (2006–2007) the maximum tuition fee per annum has gone up to £3000.

If finding an additional £3500–£4700 to complete a university course aroused this amount of passion among students when fees were first introduced eight years ago (see quotes below), just think what the reaction to top-up fees is going to be when we are talking about £9000–£12,000.

> *'Paying fees and grants should be a priority with the government – an educated society is a safer and happier one.'*
> 2nd year Biochemistry student, Kent

> *'I feel university education is becoming elitist. I know many people who are definitely intelligent enough to go to university but can't afford it, especially for a long course like mine.'*
> Veterinary Medicine student, Cambridge

> *'It makes me angry; you hear on the news we are crying out for doctors, yet I had to pay my own fees.'*
> Medical student, Imperial College, London

But others had a different point of view:

> *'Being a student, I don't like fees, but I can see that to improve universities funding is needed.'*
> 1st year Electronic Engineering student, Bristol

> *'Fees could make universities provide better facilities; after all we are now customers.'*
> 3rd year Conservation and Restoration student, De Montfort

Your living expenses

These have to be paid for largely by you. More maintenance bursaries are being given by the government and universities than ever before, so there is more help available, especially for low-income families (see Chapter 2 for full details). Things are not going to be easy, though they are far from hopeless and you should be able to manage. But wherever your money comes from, it's you who will have to eke it out and make ends meet. So here are the facts.

Accommodation – the major demand on your finances

Accommodation will probably soak up half your income. If it's full board in university accommodation you are looking at over three-quarters of your total income.

Case study

Katie Johnson from Alton College, Hants and Rob Snelgar from Guildford College, both planning to go to university this year, give their views.

Q: How do you feel about having to pay fees of £3000?

Katie: I don't think it is fair because previous uni students haven't had to pay so much.

Rob: Money like that is hard to come by – it's really unfair.

Q: Have higher fees put you off going to university?

Katie: Yes and no. £12,000 is a lot of money to find, but to be a doctor, the job I want to do, depends on getting a degree so I have no choice.

Rob: Uni is a great opportunity, so that is the price I will have to pay.

Q: What do you think will be the effect of high fees?

Katie: I know lots of my friends are having second thoughts about going to university.

Rob: People will become stressed and depressed – not much good will come of it.

Q: Does debt worry you?

Katie: Yes, the thought of owing £30,000 (fees plus loan) is inconceivable. It's not how I want to start my career.

Rob: At least with student loans it will either get written off or paid off eventually.

Finding the right place to live is important, especially in your first year. It can affect your whole attitude to your college, your course, your study, the town or city where you are staying, making the right friends, and whether you actually do well. If it's half an hour's walk, or a bus ride across town, to get to the library, you may think twice about going there. If you're stuck in a bedsit with a grumpy landlord and no other students around you, the weekends could be very long and lonely. But halls aren't right for everyone:

'It is impossible to get a decent night's sleep because of noisy students returning after a night out.'
1st year Arts student, Robert Gordon University

'Occasionally you'll hear people running along the corridor at two in the morning. But mostly people are considerate.'
Modern Languages student, Cambridge

Most institutions give first-year students first claim on halls of residence and most students jump at the chance. It gives you a circle of ready-made friends. But for some students, living with a hundred or so other people, sharing bathrooms, meal times, TV programmes, problems, passions – even bedrooms – can be an unbearable strain. Others thrive on the camaraderie. Criticising mixed halls, one student told us:

'Coping with an ex-boyfriend over cornflakes and coffee at 8am is something not to be endured.'

Where can I get information and help?

College prospectuses will generally give you details about halls of residence, though these may not be altogether bias-free. Students' unions may also have a view – ask if there's an alternative prospectus or students' union handbook. Above all, check out the accommodation for yourself if you can when you make your first visit.

Look at:

⊙ Cost
⊙ Whether rooms are shared
⊙ Eating arrangements – is it full board, half-board, kitchen/do-it-yourself?
⊙ Facilities provided
⊙ Distance from college
⊙ Transport availability – plus frequency and cost
⊙ Shops.

The college accommodation office is responsible for placing students in halls of residence, and will send you details once you've accepted a place. It will also help you to find rented accommodation.

Accommodation in halls of residence

What will it cost?

Costs vary significantly between different types of accommodation and different universities, with much higher costs in the London colleges in particular. Be aware that the number of meals per day, the number of days per week that meals are served and the number of weeks in the academic year can vary between institutions. Some establishments offer accommodation other than the norm, such as en-suite, up-to-the-minute facilities or out-of-town accommodation.

When comparing university self-catering accommodation in halls of residence with the rented sector, remember that with college accommodation gas and electricity are probably (but not always) included. This is unlikely to be the case in the rented sector.

Will I have to share a room?

Possibly. In some colleges you may have to share a room for one or two terms. If you do have to share, you will probably be sent a questionnaire designed to find out what sort of person you are and the kind of person you could live with. Typical questions are: Would you want to share with a smoker or a non-smoker? Are you an early riser?

Do you like to go to bed late and get up late? Are you a party person? What kind of music do you like? Is there any kind you can't stand? Honesty is the only way to harmony. Even if you are easy-going about smoking, do you really want to sleep in a smoky atmosphere? And, although your intentions may be very laudable at the moment, how are you going to feel about your room-mate stomping around at eight in the morning when you've been out partying until two?

'Halls are great except you don't get to pick who you live with; sharing a flat with six other people can be a nightmare, especially when food goes missing and the kitchen becomes a garbage site.'
1st year Management Studies student, Middlesex

'I'd never shared a room with anyone before and didn't really like the idea. At first it was strange, but after a couple of weeks you got used to it. Having someone around most of the time is fun.'
1st year Economics student, St Andrews

Cash crisis note

- Students in the South East, but studying outside London, are thought to be suffering particularly badly, as they are being asked to pay London-equivalent rents while not qualifying for the larger student loans given to students who study in the capital.

Accommodation in halls of residence

Average weekly cost for accommodation including two meals per day: £95.76 approx.

Average weekly cost with no food: £63.87 approx.

Amongst the lowest weekly rents for halls of residence offering two meals or possibly more a day was £50 at University College Chester, while the highest was a staggering £275 at the Regents Street Business School, London.

Amongst the lowest rents in university accommodation with no food was £32.90 at the University of Teeside and the highest with no food was £275, again by the Regents Street Business School. So you can see there is a great deal of variation in costs.

Most universities offer a range of costs for their accommodation so the highs and lows can be misleading. For example, Teesside students can find they are paying over £55 just for accommodation. The rent for college accommodation usually includes heating and lighting, and you generally only pay for the weeks you are there, which is not the case in accommodation rented in the open market. As the figures quoted here are for 2004–05 you may well find your costs are higher.

(Information based on *University and College Entrance 2006*)

How much is rented accommodation going to cost?

Average outside London: £72 pw; average in Greater London: £94 pw.

Research carried out by *Students' Money Matters* in January 2006 in higher education institutions throughout the UK revealed some interesting facts. On average, students throughout the country, excluding London, are paying £72 pw. The average rents among students in Greater London were predictably higher than anywhere else, at around £94. The Midlands was also noticeably higher at £75. The cheapest place to rent was Northern Ireland at £43. These are of course average figures; there were pockets of the country where rents varied considerably. Don't forget that on top of rent you are likely to have utilities (gas, electricity, water) to pay for. Our research estimates these costs will be around £61 per term, which is something you probably won't have to pay in university accommodation. Full details of rents in different parts of the country are shown on page 20.

Action

Check out the length and terms of your contract – is it for 52 weeks? A recent survey of university students found that more and more landlords were asking students to sign 52-week contracts for accommodation. This means they are paying rent during the Christmas, Easter and three-month summer vacations, when they are likely to be at home – something you don't have to do in university accommodation.

Another problem we encountered was that students who have to undertake a placement away from their university, such as medical students, may find they are paying for accommodation away for a couple of months while still paying for the accommodation in their university town.

Possible problems when renting accommodation

⊙ *'Landlord refused to give back deposit of £150. To my knowledge he has done the same to 15 other previous tenants – that's £2250 kept for no good reason. Easy money for some!'*
3rd year Fine Arts student, Derby

Advice note

From one who knows. 'If your landlord won't fix something, take a photograph of the problem so you have evidence that it's not your fault. With this in hand, the landlord will find it difficult to play the trick of docking your deposit when you leave. Our curtain railing has come down and the landlord won't fix it. But he won't pull a fast one over us.'

Law student, Northampton

⊙ *'Flat had no heating. Had to go to bed fully clothed complete with woolly hat.'*
4th year Information and Library Studies student, Robert Gordon University

⊙ *'Exploding shower, broken-down washing machine, dangerous housemates.'*
3rd year Entertainment Crafts student, Cleveland

⊙ *'Entertaining unwanted visitors – cockroaches from the café downstairs.'*
1st year Modern European Studies student, Thames Valley

⊙ *'Lodgings miles from anywhere. Buses stopped at 7pm so late study and going out meant paying for a taxi home.'*
2nd year Engineering student, Brunel

⊙ *'Attic room, leaking roof, clothes soaked, heating doesn't work, plug sockets hanging off the walls, landlord accepts rent in cash only – £100 a week.'*
1st year Materials student, Imperial College

⊙ *'I'm living with my landlord and a horde of mice – they eat everything – the mice I mean.'*
3rd year Mental Philosophy student, Edinburgh

But it's not all complaints:

⊙ *'Our landlord is very sweet; he bought us a huge packet of biscuits for Christmas.'*
2nd year Psychology student, Queen's University, Belfast

Foulke's story

It seemed the ideal place for a first-year student – a block of student flats opposite the university. Newly converted from a warehouse, they were modern, warm, clean. I moved into a five-bed flat with four friends. What I didn't realise was that the flats were not on the university's list of suitable accommodation for students. When there is trouble, and there was, that is very important.

Three weeks into the term and the lifts were out of action and we were three floors up. Next the security door stopped working. This meant anyone and everyone could come and go as they pleased in the building, and they did.

When we came to leave at the end of the year, though our flat was left in good condition, the owners refused to give back our deposit, saying the communal passages and stairs were in a dreadful state. They were. But whose fault was that? In our flat alone they withheld £1250 (£250 from each student) and, as far as I know, the residents of the other 150 flats haven't seen a penny back either. Uni teaches you to stand on your own two feet – but sometimes it's a hard and expensive lesson to learn.

Alice's story

Problem: my bedspring broke. Sleep was impossible. Exams were looming. I needed rest but my landlady was very slow to get things done. Strategy was called for. I invited the landlady over and got her to sit on the bed while we talked. I asked her if she was comfortable, and she had to agree she was not. I then asked her if she would like to sleep on the bed – every night. A new bed arrived within four days.

Should I take out insurance?

That's something only you can really decide.

A recent survey completed by Endsleigh shows that, on average, students now take £4244-worth of belongings to university and this is not going unnoticed by thieves. These possessions are often highly valuable and portable, for example laptops, iPods and mobiles. If you lost them, how would you replace them?

Insurance is another drain on your resources but with the free and easy living of the student lifestyle, it could be money well spent and save a lot of heartache. Endsleigh receives some £500,000 worth of claims from students during their first term at uni, which makes you think.

If you are living in halls you may find there is a comprehensive policy covering all students and this is included in your rent bill.

If you are living in rented accommodation, the landlord of the house or flat you rent should have the premises covered by insurance for fire and structural damage, but this is unlikely to cover your personal possessions. Students tend to keep open house, and because people are coming and going all the time security is often lax. If you do have a lot of expensive possessions it might be worthwhile considering your own insurance, especially if you carry your expensive belongings about. Ask yourself: What would it cost me to replace my stereo, TV, video, camera, gold watch, PC, course books, whatever? Compare that with an outlay of, say, £30 a year. Rates for personal insurance depend on where you live. It costs more if you live in a big city than a sleepy rural town. In a crime hot spot, rates can be prohibitive.

> 'Everybody round here hires a TV so if it walks it's covered by the TV rental company. The same goes for washing machines and all other appliances.'
> 1st year student, Liverpool University

> 'We had a microwave and sofa cushions stolen! But mainly it's computers, TVs, stereos.'
> 3rd year Genetics student, Birmingham

Are you covered by your parents' insurance?

If you are, that is obviously the cheapest form of cover, *but* don't assume that your possessions are covered by your parent's home insurance once you go to uni. Some standard home insurance polices specifically exclude students – I wonder why? Get your parents to check the small print.

You can also take out insurance to cover the fees you have paid, just in case you are ill – or worse – and can't complete your year.

NatWest offers a choice of packages to students: their basic 'budget' policy starts from £16. This covers your possessions against theft, burst pipes, fire, storm, vandalism and flood whilst in your room; also at your parents' home(s); in direct transit to and from home at vacations; and in locked storage on campus at any time. Items automatically included are covered for your landlord's property up to £5000, college property on loan up to £250 and accidental death of parent or guardian up to £5000. Cover can be extended to include desktop computers, accidental damage, vacation cover, legal expenses and rental protection. Their more comprehensive 'peace of mind' policy includes all these benefits plus a lot more. For more details check out www.natwest.com/studentinsurance.

Endsleigh, which specialises in helping students, offers student possessions insurance starting at under £20 for £2500-worth of cover for halls of residence, and £25 for £2500-worth of cover off-campus in a 'good' area. This rises to £68 for £2500 of cover in a grottier area. They also offer a special computer cover with premiums starting at just £6 per £100-worth of cover, rising to £10 per £100 of cover in dicey areas. (Prices correct at December 2005.)

Do you make music? Whether you play in an orchestra or drum for a rock band, or whether it's part of your course, for pleasure or to make extra money, if you lost that valuable guitar, violin, double bass or cello you'd be stuck. Insurance rates vary depending on whether you are in the UK or travelling in Europe, and what kind of instrument you have. Endsleigh offers a minimum premium of £20. The cost works out at around £1 per £100 of cover for all stringed orchestral instruments (such as violins or double basses). Shop around to get the best cover before making a decision.

Where to live?

Halls, rented accommodation with friends, at home? We asked some students what they thought.

Living in halls – Jess's story

Jess is 18 and in her first term at Cambridge University, where she is studying Modern Languages.

'I love living in halls. I have my own room, which is massive – I had 30 people to one party. Because it is so big, people tend to congregate there and my chocolate fondue parties are legendary. Cambridge is a very social place. Everything seems to be within two minutes' walk – canteens, clubs, pubs, shops, halls for other students. There are quite a few parties, but mostly we gather in the bar.

'You are never lonely. People are always knocking on your door asking if you'd like a cup of coffee, or to share a bottle of wine. My room is on a corridor with 12 other students – all girls. You share a kitchen and bathroom, which sounds horrendous, but surprisingly you never have to wait for a basin or shower.

'As an only child I wondered whether having people around all the time would be annoying. It can be noisy: sometimes I need my own space and when you get people running down the corridor at two o'clock in the morning you think "go away!". But generally people are considerate, and fortunately the guy in the room above me shares the same taste in music – indie rock – otherwise that might drive you mad.

'I eat largely in halls and it is good value – £5 for a three-course formal dinner, £1.50 for a two-course meal in the canteen, £2.50 for a hot dog from the stall outside college – a weakness but yummy! Halls without food cost £3036.

'My room is fairly rudimentary – a wardrobe, bed, three tables and four chairs and endless white wall space. A friend advised me to put some money aside (£20) to make my room mine – excellent advice. I went for humour – three large posters of the Simpsons, Little Britain and the sayings of George W Bush – a sovereign remedy if you are feeling a little down.

'I would like to stay in halls, but may find I'm sharing a college flat with up to ten other people next year. Now that could be a very different and possibly difficult experience!'

Two in a flat – Sam's story

Sam is in his second year at St Andrews University, where he is studying International Relations. He lives with Dave, another second-year student, who is studying Modern History.

'We live over a curry house – no smells, fortunately, and no free curries, just a large complimentary whisky when we eat there – malt of course – which is better.

'I prefer a flat to halls because it gives you that extra freedom, and you don't have noisy neighbours coming in at all hours of the night, or endless fire alarm tests. It took a bit of time to get used to people not being around all the time. I have to make more effort. Still, the Union is only 30 seconds away and friends not much further. I do enjoy having my own space and the kitchen.

'The flat also has a bathroom and two very large bedrooms. If we want to entertain, which we do regularly, we have to move the bed out of one of the rooms – which is not the hassle it sounds. Fortunately we have similar tastes in music.

'We spend about £35 a week between us on food and take it in turns to do the Tesco run. When it comes to bills they are divided strictly down the middle.

'If we give the curry house enough notice they allow us to hold parties in their spice garden but, with the Scottish weather, entertaining outside is rare and, since we are all into cooking, we tend to hold dinner parties when large quantities of food are consumed and even larger quantities of wine – Tesco's cheapest at under £3 a bottle.

'The rent is £3250 each for a ten-month lease. Halls were £2995 with weekday food included. Pound for pound, living in a flat is marginally more expensive. But I think we probably save on socialising.'

Sharing a house – Jono's story

Jono is in his third year at Loughborough studying Innovative Manufacturing and Technology.

'In my first year I was in halls – it's the best way to start. It's how you make friends. In my second year I shared a house with the guys who had lived next to me, above me and across the corridor in halls – it was a riot. Now I live in a mixed house with six other students, four guys and two girls. It is very civilised. Though the bedrooms are small, we have spacious living accommodation with a large sitting room and kitchen/diner, a bathroom, shower room and three toilets. No real garden, thank goodness, but a yard, which is great for barbecues in the summer.

'The five guys are all very sporty and eat huge amounts. During the week we cook and eat together and take it in turns to buy and cook the evening meal – the standard is high, haute cuisine no less. My favourite: take 8–10 chicken breasts, cut them open, stuff with herbs and spices and cheese – ideally mozzarella if you can afford it – close up, wrap in bacon and grill – very tasty. Look for the two-for-one offers. Cost: less than £6 for a meal for five. Last year we lived as students each doing our own thing, now we live as humans. I prefer this. Having a table in the kitchen we can all sit round helps. As for the girls, they cook their celery sticks together and are happy.

'We have a kitty for general household stuff – £3 each a week – and house cleaning is a group effort – 20 minutes on a Sunday morning. It works 'cos there are seven of us.

'We pay £62 each a week rent which is high for houses around here, but all our bills (gas, electricity, water) are included. The landlord probably makes a bit out of this, but not having the hassle of settling up bills is worth every extra penny we pay. I am still owed £40 from unsettled bills from my last house.

'When we arrived here we discovered we had a vast cellar stuffed with rubbish. The landlord said we could clear it out and even gave us a crate of beer for our trouble. It's a fantastic venue for parties – make a noise and the neighbours can't hear it, spill your drink and nobody minds. As we are all rather house-proud, entertaining is hassle- and trouble-free.

'It is also the perfect place for our embryo pop band to practise. We only got together last year, but have already played four gigs. Are we any good? As lead singer, I have to be positive, but to be honest, I don't see it as a future career move. But if you're coming to Loughborough, look out for Jimmy Scragg – a name chosen because we didn't want to be taken too seriously – not that anybody would. Critics' verdict? "Half-talented when wasted."'

Thrift tips

'*Book travel in advance.*'

1st year Chinese Language and History student, Sheffield

'*Work as a TV extra or catalogue model.*'

3rd year Psychology student, Wolverhampton

'*Sell your work.*'

3rd year Visual Studies student, Norwich School of Art and Design

'*Use your hobby – I photographed a family on holiday and pocketed €100.*'

Wolverhampton student

Drinking tips

'*Make your own beer – it's fun, cheap and tasty.*'

3rd year Digital Media student, Wolverhampton

'*Organise parties at home and get others to bring the drink.*'

2nd year Journalism, Film and Media student, Cardiff

'*Drink cider rather than ber – it's cheaper and takes less to get you drunk.*'

4th year Biochemistry student, Oxford

'*Become teetotal. Impossible? Try the next tip.*'

3rd year Design student, Wolverhampton

'*Learn to drink slowly.*'

3rd year English student, Wolverhampton

Living at home – Christopher's story

Christopher is in his second year at the University of the West of England, Bristol, where he is studying Business Administration.

'Money – that is why I decided to go to the nearest university and live at home. My parents don't charge me rent. I eat with the family most of the time (I have two younger brothers) and I guess it is much easier: not so much to worry about things like internet connection, doing the washing, running out of food. It works because my parents are pretty free and easy. They just let me get on with it and do my own thing.

'Of course there are drawbacks – mainly in my social life. Many people make their friends at uni, not so much on their course, but from living in halls. I have found it difficult making friends and entering into the life of the university. I live about 25 miles away and only drive in when I have lectures. I took a gap year before uni so I find I am older than many of the students in my year. The first year for many students is their first time away from home and they go wild. I had done all that.

'My biggest expense is petrol – £30 a week and insurance on my car. I have taken out a student loan – around £3000 a year – and have a job in a sausage shop during the holidays – on a busy week I can earn around £264. I draw £50 a week spending money from the bank during term time and find I am never short of cash and have no debts.

'Would I advise students to live at home? Probably not. I feel I am missing out on student life, but if you want an easy, trouble-free, debt-free way of life, there is a lot to be said for it. It's a matter of personal choice. I don't regret my decision.'

More and more students are choosing universities where they can continue to live at home because it is cheaper. In fact 64% of students responding to our survey said they knew of someone who had decided to study in their own home town for financial reasons. As you will see in the next chapter, the amount of loan you can borrow is smaller, but then that means less debt. For some students, this idea would be unthinkable. Going to university is all about gaining independence. But if that results in you having to abandon your course because of debt then you could be back where you started – at home! It's worth thinking about.

Do I have to pay Council Tax?

Students are largely exempt from paying Council Tax. Certainly, if you live in a hall of residence, college accommodation, student house or somewhere in which all the residents are students, you will be exempt. If you live in a house where there are already two adults, your presence does not add to the bill. If you live in a house with one adult, that person will not lose their 25% single occupancy discount, providing they can supply proof that you are a student.

However, things are never quite that simple, as Paul Hubert, the welfare officer at Leeds Metropolitan University, pointed out to us. 'Frequently,' he said, 'students in external accommodation do not spot the problems coming and these can prove intractable.' Some examples:

⊙ A full-time student moves into a house shared with non-students, and housemates expect them to contribute to the Council Tax bill

★
TOP*TEN* *internet spenders*

	Termly spend
Final year AIMS, Kingston	£180
1st year Law, Sheffield	£150
1st year, Media and Cultural Business, Kingston	£120
2nd year English, Queen's Belfast	£120
3rd year, Computer Science, Anglia Ruskin	£100
3rd year Business Management, Gloucestershire	£100
1st year Biology, Queen's Belfast	£100
3rd year Maths and Computing, Queen's Belfast	£100
3rd year Film Studies and History, Queen's Belfast	£100
1st year Business Studies, Bristol UWE	£80

⊙ The flatmate who drops out of their course during the summer and fails to claim benefit
⊙ The part-time student who thought they would be exempt
⊙ The student/postgrad who is writing up work and is refused student status by local authorities.

If in doubt, go to your university welfare officer – they are usually on the ball.

Other living expenses

While your accommodation will probably take at least half of your available resources, how are you going to spend the rest?

Food

Average: £36 pw.

Once you have a roof over your head, the next major expense is food, and here our survey showed that costs were fairly similar throughout the country, with an average of £36 a week – the same as last year. However, when we started to look at individual areas within the UK the picture changed. The hungriest students, with an average bill of £47 a week, appear to be in the Midlands. When you started looking at individual bills the picture changed again. Obviously some students with families had massive food bills, but a 19-year-old student (male) studying Computer Science in Games Development at Wolverhampton University quoted a weekly food bill of £140, while his colleague, an 18-year-old student (female) studying English, also at Wolverhampton, quoted a weekly food bill of £160.

Thrift tips

... for hungry students:

'Give dinner parties and charge.'
2nd year Industrial Relations and Modern History student, St Andrews

'Make your own sandwiches for lunch and sell them to friends.'
1st year Medicine student, Cambridge

'Get to like pasta!'
4th year Psychology student, Paisley

Socialising/entertainment

Average: £21pw.

Our research didn't assess how good a 'good time' students were having, or how often they went out, but on average students spend around £21 a week on entertainment and socialising, which is down on last year. The biggest spenders, with bills of around £38 a week, were in Wales. However, the highest individual spenders this year were all to be found at Wolverhampton University. Outright socialites were a 20-year-old second-year Sports Coaching student and an 18-year-old first-year Pharmacology with Human Physiology student, both male, both with a honking weekly bill of £200. A not very close second were a 19-year-old first-year student studying Computer Games and Design and a 20-year-old third-year Geography and Education student (female) who both had weekly bills of £80.

★

TOP*TEN* most popular drinks

Region	Drink
London	Gin & tonic
Oxbridge	Archer's
South	Wine
West	Vodka
Midlands	Lager
East	All equal
North	Vodka/Guinness
Wales	Carling
Scotland	Vodka
Northern Ireland	Malibu & Diet Coke

What to order where

Diesel (half a pint of lager, half a pint of cider, plus blackcurrant) is the northern name for snakebite and black and is as popular there as snakebite is across the rest of the UK. Vodka (whether in alcopops or shots plus mixers) is also high on the list. In our survey Carling was consistently mentioned as the most popular type of lager, everywhere except Northern Ireland and Scotland – where Tennents reigns supreme. Turbo shandy (half a pint of lager, half a pint of Smirnoff ice) is popular in the Midlands, along with VK alcopops. The average price of the cheapest drink is £1.22.

Books

Average: £71 per term.

All students said they spent more on books in the autumn term and in their first year than at any other time. Some reported that they'd then taken to using libraries instead of buying, as books were so expensive. It is difficult to give an average figure for books, as what you need to buy depends on your course and how well stocked your college library is in your subject. It's worth checking this out before starting your course if you can. Taking our own survey as a very general guide, the average figure was £71 per term.

Points to check

Your university or college may have a second-hand bookshop. Find out before you start purchasing: books are very expensive. Check out your college library. Is it well stocked in books on your subject? Is it close to where you study and where you live? Try looking at www.uni-trader.co.uk, a website started up by a student at Durham University, which works a little like the student noticeboard. Students with things to sell – especially textbooks – put them on the site. Initially launched in Durham in 2004, then expanded into the North East, it went nationwide last October (2005). Each university has its own designated area so you can start by trying to buy – or sell – locally. As well as textbooks we found other useful stuff for sale: lab coats, electric guitar, swivel chair, toaster, mini fridge, earrings, mobile phone, set of orange circus juggling clubs (just what you need to succeed at uni) and a Peugeot 205 for less than £100.

Course equipment

Average: £63 per term.

In subjects such as architecture, the creative arts and some science-based subjects, this can be a major item. Students on design courses were finding it particularly hard. Figures of up to £300 were often mentioned, even £1000 and £1500. Computers are a major cost for students and were also often mentioned. However, equipment isn't an issue for the many students who said they spent less than £5, or even nothing. As a rough guide for those who do have to shell out for equipment, we came up with an average of £63 per term. But the fact is, if you need the equipment, you will have to pay for it whatever the cost.

> 'I'm currently on the most expensive course – 3D Design. The financial strain of coping with the cost of materials is hindering my design capabilities and interfering with my studies; the annual cost of course equipment is £200.'

Photocopying and stationery

Average: £16 per term.

Many students mentioned the high cost of photocopying. For those on courses in which study covered topics in a wide range of books rather than majoring on a few textbooks the cost could be considerable. On average £16 per term was spent on photocopying; however, figures of £30 and £40 were frequently mentioned and one second-year student studying Psychology at Wolverhampton University had a whacking termly bill of £432.

Field trips

Average: £59 per term.

Geography, Biology, Zoology, Law, Fine Art, Graphic Design, Sculpture, IT, English, Textile Design, Drama, Psychology, Urban Studies and Planning – on all these courses field trips may be a compulsory component and could cost anything from £2 to £900. We asked for a termly figure, but these are generally annual occurrences. Actual cost depends on the course you are taking. As a rough guide we came up with an average figure of £59 per term.

'*Geology is becoming very expensive. I have two compulsory field trips a year costing £150 each.*'
3rd year student, Durham

Mobile phones

Average: £11 pw.

Most students today have a mobile. New deals have brought mobile phone bills down, but phone costs are still averaging £11 a week, and we did find students who were paying £50 or £60 a week just to chat. More and more students are relying on their mobiles rather than paying for a landline.

Clothing

Average: £73 per term.

★ best-dressed TOP*TEN* regions	
Region	Average spend per term
Scotland	£91
Midlands	£86
London	£73
South	£70
West	£65
Northern Ireland	£60
North	£59
Oxbridge	£56
Wales	£45
East	£15

Here we asked for a termly, rather than a weekly, amount. On average students spend £73 a term on clothes, which is about the same as last year. However, many students admitted to spending over £300 a term, and one 20-year-old third-year student at Wolverhampton (female) gave a figure of £600. It would seem the best-dressed students are in Scotland , where there is an average termly spend of £91, followed by the Midlands with a termly spend of £86.

Insurance

This can be a major expense, as many of you said. Figures from £0 to £900 were mentioned, so an average figure would not mean much.

Internet

Average: £37 per term.

An expense for many students is the internet. Figures given varied enormously – from £10 to £300 a term. A meaningful figure is difficult to give since so many students said they didn't know what they spent. And those in halls of residence often find broadband is included in their rent. As a rough guide for those who are web enthusiasts we came up with an average of £37 per term.

So – where is the cheapest place to study?

Our research this year puts Northern Ireland top of the league for money management. Amongst the hardest-hit students are those studying just that bit too far outside London to qualify for the higher rate of loan, yet still paying London prices.

How students budget around the country

The budgets on the next page were drawn up from research carried out in January 2006 for *Students' Money Matters*.

For students living in university accommodation, utilities (gas/electricity) are generally included. Travel costs are for using public transport only and do not include private cars etc.

Travel

Travel during term time

To survive, it seems you need to be fit. Students said that walking was their main way of getting about. For many, however, travel was a significant cost, with students in London experiencing the most severe problems in terms of expense and time taken to get to lectures. At the other end of the scale is Wales, where the average weekly spend is £2 and nothing is more than a bike ride away. Students studying Medicine and based in London can be the hardest hit, as training often involves attachments to other hospitals, which may be as much as 40 miles away (check with your LA to see if you are entitled to financial help with transport). Scottish students can claim extra for travel as a grant if costs exceed £155 pa.

About a fifth of students are thought to own a car or motorcycle. This estimate includes many mature students, who tend to drive longer distances during term. Our research showed the average cost of petrol per week during term time was £24. Cycling seems to be much less popular than it was a few years ago. Students complained that cycling was dangerous, and another gripe was having their bicycles stolen – even being mugged for a mountain bike. Students also cited pollution and traffic congestion as problems.

Travel check

⦿ The frequency of university and local bus services. A huge number of students complained of the infrequency and unreliability of bus services and the fact that they didn't run at night.

'... and when the buses do come they are often so full they don't stop. It's quite common to be late for lectures.'

2nd year International Tourism and Management student, Robert Gordon University

⦿ The last bus. A number of students complained that in many cities bus services finish early, with no regular service after 10.30pm – a major problem for sociable students in outlying districts. Check on this when choosing accommodation; you don't want to find ...

'The last bus was at 7pm. Even a modest social life was impossible.'

Law student, Bristol

Student budgets around the country

	Greater London	South England	West	East	Midlands	Oxbridge (Oxford and Cambridge)	North	Scotland	Northern Ireland	Wales
per week										
Av. rent	£94	£69	£72	£55	£75	£94	£62	£64	£43	£57
Av. food	£32	£34	£22	£30	£47	£30	£28	£37	£24	£28
Av. soc./ent.	n/a	£24	£21	£18	£23	£16	£21	£21	£9	£38
Av. laundry	£3	£3	£4	£5	£7	£1	£3	£4	n/a	£4
Av. toiletries	£4	£5	£3	£4	£9	£3	£4	£6	£5	£4
Av. telephone	£7	£9	£6	£6	£11	£6	n/a	£9	£9	£5
Av. travel (term)	£13	£8	£8	n/a	£13	£9	£7	£9	£6	£2
Total	£153	£152	£136	£118	£185	£159	£125	£150	£96	£138
per term										
Av. books	£73	£76	£56	£62	£81	£61	£56	£84	£53	£40
Av. photocopying	£13	£12	£13	£9	£12	£7	£10	£39	£6	n/a
Av. clothes	£73	£70	£65	£15	£86	£56	£59	£91	£60	£45
Av. travel home	n/a	£29	£37	£20	£22	£18	£27	£33	n/a	£34
Av. utilities	£70	£99	£41	£48	n/a	£56	£91	n/a	£55	£30
Total	£229	£286	£212	£154	£201	£265	£243	£247	£174	£287

⊙ What the area is like at night. An increasing number of both male and female students in many more universities said it was dangerous to walk alone at night: these included students from Wolverhampton, Robert Gordon, Oxford, Cambridge, Sheffield and many more. Many also said taxis were expensive.

'Taxis can cost £4 for a three-minute journey after midnight.'
3rd year English student, St Andrews

'You need a car in Bradford; walking even in the early evening is dangerous. Somebody just up my road had a gun pulled on them. Fortunately most students don't have much money.'
2nd year Technology and Management student, Bradford

But there were more positive comments:

'Taxis are in good supply in Bangor and a journey across town is cheap.'
2nd year Psychology student, Bangor

How much will it cost to get to your college from home?

Average: £26 per term.

If you live in Exeter and decide to study in Glasgow, getting there is going to be a major expense and you won't be popping home very often. But if home is Birmingham and you study somewhere close at hand, like Manchester, it's relatively cheap.

On average, students living in the UK spend £26 per term on going to the family home. Coaches are generally cheaper than trains, but they take longer and the amount of luggage you can take with you is usually limited. The most popular means of transport for students is the train. However, many students said their parents might give them a lift at the beginning and end of the year when they have a lot of luggage. If you do have to stagger home with your luggage using public transport, remember your costs may have to include taxi fares.

Thrift tips

Don't shop on an empty stomach – it's disastrous.

Always telephone during the cheap-rate period.

Watch out for special coach-company offers.

Check that water rates are included in your rent.

Look for special student nights at clubs, theatres, cinemas.

Check out students' union shops – they buy in bulk and so give good discounts. Beer, stationery, dry cleaning, even holidays could be part of their cost-cutting service.

Student rail and coach cards

Both train and coach services offer student reductions, provided you buy their special student cards. These last for a year. One longish journey will more than cover the initial outlay, which is:

Railcard: £20 pa (Jan 2006)

Reduction: one-third off all rail fares.

Travel restrictions: check with station for full details.

NX2 Coachcard: £10 pa or £25 for three years (Jan 2006)

Reduction: up to 30%.

Travel restrictions: some journeys cost slightly more at certain times.

Travel advice note

- Restrictions on cards can change, so always check what is being offered and when you can travel.
- Look for special reductions: occasionally the rail or coach companies will have special promotions such as half-price student cards, or half-price fares. They may also give discounts on things like CDs or subscriptions to magazines. Check out www.gobycoach.com.

See the table below for some comparative travel costs from London, based on return fare prices in January 2006. Prices quoted include Young Person's Railcard or Coachcard discount.

Typical fares	Train		Coach
London to	Saver Return	Booked in advance	Booked in advance
Edinburgh	£62.10	£23.10 (very few)	£31
Newcastle	£60.35	£20 (very few)	£28
Manchester	£37.50	£20	£21
Nottingham	£30.15	£7.90	£18
Birmingham	£23.90	£20	£16
Cardiff	£35.65	£24.40	£21.50
Bristol	£32.35	£19.80	£17.60
Exeter	£28.95	£25.35	£26

Many tickets have special conditions, and advance booking varies. With some rail tickets it is cheaper to buy singles, ie London to Manchester is £10 each way. Check with provider.

Coach prices: travel on Friday is generally more expensive; reduction if booked in advance.

Can I afford to run a car?

If your only income is the standard funding for students, most rational people would say no. But since so many students do seem to have cars they must be managing it somehow. A recent survey by Reaction UK claimed nearly half of all students own or use a car. Travel from your home to your university will probably be cheaper by car, but you may also find yourself coming home many more times in a term, acting as chauffeur to the party, and taking trips at weekends. And don't underestimate the maintenance bills: they can be astronomical, especially on an old car. Then there's the road tax, currently £110 pa (£60.50 half-yearly) for cars under 1549cc and £175 pa (£96.25 half-yearly) for the rest. If you are lucky enough to have a car manufactured since March 2001 then you'll be charged according to its CO_2 emission. There are seven different bands and costs range from zero for cars with very low CO_2 emissions to £210 a year for the mighty 4×4 gas guzzler. Add to that your MOT and AA/RAC membership, which makes sense if your car has a tendency to break down, and your biggest outlay of all – insurance.

How much to insure my wheels?

Two wheels or four, it's not going to be cheap or easy.

Four wheels

Students lucky enough to have a car may find they don't have much luck getting insurance, especially if they are first-time drivers and under 21. Try Endsleigh Insurance: In 1997 the NUS, worried that many students who ran cars couldn't afford the cost of insurance cover, asked Endsleigh (an insurance company that they part own) to try to find a way to reduce motor insurance premiums for students – which they did, by up to 30%.

A word of caution: think twice about 'fronting'; that's the old trick of mum taking out the insurance and naming the student as second driver. If there's a claim and it's discovered that the student is really the main driver, you could find the insurance company won't pay up.

Insurance costs vary, depending not just on who you are, but on where you live. Big-city drivers pay a higher premium than, say, those in the country. In London the costs are prohibitive. Endsleigh warns: 'Insurance premiums are based on the address that the car resides for the majority of the year. Therefore, if you are living away from home while studying, you must provide the address where you live for the majority of the year.' So even if it would be cheaper to take out insurance from, say, your parents' home address, think before you do it. Giving false information could lead to claims not being paid.

Two wheels

You might think a bicycle was much easier to insure. But any student intending to take a bicycle to university must think in terms of having it pinched, or at least borrowed without permission. Insurance companies certainly do.

Insurance advice: a good padlock and detachable wheel or saddle should be your first form of insurance. Consider exchanging that expensive mountain bike for something that looks as if it's come off the tip.

Who to try: Endsleigh has designed a special insurance scheme to help you. It's suitable for all bikes valued up to £1500. Premiums are dependent on the value of your bike and where in the country you live, ranging from £32 for bikes worth up to £149 in a fairly thief-free area, up to £194 for a £1500 bike in a higher-risk area. All bikes valued between £1000 and £1500 will automatically be registered with Stoptheft.

Also try the banks – some offer a fairly good deal.

Approximately half of all UK-registered bikes are scooters (about 0.5 million) and they have enjoyed a recent upturn in popularity because of TV stars such as Jamie Oliver. They are often regarded as a cheaper alternative to cars, but remember – they are easily stolen. Some insurers exclude theft cover unless the bike is garaged at night. Immobilisers don't always stop thieves either, as a bike/scooter can be bundled into even a small car.

Endsleigh provides insurance for scooters and small motorbikes. A lot of their enquiries in this area come from students with bikes under 250cc. They offer Comprehensive, Third Party, Fire and Theft and Third Party cover only.

Green facts

Going green has never been more popular amongst Britain's students:

- 35% reject non-green employers
- 67% recycle waste at home
- 69% choose to walk or cycle over short journeys
- 48% say they try to buy with an environmental conscience
- 38% use energy-saving devices such as wind-up radios and low-voltage light bulbs.

(Survey by Fujitsu Siemens Computers)

So how do so many students manage?

For many students, money is not just a problem – it's the major problem. Even students not in debt and apparently managing fairly well see finance as their biggest worry. But coping on a limited budget is also a test of independence and ingenuity. Here are some money-saving ideas from current students.

'Rent out any extra room space.'
1st year Contemporary Photographic Practice student, Northumbria

'Visit car boot sales to sell, buy and sell again.'
4th year Environmental Science student, Stirling

'Offer to walk the neighbours' dogs for a couple of quid an hour.'
1st year American Studies and Computing student, Wolverhampton

'Never be afraid to ask if there is a discount for students. I found my NUS card reduced my swimming sessions from £1.95 to 75p.'
Computer student, London University

'A lot of websites pay you to fill out questionnaires to receive text message advertising – you can also sign up for offers on sites such as www.britishfreebies.com and find yourself with enough free samples of shampoo for the year.'
Sheffield Hallam University student

Facts and figures

- ⊙ Students spend over half of their money on accommodation.

- ⊙ Students taking up university places in autumn 2005 were up by 7.76% on the previous year to a record number of 404,668. However, at the January closing date for applications this year (2006) there was a marked decrease of 3.4% (UCAS figures).

- ⊙ 14% of full-time students at UK universities fail to obtain a degree (down 1% on last year) (HESA figures).

- ⊙ Drop-out rates in some universities reached 31%, but in others, such as Cambridge, the figure was 1.2%.

- ⊙ The NUS believes a major cause of drop-outs is financial hardship (NUS Student Hardship Survey). Other reasons include exam failure, ill health and switching courses.

- ⊙ Britain has one of the lowest non-completion rates for degrees in the world: Italy 58%; France 41%; USA 34%; Australia 31%; Germany 30%; UK 14% (HESA figures 2005); Japan 6% (OECD, *Education at a Glance 2003*).

So how much will you need to survive as a student?

£5000? £6000? £7000? £8000? £9000? £10,000 pa?

The NUS estimated that for the last academic year (2005–2006) students would need £10,493 if living in London and £8810 in other parts of the country for the 39-week academic year. You'd be lucky if you had that. In fact, based on what you are likely to receive in funding, the NUS suggested a shortfall in funds of £6612 for students in London and £5664 for students elsewhere. And that was last year. So in reality you're going to have to survive on what you can get and what you can earn. How much is that likely to be? Read on!

Typical student budgets

Three students show how their money goes, and where it comes from.

Rachel – 3rd year Fine Art student at Nottingham Trent University

Accommodation: a large house shared with three other girls. There are four double bedrooms plus a bathroom, living room, kitchen in the basement, a spare room, which she uses as a studio, and an additional bath and shower. It is only five minutes' walk from the campus. All costs are over a nine-month academic year unless otherwise indicated.

Outgoings	Per month	Per year	Comments
Rent	£190	£1900	Despite living in same house as last year and having a 12-month lease we were not charged rent July to Sept. due to kind landlord. Expect the same this year.
Electricity	£12	£109	Have a meter.
Gas	?	No bill	Unbelievable – we haven't had bill yet – not for last year or this.
Telephone	£40	£480	Use mobile.
TV licence		£25	Shared between four.
Internet	£4	£48	Just got broadband – 12 months.
Food in	£60	£540	Shop individually, but often eat together. No kitty; we take it in turns to buy household products.
Food out	£30	£270	Eat out once a month – Early Bird offers. Avoid snacks – have late breakfast and early tea.
Laundry	£8	£72	
Cosmetics	£10	£90	
Entertainment	£15	£135	Cinema.
Clubbing	£30	£270	Deliver flyers for club nights and get in free.
Drinking	£80	£720	Drink at home before you go out – it's cheaper.
Smoking	£15	£135	Roll my own – typical student.
Yoga	£16	£144	
Travel (Nottingham)	£10	£90	
Travel (home)		£70	Richmond, Yorkshire – twice plus lift from parents.
Travel (other)		£200	To see friends.
Course trips		£100	London galleries and others.
Course equipment		£300	Digital media-photography. Not so expensive as last year when using film photography. Donation to kick start.
Fund for degree show		£100	Also organising boat party to increase funds.
My final show		£100	Expect to spend at least that.
Books/magazines	£10	£90	For my course.

CDs/Mini discs	£15	£180	Anything new – electronic stuff.
Clothes		£300	Splurge occasionally.
Gifts		£100	Friends and family.
Holidays		£1570	Budapest, Barcelona, Normandy, Holland, Paris, London/Brighton – and possibly New York – cost of this not included.
Fees		£1175	
Total		£9313	

Income	Per year	Comments
Fees	£750 app.	Parents.
	£425 app.	LA.
Loan	£4078	Student Loan – full final-year rate.
Parents	£1560	£130 a month for 12 months.
Overdraft	£1750	Extended free bank overdraft (usually £1500) to cover rent.
Job (term)	£2160	Bar work £60 a week + drinks.
Jobs (summer vac.)	£920	Richmond Yorks District Council – 4 weeks at £230 pw spent on hols.
	£230	Handing out Metro newspaper for two weeks before Spanish hols.
Grandparents	£600	
Credit card	£280	Bad move. Took it out to book some tickets. Swore I'd never use it for anything else, but was tempted.
Total	£12,753	

Rachel says: 'Live with likeminded people who you get on with so you can share – music, clothes, socialising, even staying in with a bottle of wine. Look around for the freebies – guest nights at clubs, friends who work in bars and bring food home, being a model in hair salons. When I came here I planned not to use my bank overdraft and just to get a job. I could not imagine being in that much debt. But I soon realised that if you don't use all the finance available you'll probably end up missing out on all that uni has to offer. I expect to be £12,000–£14,000 in debt when I leave.'

Ed – 3rd year History of Art student at Bristol University

Accommodation: privately rented four-bed house which he shares with three other students – another boy and two girls. It has four bedrooms (two double and two single), a bathroom, living room with a large dining table and a kitchen. It also has a massive basement which they have cleared out and use for some 'crazy' parties.

Outgoings	Per month	Per year	Comments
Rent	£325	£3900	Over 12 months. Deposit before moving in: £300.
Electricity	£67		
Gas	£85		
Water	£30		
Telephone	£30	£360	Over 12 months.
Internet	£5	£30	6 months only.
TV licence	£?	£?	Least said the better – 2 warnings so far.
Food in	£160	£1440	Cook together. Have big table and dishwasher, so give great dinner parties for 10 to 12 people – 2 a month. Get good invites back.
Food out	£20	£180	Mostly canteen.
Socialising	£200	£1800	Out once a week clubbing and taxis.
Sport		£3000+	Sailing. Training every week and weekends. Fortunately I get a grant to help.
Clothing		£100	Most from presents and sales.
Railcard	£0	£0	Free from HSBC.
Travel (term)	£20	£180	Walk mostly.
Travel (home)		£120	Stoke-on-Trent – 3 times a year.
Books		£20	Use the library. History of Art books prohibitively expensive.
Vices	£8	£72	Real coffee junkie – need 6 hits a day.
Newspapers	£1.50	£18	*Independent* – 12 months.
Presents		£60	Family, friends. House whip-round for birthdays.
Holiday		£1250	Sailing with the British team.
Interest on	£6	£72	£800 debt – 12 months credit-card debt
Fees	£1175		
Total	**£13,959**		

Income	Per year	Comments
Fees	£65	Paid by LA.
	£1110	Paid by parents.
Student loan	£3980	
Sports funding	£3000	Government funding.
Job (term)	£1280	Graduate promotions company £40 a week. But will have to quit because of pressure of work so may end up less than this ...
Overdraft	£1250	
Credit card	£800	Be warned, leave them alone. Too much temptation.
Total	£11,485	

Ed says: 'I expect to graduate with a debt of £15,000. It is quite worrying the debt you are in, but at the end of the day you are probably going to be better paid if you get a degree. Uni is such a fantastic opportunity and most of the debt isn't going to really hurt as it's a student loan and you pay it off gradually. It will just look like another tax – annoying but no more. The freedom of uni is an experience you will never have again. If you miss a lecture, it's no big deal. In your first term you do spend a lot of money. Living in halls you want to meet people and to go out. Fortunately I had saved £500 – it all went down the drain, but I think it was worth it. Don't let the thought of debt put you off. Last year I took a year out from study to work for the Students' Union, organising the university's sports activities – some 53 of them. Doing something like that has to look good on your CV.'

The first term at university is expensive – and it can be the undoing of some students, condemning them to three years of anxiety and debt. Stories abound of students spending £3000 just on socialising, though funnily enough you never seem to meet anyone who has actually done the spending. But overspending there certainly is, and once you get badly into debt it's very difficult to get out of it.

Jess – 1st year Modern Languages (French and German) at Christ's College Cambridge

Outgoings	First term	Comments
Hall fees	£1012	For whole term. Include rooms, kitchen and food/drink card – breakdown given below.
Room	(£708)	It's massive. 30 max for a party. My weekly chocolate fondue parties are popular.
Kitchen/utilities	(£104)	
Food/drink card	(£200)	Paid up front. Card is then swiped when you buy a meal or drink in the bar. Formal three-course meal in halls £5 – don't forget your gown. Two courses in the Upper Hall £1.50 Have used only £180 so am £20 in credit for next term.
Food – additional	£265	A lot more than planned. Pizzas occasionally; breakfast when late; weekend meals when Upper Hall closed. Snacks, fruit.
Fondue parties	£20	Fondue set plus chocolate – always a success.
Socialising	£120	Cinema, concert, clubbing, college shows. Most is around the college bar and goes on your card. Need to start saving for the May balls – £100 and that's just for the ticket.
Phone	£135	Catastrophe! Dropped mobile – replacement £80. Mobile calls £5 a week. Landline calls £15 a term – a bargain.
Travel (term)	£6.80	Taxi £5 to lecture from early morning rowing session. Got stuck on the river. Everything else within 2 mins' walk
Travel (home)	£0	Lift from parents – saving £40 each way
College team gear	£215	Badminton (plus racket), netball, rowing, tennis, basketball, five sports. It's not essential but you're proud to represent your college. Quality stuff will last the four years. Fortunately parents bought my gown (£55).
Badminton	£14.40	90p a session – twice a week. Other sports free.
Making room homely/ fun	£21	3 fun posters, a picture and cards. Budget for this – white walls are not study-friendly.
Washing	£55	£1 a wash, 20p for a 10-minute dry. Had to buy iron – £15.
Toiletries	£37.67	
Clothes	£40	
Insurance	£35	Covers all my stuff.
Music	£16	DVDs – indie/rock.
Craft	£2	I make my own cards.
Stationery	£20	Brought a lot with me.
Books	£96	I spent a further £250 before I came and also bought a laptop, £500.
Internet connection	£10	
Presents	£139	I always take something when invited for a meal.
Charity donation	£4.50	All students give.
Vices	£53.84	Hot dogs – there's a stall outside college. Hum! Flapjacks – two packs a week.
Fees	£392	£1175 pa. Thankfully, no top-up fees.
Total	**£2710.21**	

Accommodation: lives in halls – very large single room on corridor with 12 other students. Very basic: bed, wardrobe, three tables, four chairs. No en-suite. She shares a bathroom and kitchen with the 12 other students (all female). As an only child, she was apprehensive about living in a community, and though sometimes she says she needs her own space, she is never lonely.

Before going to university Jess drew up a budget for the term, but her money didn't stretch quite as far as she had hoped. When her phone and badminton racket broke in the first week, her calculations started to take a dive and she ended the term with an overdraft.

Jess decided she wanted to try and manage without support from her parents. She has taken out a student loan – £1245 a term (£3760 pa). This is the maximum she can have, based on her parents' income. She also has £480 from a policy her parents had been paying into for her education, £300 from working in her parents' shop during the summer, £120 her parents sent her when things started to get tight, and £60 from selling stuff on eBay. She finished the term with a £250 overdraft, which she is busy paying off by working in her parents' shop.

Jess says, 'You can't plan for uni because it is completely different from anything you have experienced before. You start with the money you have and divide it by eight (weeks in Oxbridge term) and you think "£70 a week – that's great". Then the next week you divide by seven and the next by six and so on and you find it is now £40 and then £20 and then minus £10 – now that is a bit scary. But uni is doable – just – and definitely worth doing. My advice: during the summer after your A levels, don't have a life, just work, work, work and save because nothing will ever compare with the life you have at university.'

Fact file

Great news guys, it looks as if you are going to be outnumbered yet again. Of the university applications UCAS has received so far for 2006, 56% were from females compared with 44% from males.

So now you know how much it is going to cost, but where will the money come from? Turn to the next chapter to find out.

2

Where will the money come from?

Main sources of finance for undergraduates

> **This chapter answers questions on the main sources of finance for students embarking on higher education.**
>
> ⊙ Welcome to the top-up-fee generation (page 33)
> ⊙ Fees – what you pay (page 36)
> ⊙ Maintenance – grants, bursaries and loans (page 41)
> ⊙ Applying for grants and loans (page 49)
> ⊙ Additional help (page 59)
> ⊙ Loans – paying them back (page 61)
> ⊙ The banks – overdrafts, loans, freebies (page 67)
> ⊙ Further information (page 75)

The information in this chapter is based on the funding package for students starting university in the UK in 2006–2007. Any variations in Scotland, Northern Ireland and Wales and additional help for special case students are covered in Chapter 3.

Welcome to the top-up-fee generation

The arguments are over – top-up fees or, as they are officially called, variable fees, are here, and it would seem here to stay. Students starting their first-degree studies in autumn 2006 will be the first of the top-up-fee generation. With the introduction of top-up fees many of the existing funding arrangements for students have changed. So, if you are entering university for the first time this autumn, forget everything you think you know about student funding and start from here.

Student funding – how it will look from now on

The main points:

⊙ Universities can charge different (variable) fees for courses, but it is expected most will charge the maximum.

⊙ The maximum a student starting study for their degree in 2006 can be expected to pay in fees is £3000 pa.

⊙ Students in Welsh universities will have a stay of execution for one year, paying fees of £1200 for this year only (see page 80).

⊙ Scottish students studying in Scotland do not pay fees (see page 78).

⊙ Full-time students will no longer have to pay fees before they start university or while studying.

⊙ Students can take out a loan to cover their fees, which they will pay back gradually once they have graduated.

⊙ Payback for loans will begin in the April after you graduate if you are earning over £15,000.

There will be no help with fees for low-income families. However:

⊙ Maintenance grants of up to £2700 will be available for students from low-income families. These will be on a sliding scale depending on your family income.

⊙ Bursaries will be available from universities, especially for students from low-income families.

⊙ The grant plus university bursary should equal £3000 a year for lowest-income families.

⊙ Main source of maintenance income will be a student loan available to all students.

⊙ Part of the loan will be means tested on family income and on the amount of maintenance grant students receive.

⊙ New non-repayable Special Support Grants of up to £2700 for students receiving government support – largely lone parents/disabled.

To sum up, the main change in student funding from last year is the shift in emphasis from getting help with fees, to getting help with maintenance.

Existing and gap-year students

Existing students. Fees will be £1200 pa for 2006–2007. Help will be given to low-income families, as before, including bursaries, but not of the size being offered to new students. The best news is that you too will be able to take out a loan to cover fees and pay it back after graduation.

Gap-year students, who were given exemption from paying top-up fees, will be treated as existing students and pay £1200 pa.

It's not all bad news

Although fees have gone up dramatically and help with fees has been stopped, you won't have to pay your fees until after you graduate, and then over many years. To cushion the fee blow, grants and bursaries will be given to help with maintenance on a sliding scale. The real winners are parents, whose assessed contribution has been decreased, but, since parents have generally given more than their assessed contribution, students may well be in luck too.

Should students have to pay for their education?

This book does not set out to argue the rights and wrongs of the students' situation; its function is to provide information. However, not surprisingly, our research revealed strong feelings among students. Here are a few of their more printable comments:

'This government appears to be preventing the poor from being educated, creating yet again an educated elite.'

'Lack of parental contribution already makes life impossible. I live on half what I should. Books need subsidising.'

'Student top-up fees shouldn't happen. All higher education should be accessible to all people who wish to go, even though some courses will lead to no job at the end.'

'My parents worked hard and did overtime to help me out more, only to find that my loan was reduced.'

What the government said:

'On average, a graduate earns much more than someone without a degree. Over a working lifetime, that will make a big difference in their income.'

(Graduates earn around 62% more than non-graduates – Labour Force Survey 2005.)

Looking at the detail

Am I a special case?

If you fall into any of the categories listed below, check out Chapter 3.

- ⊙ Scottish students and those studying in Scotland (see page 78).
- ⊙ Welsh students and those studying in Wales (see page 80).
- ⊙ Irish students and those studying in Northern Ireland (see page 82).
- ⊙ Students from another country in the EU or outside the EU (see page 82).
- ⊙ Refugees/asylum seekers (see page 84).
- ⊙ Sandwich/industrial placement students (see page 84).
- ⊙ Part-time students (see page 85).

⊖

- ⊙ Foundation students (see page 85).
- ⊙ Attending a private higher education institution (see page 86).
- ⊙ Nursing/midwifery students (see page 86).
- ⊙ Healthcare students (see page 87).
- ⊙ Medical/dentistry students (see page 87).
- ⊙ Trainee teachers (see page 88).
- ⊙ Physics students (see page 88).
- ⊙ Social Work students (see page 89).
- ⊙ Dance and Drama students (see page 89).
- ⊙ Married/independent (see page 90).
- ⊙ Single parents/with a family to support (see page 90).
- ⊙ Students who have been in care (see pages 54 and 59).
- ⊙ Disabled students (see page 91).
- ⊙ Students studying abroad (see page 93).

Fees – what you pay

How much will I have to pay towards my fees?

Your university will set a price for each course up to a maximum of £3000 pa. Fees are flexible, but it is thought that most universities will charge the full £3000.

However, we did find a few universities that were charging lower fees to 2006 entrants. These included:

Institution	Fee
Greenwich	£2500
Leeds Met	£2000
University College, Northampton	£2500
York St John University College	£2500
Writtle College	£2700
Thames Valley	£2700

Who will pay my fees?

You. There will be no help from the your LA* for fees and your parents will not be asked to contribute. What's more, family income will have no bearing on what you pay. Universities can charge what they like for a course up to a maximum of £3000 pa, and what they ask is what you must pay, but you may take out a loan to cover these fees.

Will every student pay the same fees?

Students from the same country on the same course at the same university will pay the same fees – they are not means-tested – but course fees can vary even in a university. Your university will decide what fees it is going to charge. However, Scottish students studying in Scotland do not pay fees at all, while non-Scottish students who study in Scotland do, but at a different rate to England. Wales has also decided to take an independent line from this year. For full details and reasons why the rates are different, see Chapter 3. The fee table below gives you an idea of fee differences throughout the country.

This is how fees look for most students.

UK Region	2006/2007	2007/2008**
England	£3000	£3000
Wales	£1200	£3000
Scotland	£1700	£1700
Medicine in Scotland (see Chapter 3, page 87 for details)	£2700	£2700
Northern Ireland	£3000	£3000
**Likely to rise with the cost of inflation*		

Will fees ever go up?

Yes. When the top-up fee programme was first mentioned, the government said that fees would not go up before 2010, but starting from 2007 they are likely to be increased in line with the rate of inflation. Actual figures for 2007–2008 will be announced nearer the time. At the time of publishing inflation is running at around 3.2%.

How you pay – fee loans

Where is a student going to find £9000 or at worst £12,000 for fees?

*LA stands for Local Authority in England and Wales. When the term LA is used in this book, please read SAAS for Scotland (Students Awards Agency for Scotland) and ELB (Education and Library Board) for Northern Ireland.

From this year on, you will be able to take out a loan to cover your fees, which you will not have to start paying back until you have graduated and are earning at least £15,000 (see page 61 for full details). So the good news is that students will no longer have to pay fees up front; there will be no getting slung out of uni for not having the money to pay fees. The bad news is that your debt will increase – substantially.

Where will the loan come from?

From the Student Loans Company.

How do I get my loan for fees?

You apply to your Local Authority at the same time as applying for your maintenance loan and a grant. It is all on the same form. They will then pass this request on to the Students Loans Company, who will then inform you that this has been done. The form is available from www.studentfinancedirect.co.uk or from your Local Authority by post.

How much can I borrow?

Whatever your course costs, up to £3000 pa.

Is it means-tested?

No.

What will happen to the money I borrow for fees?

It will be paid direct to your university.

Who can get a fee loan?

UK first-degree students, EU students and those taking a PGCE (Postgraduate Certificate in Education).

Is taking out a loan for fees a good idea?

Yes. The big plus about the new funding system is that, because students can take out a loan to cover their fees, they or their parents will not have to pay fees before they start university or while they are studying. So all of your maintenance loan, anything your parents give you and everything you earn will all go towards living. You should have fewer money worries than your predecessors during your time at university, but your debt will undoubtedly be greater.

If my parents want to pay my fees, can they do so?

There is nothing to stop parents paying your fees. Fees have to be paid at the start of each year. Most universities allow fees to be paid in tranches, but you will need to talk to your university. Some universities will give a discount if fees are paid in full up front.

Advice note

If your parents will have to borrow to pay your fees, it's worth remembering that the loan offered by the Student Loans Company is probably the cheapest money you can borrow, so it might be an idea to come to a family arrangement – you take out the loan for your fees and they pay it off for you.

Who gets help with fees?

Nobody, unless you:

⊙ Started your course last year or before
⊙ Are a 2005–2006 gap-year student with an exemption
⊙ Are a Welsh student studying in Wales from 2007–2008 onwards (see page 81)
⊙ Are a Scottish student studying in Scotland.

What happens if I drop out of my course – will I have to pay fees?

Probably, but there are no hard and fast rules. If you drop out before 1 December you may be OK as your fees won't have been paid by the Student Loans Company before that date. But generally, it will be a matter of discussing it with your university – after all they have all the expense of providing a place for you.

I want to change my course; what happens about my fees?

Again, it will be a matter of discussion with your university. If you are changing to another course in the same university, fees may not be a problem, but if you are moving to another university then it might be more difficult.

Will I be able to get a loan for fees for any course I take at college?

No. Courses for which loans for fees will be given include: full-time (including sandwich) degree, HNC, HND, Postgraduate Certificate of Education, school-centred initial teacher training, or equivalent courses undertaken at a UK university, publicly funded college or comparable institution.

Courses for which loans are not available include: school-level courses such as A levels or Scottish Highers, BTEC and SCOTVEC National Awards and City & Guilds courses for those over 19, postgraduate courses (except teacher training), all part-time courses (except initial teacher training courses), correspondence and Open University courses.

What can I do to raise funds to pay my fees if I am unable to get a loan?

1 Talk to your local authority.
2 Talk to the college where you want to take the course.
3 Apply for a Career Development Loan – see page 73.
4 Apply to professional bodies, trusts, foundations, benevolent funds – see Chapter 6.

Advice note

If a fee debt of £9000 (£12,000 for a four-year course) fills you with horror, and well it might, don't abandon your degree aspirations – yet. There are some excellent bursary deals on offer and many students, especially those from low-income families, may find they are better off than their non-top-up-fee contemporaries.

Fast facts on finance

For students starting their course 2006–2007

Fees	Max £3000 pa (except in Wales)
Student loans	£6170 in London, £4405 elsewhere, £3415 living at home (less in your final year); 25% approx., means-tested on parents' income and maintenance grant received.
Maintenance grant	£2700 for low-income families (less in Scotland and Wales). Means-tested on family income.
University bursaries	Many will offer non-repayable bursaries. At least £300 pa likely for those on full maintenance grant.
Access to Learning Fund (Contingency Fund – Wales, Hardship Funds – Scotland, Support Funds – N. Ireland)	Random distribution; given largely to help with rent and other financial hardships.
Part-time students	Increased levels of fee grants to max of £1125 plus grant towards travel and books.
Salary payback threshold for loans	£15,000
Scottish students	Don't pay fees in Scotland

Maintenance

There are three elements to students' maintenance:

⊙ Maintenance grants
⊙ University bursaries
⊙ Student loans.

Maintenance grants

What are they and will I get one?

Maintenance grants are not new: they have been creeping into the funding system since the year 2000. What is new, though, is how much is being given – up to £2700 – and the number of students who will receive them. This is not government generosity, however, because students no longer receive help with fees. Maintenance grants are means-tested on your or your family's income.

Maintenance grants – who receives what in 2006-2007	
Income	Grant
£17,500 or less	£2700
£20,000	£2284
£30,000	£832
£37,425	£50
£37,900 and above	£0

Students who started studying for their degree in 2005/2006 or before will not be eligible for the increased grant rates but will receive grants based on last year's figures of £1000–£2000 depending on UK location and family income.

How many students will receive a maintenance grant?

It is anticipated that around half of all full-time students will be eligible for a full or partial grant.

When will I get my grant?

It will be paid in three instalments, one at the start of each term.

Who will calculate how much I will get?

Your Local Authority, based on the information you supply on your application form.

University bursaries

Universities have always offered bursaries to good students but never on the scale that they are intending to do so from now on. And those from low-income families have never had it so good. The government stipulated that to charge the maximum fee of £3000 pa, universities must sign up to an Access Agreement, which says that students receiving the full £2700 maintenance grant (ie those from low-income families) must be given a further non-repayable bursary of at least £300, making a grand total of maintenance grant and bursary of £3000 – but it could be more.

Some universities are sticking to the guidelines. Others are being far more generous. Many are offering bursaries on a sliding scale to all those receiving a proportion of the maintenance grant. The average bursary from universities is expected to be around £1000 for those receiving the maximum maintenance grant. This could be given in kind – ie reduced accommodation costs. Even students who don't actually fall into the low-income category are cashing in. Here are a few examples:

University of Bath	Bursary of up to £1500 dependent on household income: bursary for incomes of £16,000 and below = £1500; £16,001–£20,000 = £1200; £20,001–£25,000 = £900; £25,001–£30,000 = £600; £30,001–£33,553 = £300. Institute of Physics Scholarships of up to £1000 pa dependent on household income.
University of Bradford	Students entitled to the full grant will be entitled to bursary of £300.
Brunel University	Students on full maintenance grant will receive £300 pa. Students in receipt of partial grant will receive £200 pa. 150 cash scholarships of up to £3000 pa will be available to students from under-represented groups: £3000 for 360 Tariff points; £2000–£3000 for 340 Tariff points.
University of Cambridge	Students in receipt of full state support will receive a bursary of £3000 pa. Students not in receipt of full state support will receive bursaries on a sliding scale. Specific college awards are also available.
Canterbury Christ Church University	£800 for students on full state support. £500 for students on partial state support. £400 for students with household incomes between £33,000 and £45,000.
University of Central Lancashire	£1000 where principal earner's salary is less than £60,000 pa. Harris Bursary Fund – additional support for local students. Excellence bursaries targeting key areas – up to £1000 pa.
City University	£800 pa for students in receipt of the full grant. Pro rata bursaries for students in receipt of partial support. Ten scholarships worth £1100 pa for students from London studying Computing, Engineering, Mathematics or Actuarial Science.

(Trotman Information Services)

Shop around. As you can see, there are some fantastic bursary deals about and every university has a different approach. Finding a university giving generous bursaries could be more cost-effective than trying to find a low-cost course and probably better educational value too.

Where will the money for bursaries come from?

Universities will be setting aside over £350 million from the increased fee money to support students from low-income families, and it is estimated that some 400,000 students will benefit from this. But many universities are already heavily endowed by generous benefactors and have always awarded scholarships, awards and bursaries to selected students.

Where can I find out about university bursaries and scholarships, and what's being offered?

- ◉ University prospectuses and websites are a good starting point and should provide plenty of information.
- ◉ http://studentfinance.direct.gov.uk.
- ◉ Course Discover, an online database listing over 125,000 courses and including bursary information, available for use in careers libraries and schools.

There is also more information on university awards and scholarships, including sports bursaries, music scholarships, location scholarships and awards for students from abroad, in Chapter 6 of this book.

To compare and contrast what universities are offering take a look at *University Scholarships, Awards and Bursaries* by Brian Heap, published by Trotman. As well as giving full information about the new bursaries for students from low-income families, it lists over 100 institutions offering scholarships, awards and bursaries. Many are for people studying specific subjects, or are travel awards. Subjects vary from the more usual (Engineering, History, Geography, Languages, Law and the sciences) to the more specialised, such as Cultural Criticism Studies, Paper Science, Rural Studies, Retail and Textiles.

Student maintenance loans

How much can I borrow?

Not enough – at least that is what most students think. The maintenance loan is reviewed annually and is dependent on where you are studying. This year the maintained rates have been increased substantially, especially for students in London. The rates for a full maintenance loan for a full-time student in England, Wales and Northern Ireland in 2006–2007 are shown in the table.

		Full year max. available	Final year max. available
Students living away from their parents' home and studying:	In London	£6170	£5620
	Elsewhere	£4405	£4080
Students living in their parents' home		£3415	£3085

'When I started uni I didn't think I'd need a student loan. I'd taken a gap year and saved and was getting £500 a year bursary, but I spent about £800 in the first term – well,

actually most in the first month – it was outrageous, it really was. Well, let's face it; the first year isn't exactly quiet. Most went on booze, pizzas and more booze. But that first month was probably the best few weeks of my life. I had worked continuously during my gap year, so when I got to uni I hit it hard.'

Jono, 3rd year student, Loughborough

Is the loan means-tested?

Yes. Not everybody can take out the full maintenance loan. It is means-tested on your maintenance grant and on family income.

Low-income families: up to £1200 of the new maintenance grant is paid in lieu of part of the maintenance loan, so those receiving the full maintenance grant, or a high proportion of the full grant, may find they are not entitled to the full loan.

Higher-income families: a quarter of the loan allocation is means-tested against your income or that of your family. It is hoped that any part of the means-tested loan you do not receive will be paid by your parents or spouse.

This is the maintenance students can expect in 2006–2007:

Family income	Assessed family contribution	Maintenance grant	Maintenance loan	Total loan + grant
Studying in London				
£17,500	£0	£2700	£4970	£7670
£20,000	£0	£2284	£4970	£7254
£25,000	£0	£1450	£4970	£6420
£30,000	£0	£832	£5338	£6170
£35,000	£0	£306	£5864	£6170
£37,425	£0	£50	£6120	£6170
£37,900	£0	£0	£6170	£6170
£40,000	£221	£0	£5949	£5949
£45,000	£747	£0	£5423	£5423
£50,000	£1273	£0	£4897	£4897
£52,530	£1540	£0	*£4630	£4630
Studying outside London				
£17,500	£0	£2700	£3205	£5905
£20,000	£0	£2284	£3205	£5489
£25,000	£0	£1450	£3205	£4655
£30,000	£0	£832	£3573	£4405
£35,000	£0	£306	£4099	£4405
£37,425	£0	£50	£4355	£4405

Family income	Assessed family contribution	Maintenance grant	Maintenance loan	Total loan + grant
Studying outside London				
£37,900	£0	£0	£4405	£4405
£40,000	£221	£0	£4184	£4184
£45,000	£747	£0	£3658	£3658
£48,000	£1100	£0	*£3305	£3305
Living at home				
£17,500	£0	£2700	£2215	£4915
£20,000	£0	£2284	£2215	£4499
£25,000	£0	£1450	£2215	£3665
£30,000	£0	£832	£2583	£3415
£35,000	£0	£306	£3109	£3415
£37,425	£0	£50	£3365	£3415
£37,900	£0	£0	£3415	£3415
£40,000	£221	£0	£3194	£3194
£45,000	£747	£0	£2668	£2668
£46,030	£855	£0	*£2560	£2560

*The point at which the 75% non-means-tested part of loan is reached

How the calculations are made

Where students receive a maintenance grant, the amount of loan for which they are eligible will be reduced, pound for pound, by the amount of grant up to £1200. Any university bursary is not included in this.

The rate at which family income between £17,501 and £26,500 is assessed is £1 in every £6 earned over £17,500. For income between £26,501 and £37,425 the rate is reduced by £1 for every £9.50 earned over £26,5000. Family income over £37,425 will not be eligible for any grant.

For students where family income is over £40,000, 25% of the maintenance loan will be assessed at a rate of £1 for every £9.50 earned.

Cash crisis note

- By 2010, graduate debt could reach as much as £33,708 for students leaving a three-year degree course, including the proposed increase in tuition fees, says Jeremy Law, head of student and graduate banking at Barclays Bank. However, Vickie, a second-year medical student at Liverpool, reckons she will have debts of around £45,000 when she graduates, and top-up fees hadn't even come in yet.

Where does the student loan come from?

The Student Loans Company, which is a special company set up by the government to provide loans for students.

Student loans – a few facts

When the student loan was first introduced in 1992 there was uproar. Many thought that higher education in this country should be completely free; others said that students should contribute to the cost of their education. At the time, the loan was around £580. People predicted student numbers would plummet. They were wrong. In fact, while the loan increased year on year, so did student numbers. Last year a record 405,369 students started a degree course, an increase of 7.4%, or 27,825 bums on lecture hall seats.

But what about this year – the year of the top-up fees? Nobody in their wildest dreams thought back in 1992, that 14 years later, students would be facing a double loan whammy. We are into new territory and the outcome is difficult to predict. Our research amongst students in December 2005 showed that around 43% of students actually knew of somebody who didn't go to university because of financial reasons, and 64% said they knew someone who had decided to study in their home town to save money. And things may get worse. Applications to UCAS by the closing date of 15 January 2006 were down by nearly 13,000 – that's a drop of 3.4% on the previous year. Applications from men were down by 4% and applications from women by 2.9%.

Whatever your views about funding yourself through university, if you are a student just starting on higher education in the UK, you will probably end up having a hefty loan. Most students – around 80% – already do.

How much do students owe?

In the first year of the Student Loans Scheme, around £70 million was paid out to fund some 180,000 students.

By its tenth anniversary £1823 million was paid out to 723,000 students.

Last year, with an estimated 81% of eligible students taking out a loan, the figure had reached £2780 million paid out to 854,645 students, which all adds up to ...

... a massive £15.9 billion currently being borrowed by some 2.6 million students and graduates. Next year, with the fee loan, these figures will go sky high.

Compared with their predecessors the debt situation students are facing now is tough and will get tougher. But the fact is that students are reluctantly learning to live with ever-increasing debt. According to Barclays Graduate Survey 2005:

- 86% owe money to the Student Loans Company, and the average debt to SLC is £10,646
- 53% borrowed an average of £4142 from their main bank or building society
- 24% borrowed from parents, relations or friends and on average owe £2428.

How do students feel about debt?

It would seem that today's students are concerned but largely reconciled to the situation of being in debt, as a survey carried out by Barclays Bank shows.

Attitude to debt by:	Students			Graduates*			
	2000	2001	2002	2001	2002	2003	2004
Worried	13%	15%	14%	9%	13%	14%	14%
Concerned	27%	25%	24%	23%	18%	28%	24%
Angry	6%	8%	8%	8%	12%	8%	6%
Resigned	21%	19%	25%	19%	20%	18%	18%
Pleased not to have much debt	6%	7%	7%	15%	19%	6%	10%
Unconcerned	27%	26%	23%	27%	18%	19%	21%

*Based on data 6 months after graduation

It's a fact – or is it?

Students have become happier, fitter and more confident, and no longer complain so much about debt, according to a campus lifestyle survey conducted by Mori for Unite, the housing provider, published in January 2005. This new breed of undergraduate is more interested in gaining good qualifications than students four years ago.

What students say

'It's quite a frightening thought when you're only 20 years old to say: "Oh, I'm borrowing all this money – what chance have I got of ever paying it back?"'

'Student debt is bad enough, but the "invisible debt" is worse – overdrafts, credit cards, borrowing from family – all of which has to be paid back.'

'Depression is a problem that hits everyone who lives on a tight budget.'

'I can't believe I'm spending so much – it's the little things which add up.'

There are students who take a different view:

'Generally, studying is an indulgent luxury which improves prospects and so people should take as much responsibility as possible.'

'Most students don't mind the thought of paying back money once they are earning.'

The argument will continue, but our aim is to give you hard information on how to juggle your finances and tap every source available so that you can cope in the current economic climate.

Who can get a maintenance loan?

Answer: UK students who undertake full-time first degree or Diploma of Higher Education courses at universities or colleges of higher education. While there is no age limit on students taking out a fee loan, maintenance loans are available to students aged under 60.

I'm an overseas student: can I get a maintenance loan?

No. Even students from the EU who are classified as 'home' students for fees are not entitled to apply for a maintenance loan. For further details see Chapter 3, page 82.

Are there loans for part-time students?

No. But there is help (see Chapter 3, page 85).

I want to do a second degree – can I get a loan for maintenance and fees?

It depends how long your first course was and the length of your second course. In general, support will be availabe for students for the length of a course plus one extra year. If that sounds like gobbledegook this is how it works: take the length of your new course and add a year, then subtract the number of years you had funding on your first course, and what you are left with are the number of years for which you could receive funding. Still confused? Try again. Say your new course is three years. Add to that one year. Subtract the length of your first course, say three years, and you would receive funding for one year. But if, for example, your previous course was three years and your new course is four years, add another year to that and you would receive funding for two years. Of course it could work the other way, if your previous course was four years and your new course was only three. Then you would end up receiving no funding at all.

I want to change my course: what happens to my loan?

If you change to another course in the same college, your entitlement to a maintenance loan may well stay the same, but your fees could be different. Equally, if you transfer to another college the fees may be different. The major problem arises if you change to a college/course that does not attract student support or there is a break in your studies before you join the new course. It is very important if you transfer from one course to another or withdraw from your current course that you not only discuss this with your college, but also talk to your LA (or the SLC if on the pilot programme) as soon as possible.

I am doing a further education course – can I get a loan?

If you are doing a course that leads to a first degree, HND, HNC, PGCE or NVQ at Level 4 you can get a student loan. The information in this book is aimed mainly at higher education students. Students in the 16–19 age group attending further education colleges may be eligible for financial help through their college.

Here's a quick guide to what you could receive.

Household income	£17,500	£26,500	£37,500	£50,000
Maintenance grant	£2700	£1200	£0	£0
Maintenance loan	£3205	£3205	£4405 (outside London)	£3305 (outside London)
Total each year	£5905	£4405	£4405 (outside London)	£3305 (outside London)
Bursaries from universities	At least £300 likely	Portion of £300 likely: could be more	Depends on university	Depends on university, but unlikely

'Get a job – the student loan seems like a lot of money, but it doesn't cover even the essentials.' (See Chapter 4)
Psychology student, Hull

Why are the loan rates lower for the final year?

Because they do not cover the summer vacation. You are expected to be working by then, or can draw Social Security. However, if your final year is longer than 30 term weeks you can apply for more loan for each week. If it lasts 40 weeks or more you can get a loan at the full rate. This is often the case for students on 'accelerated' degree courses. Rates for 2006 are:

	Full year	Final year
Home	£3415	£3085
Elsewhere	£4405	£4080
London	£6170	£5620

Applying for grants and loans
How do I get assessed for a bursary and loans?

Most students who live in England will apply to their LA. You should start thinking about applying for financial support as soon as you have applied for a place on a course. Do not wait until you have a confirmed place on a course: just quote the course you are most likely to attend. Still apply even if you don't think you will be entitled to a maintenance grant, as your LA will also assess how much loan you are entitled to and how much your family is expected to contribute (if at all). Remember that the loan is paid by the Student Loans Company, not your LA. Your LA is responsible for means-testing family income. Any problems with your loan should be addressed to the Student Loans Company (address on page 65).

There are three important steps to follow:

1 Contact your LA for an application form or download it from the web (www.studentfinancedirect.co.uk).
2 Fill in your application form and return it to your LA by post or on the web. Give all the details you are asked for and say whether you intend to apply for a loan. Remember to include your National Insurance number if you do want a loan.
3 If your application is in order, it will be sent to Student Finance Direct, who will send you details of the support you are entitled to six to eight weeks after you send your application.

If you want to discover what help you are entitled to, check out the online calculator at www.studentfinancedirect.co.uk.

Pilot application schemes

While the above is the correct procedure for most students, this year the government is carrying out two application pilot schemes to assess whether an easier applications procedure can be found. So, if you live in one of the areas listed below, your application will be dealt with by the Students Loans Company (SLC) this year and you will need to contact the SLC's Customer Support Office on 0845 607 7577 if you have any queries. These changes will in no way affect how much support you receive.

Scheme 1

Under this scheme your whole application will be dealt with by the SLC and your LA will not be involved. Councils involved:

London Borough of Brent
London Borough of Hackney
North Yorkshire Council
South Tyneside Council
London Borough of Southwark
York City Council

Darlington Borough Council
Hartlepool Borough Council
Redcar and Cleveland Borough Council
Southend-on-Sea Borough Council
Stockton-on-Tees Borough Council

Scheme 2

If you live in one of the areas of the second pilot, your application will be dealt with by the SLC. However, your LA will be responsible for assessing your application and you can call your LA if you have a detailed question about your application. Councils involved:

Cheshire County Council
Lancashire County Council
Leeds City Council
Manchester City Council
London Borough of Sutton

Students based in Wales, Scotland or Northern Ireland should turn to the next chapter for details.

Timing is important.

- ⊙ You can apply to your LA from March onwards.
- ⊙ New students – try to return your form no later than 30 June 2006.
- ⊙ Current students – return form for reassessment by 26 May 2006.
- ⊙ All non-income-assessed students should apply by 28 April.
- ⊙ Late applications may result in late payments.

Win an iPod Nano

You can apply online from mid-April onwards or complete a paper application form available for your local authority. Everyone who applies online for 2006–2007 student support between April and July will automatically be entered into a prize draw for an iPod Nano music player – six are on offer. The online application process is fast and easy. What's more, if you need to update your details, view your payment information or change your bank details, it can be done just by logging on to your account.

When and how will I get the money?

Your student loan: once you have registered your arrival at university and have started to attend the course it will be paid into your bank account.

Your maintenance grant: once you have registered your arrival at university and have started to attend your course it will be paid into your bank account.

Your fees: will be paid direct to your university.

Your university bursary: still being decided. Likely to be paid into your bank account by your university.

All payments to you will be in three tranches, made at the beginning of each term.

Advice note

You will need to have some cash in hand when you arrive at university, since your loan/grant payment will not hit your bank account on the first day.

Panic! My loan and grant cheque hasn't arrived!

It happens – not that often, but it can be dramatic when it does. In an ideal world your cheque should be waiting for you when you arrive at your university or college, but things can go wrong. Some typical reasons we discovered were:

⊙ Local authorities were behind with their workload and have not processed your application
⊙ You applied late, so the amount of the loan has not been assessed
⊙ Loans company has been inundated
⊙ Wrong information on your bank account.

Whatever the reason, it doesn't help the destitute student to eat, so ...

What can I do?

⊙ Try the bank. If you already have a bank account, the bank may help you out with a loan – most banks offer free overdrafts to students. Talk to the student adviser at the campus or local branch. This, of course, is no help to the first-year student who needs that cheque to open a bank account, so make sure you have an account before you start your course.
⊙ Try your college. Ask your college for temporary help. Most institutions have what's called a hardship fund set up to cover just this kind of eventuality.
⊙ Try the Access to Learning Funds, which have been set up to help students. Full details are given on page 59.
⊙ Friends? They may well take pity on you when it comes to socialising, buying you the odd drink, but it is rarely a good idea to borrow from friends.

How late can I apply for support from my LA?

Up to nine months after you have started your course.

Do I have to apply for my maintenance loan before I go to university?

Applications can be made at any time during the academic year. The cut-off date for a maintenance loan application is one month before the end of your academic year.

Parental involvement

What are parents expected to contribute?

Less than in past years. Parents haven't had it so good for a long time. They are expected to make up any of the means-tested portion of the loan that a student does not receive.

The maximum parents/spouses in England are expected to contribute for one student in the year 2006–2007 is:

⊙ Students studying in London: £1540*
⊙ Elsewhere: loan top-up £1100*
⊙ Living in parents' home: £855*.

*Scotland has a different system of funding for students, and parents are assessed and contribute substantially more than parents in the rest of the UK (see page 79 for further details). For Wales and Northern Ireland the figures may differ slightly.

Compare that with the maximum figures last year, which were £2470, £2225 and £2005 pa respectively. Why the cut? Last year, fees, as well as the loan, were means-tested on parents' income. Of course, parents can still pay towards fees, and in the past many have contributed more than the allocated portion.

Note to parents. No parent is expected to contribute more than the maximum means-tested portion of the loan for each student, however high their income – but many do. (See page 44 for details of what you might have to pay).

It's a fact

Parents are contributing more than ever before:

⊙ Almost a third of students regularly receive financial support from their parents
⊙ 25% get money as and when they need it
⊙ Only 29% get no assistance at all.

How do they calculate how much loan I can have?

The actual calculation of whether and how much your family is expected to contribute towards maintenance, and how much grant you are entitled to, is very complex. It is based on 'residual income': that means what's left after essential expenses have been deducted. The assessment will be on family income, so if both parents are earning, both incomes will be assessed.

So what are essential expenses? It works like this. The LA takes your parents' or parents' plus partner's gross income before tax and National Insurance and then subtracts allowances for things like pension schemes, dependants and superannuation payments that qualify for tax relief, and whether you will be receiving any maintenance grant. Having done this they then assess what your household contribution should be. It is not until the family income is around £40,000 that parents are expected to contribute.

My parents are divorced – whose income will they assess?

Your LA will decide which parent they consider you are living with, and assess their income, while ignoring the income of the other parent.

I have a step-parent – will their income be included?

Yes, the income of a step-parent, if that's the parent you live with, or a cohabiting partner, whether of the same or opposite sex, will be taken into account. However, maintenance received from an absent parent will not be considered as part of the household income when assessing income.

What happens if my parents are not prepared to divulge their income?

You will not be assessed for a maintenance grant and will only be eligible for three-quarters (the non-means-tested portion) of the maintenance loan.

What if I have a brother or sister claiming for a maintenance grant and a loan?

If there are several children in higher education in the family, the grant and loan entitlements are calculated on the same scale as for one student; those parents whose residual income is below £40,000 would not have to contribute for either student and you would both be eligible for a full loan. If the family income is over £40,000 but below £48,000 (£52,530 in London) then they would find they have to contribute no more than for one student, and any additional loan received would be divided proportionately between the students. Any parental contribution should be divided in the same way. It must also be remembered that any other dependent children they have will come into the calculation. Parents with a higher residual income will have to contribute more. The maximum parents can be asked to pay, regardless of how many children they have at university, is £7430.

Does the parental contribution ever change?

It certainly has this year with the introduction of the top-up-fee system – it has gone down. But in general, the threshold at which parents begin to contribute towards maintenance is likely to be raised each year, so if parental earnings are static they could find they contribute less next year. Remember parents are only *expected* to contribute.

What if my mum or dad is made redundant?

If your parents' income suddenly drops, then you should contact your Local Authority or Awards Branch immediately as you could be entitled to a maintenance grant and more maintenance loan.

If my parents can't afford to or won't pay the shortfall in my maintenance loan, is there anything I can do?

No. There is no way that parents can be made to pay their contribution towards your maintenance and fees, and the local authorities will not make up the difference.

Are there any circumstances in which my parents would not be expected to contribute towards my maintenance?

Yes – if you are:

- ◉ 25 or over
- ◉ Married

⊙ Have been supporting yourself for three years
⊙ An orphan
⊙ In care.

Some important questions and answers

I want to go to a university in my home town, but don't want to live with my parents – can I get the full financial package?

Students living at home are eligible for the lower 'living at home' maintenance loan only. There is no regulation preventing you from living away from home, but funding is at the discretion of your local authority.

I'm thinking of getting married – will it affect my maintenance grant and loan entitlements?

Yes. Students who get married before the academic year are considered as independent and their support is no longer assessed on their parents' income but on that of their partner, provided he or she is earning enough. This is calculated in a similar way as for parental income.

I'm not married but living with a partner – will this affect my support?

Yes – see previous question.

What is the maintenance loan meant to cover?

Lodgings, food, books, pocket money, travel, socialising – but not fees.

My academic year is longer than at most colleges – can I get extra money?

Yes. If your course is longer than 30 weeks you can claim for an extra loan, which will be means-tested, for each week you have to attend your course. Rates for 2006–2007 are:

⊙ London: £98 per week
⊙ Elsewhere: £77 per week
⊙ Living at home: £51 per week.

If your course year is 45 weeks or longer, you will receive a loan based on 52 weeks.

⭐ **What subjects are UP and what subjects are DOWN**
TOP*TEN* **with students applying for uni in 2006**

Subject	Percentage change	Subject	Percentage change
UP		**DOWN**	
Social Work	+43.0%	Information Systems	−2.5%
Medicine/Biology/ Agricultural Science/ Physics and Maths	+39.8%	Combinations of European Languages	−2.8%
Maths & Computer Science	+24.2%	Zoology	−2.9%
Academic Studies in Education	+22.4%	Geology	−3.0%
Tourism, Transport, & Travel	+22.1%	Creative Arts & Design	−5.6%
Pre-clinical Dentistry	+20.0%	Science and Engineering & Technology	−7.6%
Building	+18.3%	Production/Manufacturing Engineering	−8.4%
Business Studies & Administration	+18.2%	Electronic/Electrical Engineering	−8.4%
Sports Science	+18.0%	Human Resource Management	−9.2%
Music	+17.9%	Non-European Languages and related subjects	−20.2%

(UCAS application figures for 2006)

If I work part-time, will it affect my student financial package?

No. Students can work during their course – ie undertake vacation work – and the money earned will not be considered when their loan/grant is calculated.

Facts and figures

Eighty-eight per cent of school leavers said they expected to have to roll up their sleeves and work some 15 hours a week to make ends meet while at university. In reality fewer students actually do work – around 39%, according to a recent NatWest Student Money Matters Survey.

Cash crisis note

- Avoid being a university drop-out (14.4% of students dropped out in their first year at the last count). Freshers who think they've taken the wrong course should beat a hasty path to their course director or their Careers Service for advice as soon as possible. Nothing is set in stone. The critical date is 1 December: the Student Loans Company doesn't actually pay your fees before then.

What will happen if I drop out of my course?

You will have to pay off any loans taken out for fees and maintenance. Your LA might also ask you to repay some of the fees they have paid.

When is the best time to take out a maintenance loan?

There are three options:

1 When you need it.
2 As late as possible – because it's index-linked to inflation (see page 62).
3 As soon as possible. Some financially astute students take out their student loan, even if they don't need it, and invest it in a good interest-paying account with a bank or building society. These accounts generally pay more than the inflation rate. Make sure you know what you are doing. Check out interest rates first, and ensure you can get at your money quickly and easily if you are likely to need it – some high-interest rate accounts give limited access.

Is there any help with travelling expenses?

England, Wales and Northern Ireland: the first £285 of any travelling expenses are disregarded. Above that you can claim a grant for certain expenses if you are: disabled; attending another establishment as part of a medical or dental course; or attending an institution abroad for eight weeks or more as part of your course.

Scotland: if living away from home, three return journeys per year to your place of study can be claimed for, plus additional term-time travel to and from your

Cash crisis note

- As your loan cheque will not be banked until you have arrived at your university or college, you will need to have some money of your own to get yourself there, and possibly to maintain yourself until the cheque is cleared. Check out the cost of train fares.

- If you are living in halls of residence, your college will probably be sympathetic if your cheque hasn't arrived and will wait until it does. But don't be too sure about this – check it out. Some colleges will add a penalty to the bills of students who don't pay up on time. And if you run out of money and can't pay your bill at all, you will not be allowed to re-register for the next academic year. If it's your final year, you will not get your degree until the bill is paid.

- If you are living in rented accommodation, you can expect no leniency. Landlords expect to be paid on the dot, usually ask for rent in advance and may request an additional deposit. You will need funds to cover this.

Advice note

Postgraduates are not entitled to a student loan. So if, as an undergraduate, you do not need the loan or all of the loan now, but are thinking of going on to do a postgraduate course, it might be worth your while taking out the student loan and investing it, so the money is there to help you through your postgraduate studies later on. If you are not a financial whiz-kid, take advice. The student loan is a really cheap way of borrowing money but you don't want to build up debt unnecessarily.

---

institution. (This does not include students whose parents live outside the UK.) The first £155 of any claim will be disregarded. Only the most economical fares will be allowed. (Cost of student railcard or bus pass may also be reimbursed.)

'Because I had sponsorship, had worked for a year before uni and had a Saturday job, I didn't need a student loan, but I took it out anyway, and put it in a good building society account, just in case I wanted to go on to do further study. As it is, my sponsor has offered me a job that's too good to turn down, so I won't need it, but it was nice to have that security cushion there. I haven't checked it out yet, but I think the loan has actually made me money; at least it hasn't cost me anything, which has to be good.'
3rd year student

Do I have to take out the whole maintenance loan amount?

No. You can take out however much you want, up to the maximum for which you are eligible that year. If you do not apply for the full amount at the start of the academic year you can apply for the rest later.

Will the loan be paid all at once in a lump sum?

No. The loan will be paid termly, in two or three instalments depending on when you apply for it.

What students owe

⊙ 86% borrowed from the Student Loans Company – average debt £10,646
⊙ 53% borrowed from their bank – average debt £4142
⊙ 24% borrowed from parents, family or friends – average debt £2429.

(Barclays Bank Graduate survey, published spring 2005)

Fact check

Of the students graduating last year:

- ◉ 306,365 first-degree students obtained a degree.
- ◉ 11% of first-degree students who graduated were part-time.
- ◉ 11% of students obtained a first-class degree.
- ◉ 43% of first-degree students gained a 2:1 Honours award.
- ◉ 56% of first-degree graduates were women.
- ◉ 42% of students received a science degree, of which 49% were women.
- ◉ 191,820 students obtained a postgraduate qualification.

(HESA statistics January 2005 for academic year 2004–2005)

Additional help

Access to Learning Fund

What is it?

This is a special fund available through your college, which provides help to students who may need extra financial support to stay in higher education.

Who gets Access help?

If you are in real financial difficulty this is the source to tap. The fund is open to both full- and part-time students studying 50% of their time on a full-time course. It is there to help those facing particular financial hardship, those in need of emergency help for an unexpected financial crisis and those who are considering giving up their studies because of financial problems. Priority is given to students with children, mature students, those from low-income families, disabled students, students who have been in care, and students in their final year.

How much can you get?

That depends on your college. Students taking part in the *Students' Money Matters* survey said that under the previous Access/hardship scheme they were receiving around £300. There is no ceiling figure: it could be £3000. Your college will use its discretion. The amount given will depend on a number of factors – your circumstances, how many other students are applying and how much they have in the kitty. You can apply for help more than once in a year.

Wales: similar payments are made through the Financial Contingency Funds (FCFs) scheme.

Scotland: provides help through Hardship Funds.

Northern Ireland: provides help through Support Funds.

Will I have to pay the money back?

Payments are usually given as a grant, but they could be given as a short-term loan.

'I tried to get funds from Access but felt I was on trial.'
Mature Physics and Engineering student, Heriot-Watt

'The college hardship fund is a wonderful scheme to help you survive.'
Mature Midwifery student with four children, Canterbury Christ Church

How do I set about getting money from the Access to Learning Fund?

Apply to your college. Every institution will have a different procedure and different criteria for measuring your needs. You will most probably have to fill in a form giving details of your financial situation. Most institutions will have somebody to help and advise you. They may even have a printed leaflet giving you details.

When should I apply for Access funding?

As soon as trouble starts to loom. The fund is limited to the amount that is allocated, so it is largely first come first served. We have heard of institutions that have allocated most of their funds by the end of November of the academic year.

I'm a student from abroad – can I apply for Access money?

Sorry, but no. The Access to Learning Fund is restricted to 'home' students only, so overseas students are not eligible.

Are there any other hardship funds?

Some institutions, and also some students' unions, have resources to help students in real financial difficulty. They all vary depending on the institution, and they will pay out money for a variety of reasons. Funds are generally given when all official avenues are exhausted. Priority is often given to students who are suffering financially because of unforeseen circumstances such as a death in the family or illness. Sometimes small amounts are given to tide you over or to pay a pressing bill. Increasingly, hardship payments are taking the form of an interest-free loan, which can be especially useful if your grant/loan cheque doesn't arrive on time. They may also offer help to students from abroad.

Leeds University Union, for example, offers a range of financial assistance to students who find themselves in difficulty. There is a Fundraising Group, which considers all applications. As the money mostly comes from external charitable trusts, their hands are tied to some extent because they are governed by each individual trust's guidelines and criteria. But they are successful and offer much-needed support.

Are there any other allowances, grants and bursaries I could apply for?

Yes. Check the next chapter: you might fall into a special category. Otherwise try Chapter 6, 'Other sources to tap'.

Gordon's story

Latin American Studies student, Glasgow

When I came to university I had an electric guitar, an amp, a bass guitar, a stereo and a camera. In times of financial need these have all had temporary lodging in the pawnshop. Gradually this became less and less temporary so that now I no longer have a bass guitar, a camera or a stereo. The loss of the latter is no great hardship as I have already sold my CDs/DVDs one by one to the second-hand record shop.

Thrift tips

'Try the Access to Learning fund: it isn't widely advertised. I got £200.'

3rd year Sociology student, Aberdeen

'Try to get your booklist early and be first in line for second-hand books.'

4th year Dentistry student, Dundee

'Take a gap year and save.'

3rd year Geography Management student, York

'Find food nearing its sell-by date and being sold off cheaply, then freeze it.'

1st year Social and Political Science student, Cambridge

(NatWest Student Money Matters Survey 2005)

Loans – paying them back

Will I be able to afford to pay back my loans?

Yes. It may take a long time, but a system has been worked out that allows you to pay back what you have borrowed in line with what you earn.

When do I have to pay back my loans?

You repay nothing until the April after you have graduated, and then only when your income is over £15,000 pa will you begin to pay off the loans. The amount you pay is related to your salary, so whether you have borrowed £1000 or £25,000, have had a maintenance or fee loan, or both, your monthly repayments will be the same if you stay on the same salary. You will go on paying until the debt is paid off. However, if after 25 years you still haven't paid it all off, the government will write off anything left outstanding (except arrears). Rates are currently worked out at 9% of income over £15,000. So the current scale looks something like this:

Annual income up to	Monthly repayments	Repayment as % of income
£15,000	£0	0
£16,000	£7	0.6
£17,000	£15	1.1
£18,000	£22	1.5
£19,000	£30	1.9
£20,000	£37	2.3
£21,000	£45	2.6
£22,000	£52	2.9
£23,000	£60	3.1
£24,000	£67	3.4
£25,000	£75	3.6

How will I make the repayments?

Repayments will be collected through the Inland Revenue and will be deducted from your pay packet at source. Probably all you will know about it is an entry on your pay slip.

Will I have to pay back more than I borrow?

In real terms, no. The interest rates on loans are linked to inflation, so while the actual figure you pay will be higher, the value of the amount you pay back is broadly the same as the value of the amount you borrowed. The interest rate last year was 2.6%; the rate at the time of writing is 3.2%.

Will all students graduate with a huge debt?

Most students starting a course now will have to face up to the prospect of starting work with a debt to pay off, and this could be substantially more than the amount totted up under the Student Loans Scheme. Our research shows that 71% of students had overdrafts, some 75% had student loans, and a massive 89% expected to be in debt either to the bank or to the Student Loans Company, or possibly both, by the end of their course – from a few hundred pounds to over £16,000. (The most quoted figure over £16,000 was £20,000 plus.)

Estimated student debt	
13%	No debt
4%	Less than £1000
5%	£1000–£2000
5%	£2000–£4000
4%	£4000–£6000
3%	£6000–£8000
10%	£8000–£10,000
17%	£10,000–£12,000
20%	£12,000–£14,000
8%	£14,000–£16,000
10%	Over £16,000

Cash crisis note

- Check out Chapter 8 on budgeting – it might save you a few sleepless nights.
- Compare current bank overdraft rates for newly qualified graduates.

Do the pay-back rules ever change?

They are reviewed every year to make sure graduates can realistically pay back what they owe. Last year the payback threshold went up to £15,000.

Will I be able to pay it all back?

As well as the possibility of graduating to a massive debt, most students graduate to a fairly substantial salary. Starting salaries for graduates with good second-class Honours degrees in a blue-chip company in 2006 are expected to be around £23,000 (median figure – AGR survey 2006). If you are earning around £1916 a month, the repayments won't seem quite so grisly. But will you find a job? Are you going to be a 2:1 success story? Many graduates start work on salaries of less than £15,000. At the time of writing this book, the employment market for graduates in the UK is good. Graduate vacancies are expected to rise by a massive 14.6% in 2006 (AGR Graduate Salary Winter Review).

It's worth remembering that if you can't find work, the Student Loans Company will wait for repayment; the banks, however, may not be so sympathetic, though most do offer special overdraft facilities to graduates, which you should investigate.

I'm a graduate with £20,000 student-loan debts to clear – is my new employer likely to pay this off?

When the loan scheme first came in, many employers thought they might need to offer the 'carrot' of paying off students' loans if they wanted to attract the best graduates. Whether the government was hoping that employers would step in and clear students' debts in this way was a question often discussed in the national press. In fact, at least one major company did draw up contingency plans for a 'golden hello' scheme, and a number of companies we contacted said they were watching the market and their competitors very closely.

Then the recession hit the UK hard, graduate openings were in short supply, and graduates were competing for jobs rather than employers competing for graduates. Employers put all ideas of 'loan pay-off schemes for students' on the back burner. However, market trends and influences change very rapidly. Good quality graduates are seen to be in short supply again and employers are quite genuinely concerned about the amount of debt graduates have. So the 'golden hello' has quietly materialised. I say 'quietly' because few employers are keen to call it that. According to the 2006 Association of Graduate Recruiters Survey of their members, 38% of graduate recruiters offer 'golden hellos', and the median level of payout was £2000.

Cash crisis note

- Don't forget, when anticipating a 'golden hello', that the taxman will expect his cut.

Where are the big graduate starting salaries to be earned?

(Median starting salaries in 2004 by type of organisation)	
Investment banking	£35,000
Legal work	£29,000
Consulting	£28,500
Actuarial work	£25,000
Accountancy	£25,000
Financial management	£24,000
IT	£22,000
Mechanical engineering	£22,000
Marketing	£22,000
Manufacturing engineering	£22,000
Human resources	£21,000

(AGR Graduate Recruitment Survey 2006)

Can I get out of repaying student loans?

Yes:

- ⦿ If you never earn more than £15,000
- ⦿ If you become permanently disabled
- ⦿ If you die!
- ⦿ After 25 years it will be written off.

Is bankruptcy an option?

Not any longer.

A couple of years ago we reported that some 9000 students and graduates were considering making themselves bankrupt to avoid debt. New laws to make it easier to become bankrupt were being introduced, and in straightforward cases you could probably clear your debts within 12 months.

The government, it would seem, were hot on their heels, moving rapidly to close this obvious loophole in its system of student finance, and today the Student Loans Company tells us that making yourself bankrupt to avoid debt is not an option for clearing your student loan. Well, at least your good reputation will be intact.

Cash crisis note

It's official ...

The great British entrepreneurial spirit is not dead and only slightly dampened by rising student debt. The number of students planning to set up their own business after qualifying remains consistent at 4%, or around 30,000 students.

However, student debt is likely to slow down their plans: while 75% of students with ambitions to go it alone would either scale back or defer their plans until their debts were paid off, a brave (possibly foolish) quarter would carry on regardless.

(Survey commissioned by the National Council for Graduate Entrepreneurship (NCGE) in conjunction with Barclays)

Where can I get more information on student loans?

- ⦿ The Student Loans Company is based at 100 Bothwell Street, Glasgow G2 7JD. It has a free Student Loans Scheme help line on 0800 405010. Website: www.slc.co.uk.
- ⦿ Full information about the Student Loans Scheme is set out in its own leaflet, issued free and updated each year.
- ⦿ There are many anomalies within the scheme that we have not touched on here. For details see 'Further information' at the end of this chapter (page 75). Do also

take advice from your local authority and college so that you know exactly what you are getting involved in.

Is the Student Loans Scheme better than borrowing from the bank?

Most banks and building societies will give students overdraft facilities on special terms, usually including an interest-free £1000–£2000 overdraft facility (see page 68). This is intended mainly to help you during that difficult period when your loan hasn't yet arrived or you've run out of cash at the end of the term. The overdraft is wiped out as soon as the loan cheque is cashed. It is better to use the bank's 'interest-free' facility if your financial problems are temporary or you are certain you will be able to pay it back once you graduate. Most banks don't start charging interest on student overdrafts immediately you graduate, giving you time to get a job. This can be several months, but check it out with your bank. Banks also offer students longer-term loans at competitive rates, which should be investigated.

But, in general, banks are not the best bet for long-term borrowing for students – the Student Loans Scheme is, since the interest rate is no more than inflation, and payback is related to your salary. (See details on pay-back arrangements in previous questions.)

It's worth remembering, however, that to get a loan you have to have a bank or building society account. As mentioned, if you already have an overdraft with your bank, as soon as the loan hits your account it will automatically be used to pay off the overdraft, so you might not actually find that you have more cash in hand to spend, though you'll certainly have more peace of mind.

The banks – overdrafts, loans, freebies

Which bank? What's the carrot? What will they do for me?

Despite all the talk of students and their financial difficulties, and our research showing that most students are likely to be in debt by the time they qualify, banks are still falling over themselves in an effort to gain your custom. Nearly all offer students some kind of carrot to get them to open an account, and promise some kind of interest-free loan. Their reasoning isn't difficult to fathom. Banks are in the business of long-term investments. Students are the country's potential high earners. Statistics show that people are more likely to change their marriage partner than their bank. The strategy is: Get 'em young and you've got 'em for life.

So what's on offer?

Overdraft

The most useful offer made by banks to students is an interest-free overdraft. Our research showed that 70% of students took advantage of this. As you will see from our chart it could add another £1000–£2000 to your spending power. But it eventually has to be paid back. And don't assume it is yours as a right: you must ask first. Most banks also offer special arrangements for paying the overdraft off once you graduate. Again, check what these are before you step on the slippery slope to debt. How long will they give you to pay it off? What will the charges be then? How long does the interest-free loan last? These are the questions to ask.

Freebies

Most banks keep their new student offer under wraps right until the very last minute – largely so that their competitors can't top it with a better inducement. This means the new offer is on the table from around June/July. Some banks have a closing date for their offers, which could be as early as November, when the first loan cheques have been happily banked. The offer is generally open only to first-year students. Before giving you the benefit of their freebies, the bank of your choice will ask for some proof of your student status such as your LA award letter or your first term's loan cheque.

To give you some idea of what you can expect, and to check the next round of offers, we looked at how students fared in 2005–2006.

Cash was always considered to be the biggest draw, and not so long ago HSBC was offering a £50 cash incentive to students – but not any more. Last year NatWest's offer of a free five-year student railcard worth £100 was probably one of the better offers. And the restaurant, book and mobile phone insurance from Barclays sounds like a good deal. Lloyds TSB said their new offer was going to be so different from anything they had done before, they didn't want us to feature what they offered last year – which sounds interesting. Who is offering the best deal depends on what you are looking for – see our comparison chart on page 71.

What's the best banking buy?

Compare the current facilities offered by some of the major banks. NB Student packages are usually revised each summer, so check with the banks for the latest information on their websites.

	Bank of Scotland	Barclays	Halifax	HSBC	Lloyds TSB	NatWest	Royal Bank of Scotland
Free banking:	Yes, if in credit or within agreed overdraft of up to £2100.	Yes, if in credit or within agreed overdraft.	Yes, if in credit or within agreed overdraft of up to £2100.	Yes.	Yes, if in credit or within agreed overdraft.	Yes.	Yes, provided you stay within credit limit of arranged overdraft.
Interest on current account:	Yes, paid monthly (and calculated daily). Currently 2.02% (2.00% gross).	Yes, paid quarterly.	Yes, paid monthly (and calculated daily). Currently 2.02% APR (2.00% gross).	Yes, paid monthly.	No.	Yes, paid monthly.	Yes. Currently 2% paid monthly.
Free overdraft:	Up to: 1st year: £1750 2nd year: £1900 3rd year: £2100 4th year: £2100 5th year and postgraduates: £2100	Up to: 1st year: £1000 2nd year: £1250 3rd year: £1500 4th year: £1750 5th year: £2000	Up to: 1st year: £1750 2nd year: £1900 3rd year: £2100 4th year: £2100 5th year and postgraduates: £2100	Up to: 1st year: £1000 2nd year: £1250 3rd year: £1500 4th year: £1750 5th year: £2000	1st year: £1000 2nd year: £1250 3rd year: £1500 4th & 5th year: £2000	Up to: 1st year: £1250 2nd year: £1400 3rd year: £1600 4th year: £1800 5th year: £2000	1st year: £1250 2nd year: £1400 3rd year: £1600 4th year: £1800 5th year: £2000
Student adviser:	No.	Yes, in all major campus branches or university towns.	All branch advisers can help.	Yes.	Yes, dedicated telephone contact: 9am–7pm Mon–Fri. 9am–1pm Saturday.	Yes.	Yes. In most branches – called Student Champions.

Low-cost graduate loan:	No.	Yes, up to £10,000 for up to 7 years fixed rate at 8.9% APR, repayments.	No.	Yes, up to £25,000 at preferential rate available up to 5 years after graduation. A range of repayment periods.	Yes, up to £10,000 at preferential rate of 7.8% typical APR with up to 5 years to pay it back. Optional 4-month repayment holiday. Free overdraft up to £2000 for 3 years.	Yes, up to £15,000 at preferential rate over 7 years (5 years for loans of £10,000 or more). Optional 4-month repayment holiday. Contact bank for details on interest-free overdraft/credit zone/repayment plans.
Professional study loan, ie Medicine, Dentistry, Optometry, Veterinary, Science, Legal:	No.	Professional Study Loan up to £15,000. Up to £25,000 for Law.	No.	Considered on individual basis. Excellent rates given.	Up to £10,000 with a 48-month repayment break. 7.8% APR.	Up to £20,000 with a Professional Trainee Loan Scheme (full-time trainee Barristers and Solicitors can borrow up to £25,000). MBA Loan available.
Career development loan:	No.	Yes, up to £8000.	No.	Professional study loans considered on individual basis.		

Yes, £1000-£15,000 at 2.5% over base rate with 7 years to pay if amount £10,000 or over. If for refinance maximum 5 years repayment. Can be deferred for 9 months. Also £2000 interest-free loan to repay student/graduate overdraft.	(Low-cost graduate loan)
Up to £15,000 (Medical, Dentistry, Law, Osteopathy, Veterinary, Chiropractic only) repayable over 7 years.	(Professional study loan)
Yes, up to £8000.	(Career development loan)

What's the best banking buy? Cont.

	Bank of Scotland	Barclays	Halifax	HSBC	Lloyds TSB	NatWest	Royal Bank of Scotland
Cashpoint outlets:	Free if you take money out of your account using Bank of Scotland/Halifax or LINK machines.	Barclays and free access to over 39,000 cash machines in UK.	Free if using Halifax/Bank of Scotland or LINK machines.	Free use of HSBC cash machines.	Access to over 32,000 cash machines via the LINK network. Also any Post Office branch to cash cheques and pay money into account.	All major cash machines in UK.	All major cash machines in UK.
Insurance:	10% off World Explorer Travel Insurance package.	No special package.	10% off World Explorer Travel Insurance.	Special student package. Four levels of cover from £2000 to £5000. Covers possessions in student accommodation when away for up to 30 days. Optional cover for your PC up to £2000.	None.	Student Possessions Insurance.	Special student package only available online.

Freebies:						
Commission-free traveller's cheques and foreign currency. 10% off World Explorer Travel Insurance. Bank of Scotland Current Account Visa Debit card. 24-hour telephone and internet banking.	Restaurant and leisure discounts worth £28. Mobile phone insurance worth £60. 15% discount on Blackwell's books on line. All Sports discount worth £24. 3-year National Express coach card worth £19.	Commission-free traveller's cheques and foreign currency. 10% off World Explorer Travel Insurance. Halifax Current Account Visa Debit card. 24-hour telephone and internet banking.	Fee-free credit card with £500 limit. Banking 24/7 via internet banking. Automatic transfer to 3-6-year graduate service depending on length of study.	Watch this space – radical new offers on the way!	Free 5-Year Young Person's Railcard worth £100. Apply for a credit card with no annual fee. Online banking. Commission-free traveller's cheques and foreign currency (purchase only). Automatic transfer to 3-year preferential graduate service.	3-in-1 Highline card or Cashline ATM. ATM mobile phone top-up facility. 24-hour telephone and internet banking. Fee-free credit card. Commission-free traveller's cheques each year, discounts on books, CDs, videos, computer games, concert tickets, travel, plus extra protection.

But should one be bribed into choosing a bank? Forward-thinking students may well decide that interest-free overdraft facilities carry more weight in making the choice than a paltry one-time cash offer. Here you would do well to look carefully at the small print before making a decision. Some banks offer more in the second and third years. But do you want that kind of temptation?

'I went for the freebies – rather than the most sympathetic bank manager – bad move when debt loomed.'
3rd year student, Glasgow

Before deciding which bank to choose, check out:

- ⊙ Ease of getting an overdraft
- ⊙ Rates of interest charged if overdraft goes beyond limit, and ease of extending it
- ⊙ Interest rates on graduate loans – some are much better than others
- ⊙ What happens to your overdraft once you graduate
- ⊙ Proximity to university/lodgings of local branch
- ⊙ Reciprocal cash point facilities close to your institution – otherwise you could be charged for making withdrawals.

Cash crisis note

- Even though for over 86% of students debt is a way of life, most are at least opting for the cheapest way of borrowing, with the majority going to the Student Loans Company before seeking other sources of cash. However, *Students' Money Matters* research showed that 70% did have bank overdrafts.

What is a bank student adviser?

A student adviser ('student champion' at RBS) is somebody in the campus branch of the bank, or the branch closest to your college, who has been earmarked to deal with student problems. They are usually fairly young, and they are always well-versed in the financial problems students face. Certainly you will find them sympathetic, and full of good advice on how to solve your particular problems. But you won't find them a soft touch, as one student adviser pointed out: 'It's no good us handing out money like confetti – it just builds up greater problems for the student later on.'

What is a low-cost graduate personal loan?

This can be a life-saver for the newly qualified graduate. It is a special personal-loan scheme offered by some banks to graduates to help tide them over the first few months while they get settled into a job. Most banks offer anything up to £10,000, some up to £15,000 and more, and some up to 20% of your starting salary. A graduate loan can be individually negotiated. The loan could be used to pay for suitable clothes for work, a car, advance rent – whatever you need. But remember: nothing is for free; you will have to pay interest, and if you already have a student loan and a substantial overdraft, this might be just too much debt. The graduate loan should not be confused with the many other types of loan banks offer to postgraduates to assist with study. (See Chapter 6, page 192.)

Banks' websites

Check out the banks' websites for the latest information and offers.

Abbey	www.abbeynational.co.uk
Bank of Scotland	www.bankofscotland.co.uk
Barclays	www.barclays.co.uk
HSBC	www.banking.hsbc.co.uk
Lloyds TSB	www.lloydstsb.co.uk
NatWest	www.natwest.com
Royal Bank of Scotland	www.rbos.co.uk

Cash crisis note

- Never run up an overdraft without asking the bank first. They are much more sympathetic if you put them fully in the picture. And unless they know you are a student, you could find you miss out on the interest-free loan. Talk to your bank's student adviser – ideally before you hit a problem.

What are career development loans?

They are designed for people on vocational courses (full-time, part-time or distance learning) of up to two years where fees aren't paid, and you can't get support from your LA. They cover course fees (only 80% given if you are in full employment, 100% if you have been out of work for three months or more) plus other costs such as materials, books, childcare and living expenses. You can apply for £300–£8000.

The scheme is funded by a number of high street banks (Barclays, the Co-operative, the Royal Bank of Scotland) and administered by the Learning and Skills Council (LSC), who will pay the interest on your loan during training and for up to one month afterwards. If the course you take lasts more than two years (three years if it includes work experience) you may still be able to use a CDL to fund part of your course. Shop around the different providers and compare the terms offered before making a choice.

For a free booklet on career development loans phone 0800 585505. More information can also be found on www.lifelonglearning.dfes.gov.uk/cdl.

Health check

I'm sick and myopic, and I've got toothache – can I get free treatment?

As a student you don't actually qualify for any help, but as someone on a low income you could qualify for free or reduced:

⦿ Dental charges

⦿ Glasses

⦿ Eye tests

⦿ Prescriptions.

Form HC1 ...

... is the starting point, available from high street opticians, the Benefits Agency or Post Office. That will probably send you off on a trail leading to form HC2 or HC3; if you haven't received either of these items you will need form HC5, and don't forget to ask the chemist for receipt form FP57 (EC57 in Scotland) to claim for free prescription charges. If you are confused – and who isn't? – then leaflet HC11 will put you straight on the NHS in general and an HC12 on costs – both available from your Benefits Agency or by phoning 0845 850 1166 (local rates) or 0191 203 5555.

Try to get things going before treatment begins, or at least before you need to pay up. Otherwise, make sure you keep all bills and receipts, as evidence of costs. If after filling in HC1 you are told you are not entitled to any help and you think you are, give the Department of Health a ring on their freephone advice line 0800 917 7711. It could be that the computer is 'confused' as well – it has been known! It can be a long process, but it's often worth the effort.

For immediate medical advice, phone NHS Direct on 0845 4647.

It's serious – I could be off sick for weeks. What should I do?

If you become seriously ill and are likely to be off sick for months then you should obviously let your university department know, but also your LA and the Student Loans Company, since your student loans might be affected if you are off for more than 60 days.

Thrift tips

'Spend time in the library in winter as it's warm and saves on heating bills.'

2nd year Politics and History student, Aberystwyth

'Take all the food you can at breakfast, which is free, and eat it for lunch.'

1st year Medical student living in halls of residence at Dundee

'If you think £1 is nothing, try saving one a day for a year. £365 is two months' rent.'

2nd year Electronics student, Robert Gordon University

Further information

Who to contact/what to read

Contact the Student Loans Company support line on 0845 607 7577 for what financial help is available, the application process and paying off your loan.

Contact the DfES help line on 01325 392822 between 10am and 3pm for more detailed questions on student finance and eligibility.

Full information about fees, maintenance grants and loans is given in the following free booklets, which you would be well advised to get and study:

- For students in England: *A Guide to Financial Support for Higher Education Students in 2006/7* (which is the source for the loan statistics in this chapter), Department for Education and Skills (DfES) Publications Centre (Braille and cassette editions also available). Tel: 0800 731 9133. Fax: 0845 603 3360. Website: www.dfes.gov.uk/studentsupport. General enquiries: 01325 392822.

- For students in Scotland: *Student Support in Scotland: A Guide for Undergraduate Students 2006/7*, available from any Scottish university or the Student Awards Agency for Scotland (SAAS), 3 Redheughs Rigg, South Gyle, Edinburgh EH12 9YT. Tel: 0131 476 8212. Email: saas.geu@scotland.gsi.gov.uk. Website: www.student-support-saas.gov.uk.

- For students in Northern Ireland: *Financial Support for Students in Higher Education 2006/7*, Student Support Branch, Department for Employment and Learning (Northern Ireland), Rathgael House, Balloo Road, Bangor, Co. Down BT19 7PR. Tel: 028 9025 7710. Website: www.delni.gov.uk/index.htm.

- For students in Wales: National Assembly for Wales, Higher Education Division 2, 3rd floor, Cathays Park, Cardiff CF10 3NQ. Tel: 029 2082 5831. Fax: 029 2082 5823. Website: www.learning.wales.gov.uk.

Cathy's story

In my first year at Leicester I went mad and spent loads of money visiting friends in Birmingham. I soon regretted this as I was already getting into debt. During the next year I moved three times and had to buy expensive equipment for my course. By the end of my second year my loan had gone and I was so poor I lived on rice and gravy for two weeks. All my rent cheques bounced, and I had my Switch/Maestro cards and cheque book taken away. I couldn't go to my parents as they couldn't afford to support me. I have never been so scared in my life. I had to borrow from friends to pay my rent and barely got through. To make matters worse, I kept getting letters from my bank saying – surprise, surprise – I was overdrawn and charging me £27.50 for the privilege of doing so. To rectify this seemingly hopeless situation, I took a year off, and worked for the students' union, and am now back in uni (De Montfort) and back on track.

Cash crisis note

- Can't face all this debt? There's always the Open University. More and more young people are choosing the Open way. Last year 17,600 under-25s, the equivalent of a good-sized university, signed up to take an OU degree course – that's a three-fold increase in the last eight years. And of those, a third were aged 21 and under. Most students in our universities would probably tell you the OU route is not so much fun, but then debt isn't a bundle of laughs either. For information check their website (www.openuniversity.ac.uk) or phone 0870 333 4340.

TOP*TEN* lowest drop-out rates

Royal Veterinary College	0%
Cambridge	1.2%
Courtauld Institute of Art	1.3%
Oxford	2.3%
St Andrews	2.4%
Royal College of Music	2.7%
Stranmillis, Belfast	2.8%
Durham/Imperial College	3.7%
Bath Spa/Nottingham	3.9%

(HESA performance indicators for UK universities and colleges – full-time study, published September 2005)

TOP*TEN* highest drop-out rates

University of Bolton	31.0%
University of Derby	27.0%
Sunderland	26.8%
University of East London	26.0%
Trinity College Carmarthen	25.8%
London South Bank	25.6%
Middlesex	25.1%
Thames Valley	25.0%
London Metropolitan	24.7%
North East Wales Institute of HE	23.9%

(HESA performance indicators for UK universities and colleges – full-time study, published September 2005)

Am I a special case?

Funding for students in special categories

This chapter looks at various special categories and funding options

- ⊙ Geographical – Scotland, Wales, Northern Ireland, students from abroad (page 77)
- ⊙ Courses with a difference – sandwich/industrial placements, part-time courses, foundation courses (page 84)
- ⊙ Attending a private higher education institution (page 86)
- ⊙ Healthcare courses – nursing, midwifery, paramedics, medicine, dentistry (page 86)
- ⊙ Other subjects – teaching, physics, social work, dance & drama (page 88)
- ⊙ Additional help – mature students, students with dependants, disabled students (page 90)
- ⊙ Studying abroad (page 93)
- ⊙ Further information (page 98)

This chapter looks at the funding and extra help that is available for students in special categories. In some cases this is in addition to the funding outlined in the previous chapter; in others it is a completely different system or sadly there is no funding at all.

Geographical

Not all regions of the UK follow the same student funding system. Scotland, for example, decided to introduce its own no-fees funding solution for its own students soon after the new Scottish Parliament was set up. Now Wales has decided to take a more independent line.

Scotland – what's the deal?

In brief:

- If you live and study in Scotland you pay NO FEES for your university education, and because of EU regulations, this also applies to EU students.
- Students from the rest of the UK who study in Scotland do pay fees but less than in the rest of the UK.
- Scottish students attending universities in England, Wales and Northern Ireland pay fees and will have to pay the new top-up fees of up to £3,000.
- As in the rest of the UK, those paying fees will now be able to get a loan to cover their fees.
- All students studying in or outside Scotland can apply for a maintenance loan.
- Non-repayable bursaries will be given to students from low-income families. These will replace part of the loan so you will not incur too much debt.
- Before Scottish students start celebrating, there is a sting in the tail. Scottish and EU students who study in Scotland have to pay a one-off endowment once they graduate. A loan can be taken out to cover this.
- Scottish parents will be assessed to contribute more than in the rest of the UK.

I'm a Scottish student studying in Scotland

If you are a Scottish student studying in Scotland you are eligible for:

Non-repayable Young Students' Bursary (on family income of up to £31,775)	Up to £2455	
Student's loan:	Min	Max
Living in parental home	£560	£3405
Living elsewhere (loan rates for final-year students are slightly less)	£850	£4300
Additional loan for low-income families (on family income up to £20,225)	Up to £560	

How much is the endowment?

This was originally set at £2000, but it is index-linked so it is gradually increasing:

- 2001/2002 – £2000
- 2002/2003 – £2030
- 2003/2004 – £2092
- 2004/2005 – £2154
- 2005/2006 – £2216
- 2006/2007 – Announced October 2006

The endowment figure to be paid is fixed at the start of your course and will not change. If you think paying an endowment is unfair, remember: it is a lot less than the fees students in the rest of the UK are paying. You can either pay the endowment in a lump sum or take out an additional student loan to cover it. Repayments start the April after you graduate.

Some graduates will be exempt from paying the endowment: they include mature students, lone parents, disabled students, part-time students, those who don't graduate and, of course, students studying outside Scotland.

I'm a Scottish student studying outside Scotland

If you are studying in the UK but outside Scotland you will have to pay the full fees demanded by the university for your course, up to £3000 pa.

To help finance your studies you are eligible for:

Student fee loan to cover fees	Up to £3000	
Non-repayable bursary (on family income up to £31,775)	Up to £2000	
Student maintenance loan:	Min	Max
Living away from home in London	£850	£5305
Studying elsewhere	£850	£4300
Studying outside Scotland but living at home (loan rates for final-year students are slightly less)	£560	£3405
Additional loan for low-income families (on family income up to £20,225)	£560	
No endowment will be paid		
You may be eligible for a bursary from your university, see page 42.		

What parents in Scotland are expected to pay.

This table will give some idea of what Scottish parents could be in for.

Residual income	Assessed contribution
£22,560	£45
£25,000	£316
£30,000	£872
£35,000	£1427
£40,000	£1983
£45,000	£2538
£50,000	£3207
£55,000	£3976
£60,000	£4745
(NB figures for a spouse are slightly higher)	

A deduction of £180 will be made from the assessed contribution for every dependent child other than the student. No parent is expected to contribute more than £4455 pa for one child if studying in London, £3450 pa if the student is living away from home and studying anywhere else, and £2845 pa if the student is living at home. These figures are based on the full loan minus minimum loan that a student can take out, regardless of parental income. If there is more than one child at university the maximum contribution a parent can be expected to make is £7430 pa regardless of how many offspring they have at university. Although Scottish parents may look with envy at parents in the rest of the UK, who will be assessed to contribute considerably less than those in Scotland, English students will be totting up a great deal more debt than their Scottish counterparts.

I'm a student from outside Scotland studying in Scotland

If you are from outside Scotland you will pay a set fee of £1700 pa. This may seem like a lot less than the £3000 students are paying in other parts of the UK, but the reasoning is that Scottish degree courses last four years whereas degrees in the rest of the UK generally last three years. If you multiply £1700 by four you'll see you're paying a lot less than the £9000 some students will have to find. But Scottish universities will be under no obligation to pay bursaries to students from lower-income families and are unlikely to do so. See previous chapter for details on fee loans (page 37), maintenance grants (page 41) and maintenance loans (page 43).

Emma's stand

Is it fair that English students pay fees when attending Scottish universities but EU students don't?

Emma Block, an English student who was studying Philosophy at Glasgow University, certainly didn't think so and decided to challenge the system, claiming that in law the extra fees were a breach of her human rights and discriminatory under the race relations legislation. This was over a year ago.

Her case, which was taken up by one of Britain's top education lawyers, was the first legal challenge to the Scottish parliament's powers to impose higher charges on undergraduates who come from other parts of the UK.

Emma is understandably angry that she is having to pay more for her degree than undergraduates from France and Germany.

The case will initially be filed in the Scottish courts, but lawyers believe it may only be resolved by the European Court of Human Rights.

Around 20,000 English students currently studying at Scottish universities are watching this case with interest, in the hope it might result in a rebate – but there's a long way to go yet.

Wales – what's the deal?

Studying in Wales in 2006–2007

The Welsh Assembly has decided not to bring in flexible fees (or, as most people call them, top-up fees) until 2007–2008. So all students starting a degree course in a Welsh university in 2006–2007, including EU students, will pay a fixed fee of £1200. This is the same fee figure that existing students will be paying. To cover your fees you will be able to take out a loan. You will also be eligible for a means-tested maintenance grant (see page 41) and a maintenance loan (see page 43). After that, things change. From autumn 2007, Welsh universities will be able to charge students fees of up to £3000 pa for courses. But it's not as simple as that.

Welsh students studying in Wales from 2007–2008

While UK students from outside the principality will have to pay in full the top-up fees asked by universities, students who normally live in Wales and choose to study in Wales, along with EU students, will receive a fee grant of £1800 pa to offset the increase in fees. This is not means-tested, does not have to be repaid and will have the effect of keeping the fees Welsh students pay in Wales down to £1200 pa. Welsh students from lower-income families will be able to apply for a Higher Education Assembly Grant of up to £2700 to help with maintenance. This is means-tested and operates in a similar way to the grant in England (see page 41). To cover the portion of the fees you do have to pay, you can apply for a loan. You can also apply for a maintenance loan (see page 43).

Students from outside Wales who study in the principality

In 2006–2007 fees will be £1200. From autumn 2007 onwards Welsh universities will be able to ask for up to £3000 in fees and those from outside the principality will have to pay whatever the university asks. You will not be entitled to the fee grant given to Welsh students, but you will be able to apply for a fee loan to cover costs (see page 37). Maintenance grants of up to £2700 will be available for students from lower-income families, as in England (see page 41 for details). As we publish, heated discussions are under way as to whether Welsh universities will be giving bursaries to students from low-income families, as in England. You will be able to take out a loan to cover the cost of your fees (see page 37) and a maintenance loan (see page 43).

Welsh students studying outside Wales

If you normally live in Wales but are studying outside the principality you will *not* be entitled to a fee grant and will have to pay the fees demanded by the university of your choice – up to £3000 pa – from autumn 2006; so there will be no fee holiday this year. However, you will be entitled to take out a loan to cover fees (see page 37) and a maintenance loan (see page 43). You may also be entitled to an Assembly Learning Grant of up to £2700, similar to that available to students in England. This is given on a sliding scale depending on family income (see page 41). You may also be entitled to a bursary from your university (see page 42). In other words you will be treated in the same way as students from England.

All students in Wales

As in the rest of the country, from 2006:

⊙ All UK students from Wales or studying in Wales, along with EU students, will be able to take out a loan to cover fees while studying and pay it back when they start earning.

⊙ Fees will no longer be means-tested.

⊙ A means-tested maintenance grant will be available to all UK students but not those from the EU.

⊙Maintenance loans of up to £5620 (£6170 in London) will be available to UK students. Part of this will be means-tested on family income and how much maintenance grant you receive.

Northern Ireland – what's the deal?

Northern Ireland generally follows the same system as in England (see Chapter 2), but there are a few differences.

1 The maintenance grant is much higher in Northern Ireland (£3200) than in England (£2700). It is non-repayable and, of course, means-tested. But, as you will see from the chart below, the amount of loan that students from lower-income families are able to take out is also reduced, so what you will have to spend will be the same as your English counterparts, except you will have less loan debt. Once the family income reaches £30,000 the available grant is the same as in England.

| Maintenance grants and loans – assuming student is living away from home and not studying in London | | | |
Income	Grant	Maintenance loan	Total
£17,500	£3200	£2705	£5905
£20,000	£2644	£2844	£5488
£23,000	£1978	£3011	£4988
£25,000	£1534	£3121	£4655
£26,000	£1200	£3205	£4405
£30,000	£832	£3573	£4405

2 New students from Northern Ireland starting courses in the Republic of Ireland in September 2006, where the funding system is quite different from in the UK, will have their registration fee (€775, 2005/06 rate) paid by their ELB (Education and Library Board), and will be eligible for a Higher Education Bursary and maintenance loan for the balance of their support based on the support offered to existing students.

3 Extra help if in a sticky situation: Support Funds are available through your university in Northern Ireland. These operate in a similar way to the Access to Learning Fund in the UK. See page 59 for details.

Students from abroad – what will it cost, who will pay?

EU students

EU students will be treated on a similar basis to UK counterparts regarding fees.

⊙If studying in England or Northern Ireland you will be expected to pay up to £3000 pa towards your fees.

⊙If studying in Wales you will pay £1200 this year (2006–2007) and will receive a fee grant of up to £1800 next year (2007–2008) when top-up fees are introduced. This will in effect keep your fees down to £1200. (See page 81.)

⊙ If studying in Scotland you will pay no fees, but you will pay an endowment of around £2250 on completing your course.

All EU students will be able to take out a loan to cover their fees or endowment payment and then pay them off gradually once they graduate.

EU students are not entitled to apply for a maintenance loan or a maintenance bursary.

Non-EU 'overseas' students

Even though most UK students pay fees, the full cost of a course is subsidised by the government. Students from countries outside the EU will be charged the full cost of the course and can legally be charged higher tuition fees than UK students – so for a first-degree course you can think in terms of:

⊙ Arts course/classroom: £8100
⊙ Science-based course: £9900
⊙ Clinical course: £20,100.

(Figures are averages for the year 2005–2006.)

You will not be eligible for a fee loan, a maintenance loan or grant or any help with funding. Some universities do give bursaries to overseas students, and some charities have special funds for overseas students. See Chapter 6, page 162.

Fee rates for postgraduates can be higher (see page 174). Most universities and colleges do have a designated overseas adviser whom you could ask for help.

For details on living in the UK try the educational enquiry service at the British Council Information Centre (Bridgewater House, 58 Whitworth Street, Manchester M1 6BB; tel: 0161 957 7755; email: general.enquiries@britishcouncil.org; website: www.britishcouncil.org) or UKCOSA (website: www.ukcosa.org.uk; Advisory Service tel: 020 7107 9922 – open 1pm–4pm Monday–Friday), whose Council for International Education handles around 10,000 enquiries from students a year. Otherwise, try the British Council, High Commission or Embassy in your own country. A booklet called *Investing in the Future: Help with Tuition Fees for European Union Students* is available from the DfES Publications Centre (see page 75 for contact details).

'Please give EU students loans and sponsorship – we need help too!'
Christopher, Physics student, Oxford

It's a fact!

45,125 students from overseas were accepted onto degree courses in UK universities in 2005 – up by 4.3% on the previous year.

(UCAS figures)

Refugees and asylum seekers – what help is there?

Very little!

If you have the right qualifications, and can afford it, you are free to apply to any UK university. But any funding, and how much you must pay, will depend on your immigration status and how long you have been in the UK. Most refugees and asylum seekers do not qualify for funding and are considered 'overseas' students. (See previous page.)

If you have already lived in the UK for three years, funding concessions are occasionally available, but don't expect it.

★	countries sending students		
TOP TEN	**to study in the UK**		
Country	2005	2004	Change
China	4885	6324	−22.8%
Ireland	3177	3384	−6.1%
Nigeria	3097	1925	+60.9%
France	2188	2149	+1.8%
Hong Kong	2145	2202	−2.6%
Germany	2001	1722	+16.2%
Malaysia	1878	2076	−9.5%
Cyprus	1730	1332	+29.9%
Greece	1499	1552	−3.4%
India	1365	1214	+12.4%
Pakistan	1365	1230	+11.0%
(UCAS application figures for 2005)			

However, if you are granted full refugee status, then you will be eligible for the same funding as UK students – see previous chapter. If you have already started your degree studies and your immigration status changes it is important to tell your university as soon as possible. You must apply for any support within four months.

So where can refugees and asylum seekers not entitled to funding find help?

⊙ Some universities offer bursaries to students from overseas – see *University Scholarships and Awards* by Brian Heap, published by Trotman.

⊙ There are many trusts and charities in this country that have funds to help students from overseas – see Chapter 6.

⊙ Check out the following websites: www.info-for-asylumseekers.org.uk; www.heran.org.uk; www.ukcosa.org.uk; www.refugeecouncil.org.uk.

'You think you've got it hard. As an overseas student I get no government support and I'm working my ass off to support myself.'
Connie, a Physics student at Imperial College London, earns £84 a week during term time and £175 a week during vacations as a Sales Assistant

Courses with a difference

Sandwich/industrial placement

Will I have to pay fees during my industrial placement?

Yes. Whether it is a thick or thin sandwich placement, all students will have to pay fees. Those who spend an entire year of a course on a industrial/sandwich placement at home or abroad will have to pay reduced fees. For those already on a university course the figure for 2006–2007 is likely to be £600, which is about 50% of the current fee. Top-up-fee students will find that universities can set their own figure, and many universities are still making up their mind what to ask. Loughborough, for example, said it was unlikely to be much more than the figure asked of current students, and certainly nowhere near 50%. The University of Central Lancashire has set a figure of 20% of the top-up fee, which works out at about £600. But why, you might ask, do you have to pay fees when you are not enjoying the advantage of university? This is said to be a contribution towards the cost to the institution of administrative and pastoral arrangements relating to the placement. If the placement is for less than a full year, full fees will be charged of up to £3000 pa (£1200 in the case of current students). You may apply for a fee loan (see page 37) and also for a maintenance loan (see page 43). If you are on a full year's industrial training you will only be eligible for the reduced rate of loan – see rates below.

	Full year	Final year
London	£3030	£2320
Elsewhere	£2160	£1680
Parental home	£1620	£1230
Overseas	£2585	£1885

(Rates for 2005–2006)

I'm a part-time student – will I get a grant?

Yes. Part-time students in England and Wales doing 50% or more of a full-time course can apply for an income-assessed fee grant towards fees and a course grant to help with travel and books. Both are means-tested.

Course	Fee grant max available	Course grant max available	Max total support
50–59% of the full-time course	£750	£250	£1000
60–74% of the full-time course	£900	£250	£1150
75%+ of the full-time course	£1125	£250	£1375

There are around 500,000 part-timers in higher education in England, and the government expects around 85,000 to benefit from this financial package.

I'm going to take a foundation course – will I get funding?

Some courses include a preliminary or foundation year. These are designed to prepare students for study in their chosen subject if their qualifications or experience is not sufficient to start a degree-level course of study. The same support is available to students on a foundation year as for undergraduates if, and this is crucial, the following conditions are met:

⦿ The foundation year is an integral part of the course

⦿ The course as a whole is eligible for student support

⦿ You enrol for the whole course and not just the foundation year.

For full details of funding, see page 33 (England), page 78 (Scotland), page 80 (Wales) and page 82 (Northern Ireland).

It's a fact!

The number of students who started foundation degrees in 2005 was up by a massive 42%, from 6227 in 2004 to 8870. Most popular courses: Design Studies, Computer Science and Sports Science (UCAS figures).

Some universities charge lower fees for foundation courses.

Attending a private higher education institution

From September 2006, students attending a private higher education institution which has been designated by the DfES should be able to take out a loan to cover fees of up to £3000. This will not be means-tested. It may not be enough to completely cover your fees, as these can be higher than in other types of universities. You may also be able to take out a maintenance loan and could be eligible for a maintenance grant. Non-means-tested grants are no longer available. The course could cover any topic – Theology and Complementary Medicine for example. See also the Dance and Drama entry on page 89.

Healthcare courses

What's the package for those taking nursing and midwifery courses?

You will not have to pay fees and will receive a non-repayable, non-means-tested bursary, providing you have been accepted for an NHS-funded place. If you receive a bursary you will not be able to apply for a student loan.

England and Wales

Bursary rates for nursing and midwifery DipHE courses for 2005–2006, based on 45 weeks' attendance:

- Studying in London: £6859
- Elsewhere: £5837
- Living in parental home: £5837.

Scotland and Northern Ireland

Bursary rates for nursing and midwifery DipHE courses for 2005 –2006, based on 45 weeks' attendance:

	Scotland	Northern Ireland
Under 26 years	£5845	£5495
26 years and over	£6580	£6185

I'm taking an allied health professional course – what support is there for me?

The UK health authorities pay the fees of full- and part-time pre-registration students on courses in: Audiology, Chiropody, Dental Hygiene, Dental Therapy, Dietetics, Occupational Therapy, Orthoptics, Physiotherapy, Prosthetics, Radiography, and Speech and Language Therapy. A maintenance bursary is available, but means-tested on family income. It is, however, a bursary and not a loan, so what you get is non-repayable. You will also be able to apply for a lower-rate student loan to make up the balance of your living costs, and you may be eligible for help from the Access to Learning Fund (see Chapter 2, page 59).

Bursary and loan rates					
	Bursary rates			Reduced loan rates	
	England/ Wales	Scotland	N. Ireland	England/Wales/ N. Ireland	Scotland
London	£2837	£2810	£2700	£3030	£2605
Living away from home	£2309	£2280	£2195	£2160	£2105
Living in parents' home	£1889	£1735	£1790	£1620	£1615

Extra allowances may be available for older students, overseas students, single parents, those who have dependants, or students who incur clinical placement costs.

Medical and dental students – is there any extra help?

England, Wales, Northern Ireland, Scotland

Medical and dental students who are on standard five- or six-year courses will be treated as any other student in that area for the first four years of their course and have to pay the fees required. Those from outside Scotland who are studying in

Scotland will be charged standard fees of £2700. Scottish students studying in Scotland will not be charged fees. See page 80 for fees in Wales. In your fifth and any subsequent years, funding will be provided by the NHS, which means your tuition fees will be paid and you will be eligible to apply for a means-tested NHS bursary and a reduced maintenance loan from the Student Loans Company (see details on allied health professionals above).

If you live in England and want to study in Scotland, Wales or Northern Ireland the NHS Student Grants Unit will assess and pay your bursary.

If you live in Scotland, Wales or Northern Ireland and want to study in England you should consult the relevant national authorities.

Graduates taking the four-year accelerated course in medicine for graduates should see Chapter 7, page 188.

Other subjects

What's the deal for trainee teachers?

If you already have a degree and are considering a postgraduate course of initial teacher training (ITT) turn to Chapter 7, page 188, for details of the new incentive package that is being introduced. You could be in for a nice surprise.

There are no special incentives for undergraduates any more. Undergraduate trainee teachers receive the same funding as other students – sorry!

Trainee teachers in Wales

In Wales there's a special deal called the Secondary Undergraduate Placement Grant, which is available on an annual basis to support you during schoolteacher training experience. £1000 will be paid to undergraduate students who are on a secondary Initial Teacher Training course specialising in one of the secondary shortage subjects (which are: Design and Technology, English (including Drama), Information Technology, Maths, Modern Languages, Music, RE, Sciences and Welsh). A grant of £600 will be paid on an annual basis to those on other secondary subject courses. Small hardship grants are also available for those who get into unforeseen difficulties that might prevent them completing their course. Postgraduates see Chapter 7 page 187 for more funding information.

Special bursaries for physics students

To increase the number of students studying physics, especially amongst those who would not traditionally choose it as a subject to study, the Institute of Physics is offering 300 new bursaries a year. Each student would normally receive £1000 pa for the duration of their course. Where degrees differ from the standard UK three-year Bachelor's and four-year integrated Master's (in Scotland for example), the overall amount awarded would be £3000 for a BSc and £4000 for an MPhys/MSci.

The bursaries are not necessarily aimed at the high-flyers and not all physics students will receive one. Universities will allocate the bursaries, and will select the students who receive them according to certain criteria, such as financial hardship, coming from a school with a poor record of university entrance, or being a mature student with a family. Academic performance will be used as a deciding factor only when the number of deserving candidates outstrips the number of awards available in a university. Physics bursaries will be given in addition to any other grant or bursary students are entitled to receive, and will not replace them. Bursaries are also available to part-time students on a pro rata basis. To find out more, talk to the university where you want to study.

I'm taking a degree in Social Work – can I get a bursary?

A Social Work bursary is available to undergraduates taking a degree in Social Work (full-time or part-time) who are normally resident in England. The bursary is non-income-assessed, which means that earnings, savings, and other sources of income such as LA grants and university bursaries, are not taken into consideration. Funding includes a grant of up to £2900 depending on: individual circumstances; the reimbursement of certain expenses relating to practice learning opportunities; and possible help with tuition fees. At the time of going to press, the level of tuition fee support for 2006–2007 has not been decided.

For full details on eligibility criteria, financial values and an explanation of the application process, download an application pack from www.gscc.org.uk, email bursaries@gscc.org.uk or call the Bursaries Customer Service Team on 020 7397 5835.

I want to study Dance and Drama – will I get funding?

A majority of accredited Dance and Drama courses at private HE institutions offer some form of funding to help with fees and living expenses.

If you are offered a state-funded place on a higher education course then you should be eligible for the same funding as students on degree courses. RADA, the Guildhall School of Music and Drama, the Central School of Speech and Drama, Bristol Old Vic Theatre School, Rose Bruford College and many other institutions fall into that category. (See previous chapter.)

If you are offered a place as a private student by your college and it is not funded you will have to pay the full cost of the private tuition fee. For those who do not receive an award, a three-year course (including living costs) could set you back £50,000. However, you should still contact your LA (or the SLC) for details of how to apply for help as a private student on a designated course, as some might be available. While Higher Education courses in Dance or Drama no longer offer Dance and Drama Awards (having introduced the 'state-funded places' scheme), awards are given by 20 performing arts schools. Competition for all these awards is very fierce – not all students who achieve a place will receive an award.

Not all accredited courses attract government funding, so if funding is essential, check the status of a course before you start applying. The DfES booklet *A Guide to Vocational*

Training in Dance and Drama is full of useful information including a full guide to funding. Phone 0845 602 2260 or see www.dfes.gov.uk/studentsupport/dancedrama.

Additional help

I'm a mature student/independent/married; is there any special funding or advice for me?

An independent student is someone who no longer lives with their parents, has been working for at least three years, or is over 25. As an independent student you are entitled to the general funding package for students (see Chapter 2 or the beginning of this chapter if you're based in Scotland or Wales) and you can earn up to £17,500 before you start losing any of your funding benefits. There is no age limit on taking out a fee loan, and the cut-off point for taking a maintenance loan is now 60. If you are married, or living with someone in a stable relationship, your partner's income may well be means-tested if you apply for a maintenance loan.

It's a fact!

The number of mature students starting a degree in UK universities in 2005 was up by 6.2%. (UCAS figures)

If I become a student will I still receive benefits such as income support?

In order that students receiving benefits such as income support or housing benefits can still receive these payments, a new non-repayable Special Support Grant has been introduced of up to £2700 pa. This works in a similar way to the Maintenance Grant (see Chapter 2, page 41) – it is given to low-income families. If you receive the Special Support Grant you will not be eligible for the Maintenance Grant.

I have children to support – are there any other allowances, grants and bursaries I could apply for?

⊙ A new non-repayable Special Support Grant of up to £2700 a year is available for new full-time students who are eligible for benefits such as Income Support or Housing Benefit while they are studying. Main beneficiaries are likely to be lone parents, other student parents and students with disabilities. The grant is based on household income and does not have to be paid back. If you're eligible for the Special Support Grant you will not be eligible for the Maintenance Grant. This will not affect any university bursary you are offered.

⊙ The Parents' Learning Allowance: up to £1400 pa for help with course-related costs for students with dependent children. Income is assessed.

⊙ Childcare Grant: up to £148.75 a week for one child and £255 for two or more.

Amount given based on 85% of actual childcare costs. Paid in three instalments by the Student Loans Company but does not have to be repaid.

⊙ Child Tax Credit: available to students with dependent children and paid by the Inland Revenue. Students receiving the maximum amount will be entitled to free school meals for their children. Amount you get will depend on circumstances. Call 0845 300 3900 for more details or contact www.inlandrevenue.gov.uk/taxcredits and check out how much you could get.

⊙ Adult Dependants' Grant: up to £2455 pa for full-time students with adult dependants. Paid in three instalments.

⊙ Access to Learning Fund: see page 59. Universities generally look very favourably on mature students when allocating access funds.

I'm disabled and I want to go into higher education – can I get extra help?

There are a number of ways you can get extra help, depending on your disability. If you follow up every lead offered here, it's going to take time, but the results could be well worth while.

What's the starting point for somebody who's disabled?

First choose your course, then choose the university or college where you would like to study. Next check out the college facilities, and their ability to cope with your specific disability, by:

1 Writing for details of facilities
2 Visiting suitable institutions
3 Having a 'special needs' interview with the institution.

Then fill in your UCAS application.

When should I start getting organised?

It's a good idea to start getting organised in the summer term of your first A level year, as you may have to revise your choice of institution several times.

What financial help can I expect from my local authority?

Like most students on full-time higher education courses in this country, as a disabled student you would be eligible for the full financial support package for students described in the previous chapter.

I am severely disabled – can I get a student loan?

Yes. As an undergraduate you would be eligible for a student loan. In fact, the regulations laid down when the Student Loans Company was set up allow for the loans administrator to delay the start of repayment for people with disabilities, and any disability-related financial entitlements you receive will be disregarded when calculating your repayment amounts. Phone the Student Loans Company helpline free on 0845 607 7577.

Can I apply to the *Access to Learning* Fund?

Yes. Each institution decides its own criteria for payments – there are no set rules. You might find being disabled gives you more entitlement (see details on page 59).

What extra money is available for disabled students?

There are Disabled Students' Allowances (DSAs) for full- and part-time students, which offer support to those with a disability or specific learning difficulty such as dyslexia.

There are four Disabled Students' Allowances (2006–2007 figures):

1 Up to £12,135 per year for non-medical personal help – eg readers, lip-speakers, note-takers. Up to £9105 if studying part-time.
2 Up to £4795 for the whole course for specialist course equipment – eg computer, word-processor, Braille printer, radio microphone, induction loop system.
3 A general Disabled Students' Allowance – up to £1605 pa (£1200 for part-time study) for minor items such as tapes, Braille paper, extra use of phone.
4 Extra travel costs incurred as a result of your disability.

Distance learning

Full-time undergraduates who cannot attend their course because of their disability will be eligible for full-time student support in addition to DSAs.

Can I get help with travel?

The loan for students includes a set amount for transport costs (£285) – as a disabled student you can claim for extra travel expenses incurred over this amount if your disability means, for example, that you are unable to use public transport and must travel by taxi (see point 4 above).

What about Social Security benefits?

Most full-time students are not entitled to benefits such as Income Support and Housing Benefit. However, such benefits can be available to students in vulnerable groups such as students with disabilities, but the situation is complicated. The people to put you in the picture are your Jobcentre/JobcentrePlus or Skill: The National Bureau for Students with Disabilities (see page 100); alternatively phone the Benefits Inquiry line on 0800 882200; minicom users 0800 243355. Opening hours: 8.30am–6.30pm Monday–Friday; 9am–1pm Saturday.

Can I get a Disability Living Allowance?

Yes. This allowance is available to you as a student. It provides funds on a weekly basis for those who need help with mobility – eg the cost of operating a wheelchair or the hire or purchase of a car. It also covers those who need care and assistance with any physical difficulties such as washing or eating, or continual supervision. The allowance will not affect your Disabled Students' Allowances in any way. See previous question for people to contact.

Studying abroad

I have to spend part of my course studying abroad – will I get extra help?

Yes, but it will be a loan. If you study abroad for at least eight weeks as part of your course you are eligible for an overseas rate of loan, which for 2006–2007 is £5255 max (£4578 for final-year students).

Don't forget, if you spend a year away in another country you will still have to pay reduced fees of around £600 unless you're on an Erasmus exchange (see page 94).

Scotland: pay rates differ by country so you might get more or less than the stated figure.

My course abroad is longer than my course in the UK – can I get more money?

Yes. The rate given is worked out on a year of only 30 weeks and 3 days. If you need to stay longer, you can increase your loan.

The rate for 2006–2007 is £107 per week (rates may differ in Scotland).

'Students who have a compulsory study period abroad can get into serious financial difficulties. Nobody warns you of the cost of this before you choose a course such as European Studies and Modern Languages.'
3rd year French and Russian student

It's going to cost me a lot more to fly to Tokyo than to take a train to Leeds – can I get any help with travel?

Yes, but not for the full fare. Your loan already includes some travel element (£285 in England/Wales), and this will be taken into consideration in calculating how much you receive. It is probably best to let your local authority calculate what you are entitled to. Remember when putting in for costs to give all the facts – the journey from your home to the airport costs something, too.

Is there any other help for students who want to study abroad?

Two organisations have been set up to assist students wanting to study in the EU:

⊙ Erasmus (sometimes known as Socrates-Erasmus), the European Community Action Scheme for the Mobility of University Students, is designed to encourage greater co-operation between universities and other higher educational institutions in Europe. Under this scheme students taking courses, including foreign languages, in other European countries may be given a grant towards extra expenses while studying abroad for a period of 3 to 12 months. These could include travel expenses, language courses, or living and accommodation costs. If you're part of this scheme you should also be exempt from paying the reduced fees that sandwich students taking a year out have to pay. This is around £600. For more details phone 01227 762712, email info@erasmus.ac.uk or visit www.erasmus.ac.uk.

⊙ The Leonardo da Vinci scheme provides opportunities for university students and recent graduates to undertake periods of vocational training of up to 12 months with organisations in other member states; placements are largely technology based. While individual employers will provide any salary, the Leonardo scheme can make a contribution towards language tuition and expenses. For more details phone 020 7289 4157.

Who to contact

Funding from these organisations is arranged mainly through your university or college. They should have full information and should therefore be your first point of call. Otherwise, contact the European Commission (8 Storey's Gate, London SW1P 3AT).

What happens if I get sick while studying abroad?

Don't wait until you get sick: take out health insurance cover before you go. (See information about travel insurance on page 138.) Your local authority will probably reimburse the costs of health insurance, providing they consider it 'economical'. Check out the situation with them first. If you are going abroad as part of your course, seek advice from your university; they will know the score. You may have to pay a social security charge. (See page 96, 'Focus on three popular places for studying abroad'.) Remember, above all else, to hold on to your receipts. Without those you are unlikely to get reimbursement from your local authority.

If you have to take out medical insurance, you can also get help to cover the cost of the insurance.

Can I study for my whole degree abroad?

You can, but it's not going to be cheap because you won't be entitled to a student loan. But you may not have to pay fees. If you go to an EU country, as a resident of the UK you will be treated like the students in that country and will normally pay no tuition fees. In most European countries higher education institutions do not charge tuition fees; if they do, then they are generally set at a nominal rate.

But a number of universities do have registration fees, and there are additional health and personal insurance costs, students' union fees and other expenses to consider. Many countries have special concessions for their students, ie concessionary rates for meals, transport and accommodation. As an EU student you would benefit from these.

The most expensive part of your stay will be maintenance costs, and because you are not taking any part of your course in the UK, you will not be eligible for the student loan.

Living costs

These vary depending on where you are studying. As in the UK, capital cities are more expensive places to live than country towns.

When it comes to the price of food in the EU, the UK is amongst the more expensive places. If you are thinking of studying further afield than Europe, the cost factor is appreciably higher as it is unlikely that you will get your fees covered for a full degree course, and travel will be a major expense.

Will studying abroad be very different?

Every country has its own particular approach to study and its own characteristics. In Europe, for instance, individual universities tend to cater for a greater number of students. Lecture classes and seminars are more crowded and there is a greater dependence on printed course material. There is less contact between tutor and student and the system generally is more impersonal.

Another major difference is the exams. Often there is a greater reliance on oral examinations. In Italy, for example, the majority of the exams are oral. While this tends to give students additional self-confidence and make them more articulate, it is something new to UK students and something they need to get accustomed to.

European students are more inclined to attend their local university, and many live at home. As a result, universities do not provide the wide range of social and recreational facilities you would expect to find at a UK university. Students use the facilities of the local city or town, which can be expensive.

Tip from a student

'The fourth year of my degree is in France. Even though I don't need a student loan at the moment, I have taken it out and put it in a high-interest account because I know I will want to travel once I get to Europe.'

1st year Chemistry student, Imperial College, London

The universities of Europe are often situated in fine old towns and in regions you will want to explore, which again will be a drain on your (limited) resources.

'My third year was spent abroad, but I still had to pay half tuition fees – for what? It's outrageous!'
4th year Languages student, Durham

Focus on three popular places for studying abroad

(Please note: all figures are approximate.)

France

You need to prove you have sufficient resources to maintain yourself while studying in France. Minimum threshold level is about €5160, with a minimum of €430 a month, but this will be barely enough to cover your living expenses. What are these likely to be?

⊙ Annual cost of a course: €150–€900 in a public institution and €3000 to €7000 in a private university
⊙ Accommodation: €150 in the university, €300 for a studio in the city
⊙ Food: €215
⊙ Transport: €20
⊙ Course charge: €92
⊙ Telephone: €30.

For the first month it is estimated that you will need around €1500. This will cover:

⊙ First month's rent: €150–€300
⊙ Deposit for lodgings (2 months): up to €600
⊙ Annual insurance for lodgings: €50
⊙ Social security: €180
⊙ Health insurance: €70–€285 depending on risk taken.

Scholarships: very few available. Try the Entente Cordiale Scholarships for Postgraduates. Contact: the French Embassy in London. Helpful website: www.cnous.fr.

Germany

A degree in Germany takes between four and six years so you must anticipate a long stay. Each year is divided into two semesters. The first hurdle is registration: this gives you that all-important student card which will entitle you to special rates on local transport, reduced rates for cultural events and use of the refectory. While tuition in universities is free, foreign students need to prove they have sufficient funds for their stay – up to €700 per month in the former West Germany, €537 in the former East. As a rule, higher education institutions and international visitors' registration offices will require you to prove you have at least €466 per month for living costs. Though EU students are allowed to work in Germany this is not a good way to fund your studies, as unemployment is high at the moment. Expenses will include:

⊙ Contribution to university services: €18–€46 per semester
⊙ Semester ticket: for travel (some universities) €92 approx.
⊙ Matriculation fee: (some states) €55 per semester
⊙ Student-rate statutory health insurance: around €281 per semester
⊙ Halls of residence: €75–€225 per month; accommodation is difficult to find since German universities do not generally have a campus system
⊙ Rent of room/flat in public sector: €155–€310 per month
⊙ Study materials: depending on course, €230–€300 per semester, possibly more.

Scholarships: German institutions do not generally award scholarships and grants. The most extensive scholarship programme is organised by the German Academic Exchange Service (DAAD) but only for postgraduates.

United States

Students are responsible for paying both their fees and living expenses. These vary enormously depending on individual colleges and whether they are state- or privately run. Tuition fees range from around $1500 to $35,000, with books and equipment adding sometimes as much as $2000 pa. On top of that you have living costs, which could add another $4000–$14,000 to your bill each nine-month academic year. You will also need money for travel from the UK and back, health insurance and personal expenses. Some financial aid is granted: in most institutions it is based on academic merit, though some colleges may give funding based on need. Full scholarships are rare. Because of this, students often have jobs during term time and work their way through college. Students can work on campus for up to 20 hours a week, but this cannot be listed as a source of income for visa applications. Other forms of funding include scholarships for special talents such as athletics. (Contact the Fulbright Commission, 62 Doughty Street, London WC1N 2JZ. Tel: 020 7404 6994. Fax: 020 7404 6874. Email: education@fulbright.co.uk. See also their website: www.fulbright.co.uk.) Special loans are available for all students.

Many universities in the USA are vast and can resemble small cities, with their own post office, grocery stores and shopping centres; they can dominate the local community and its economy. The US does not have a system like UCAS, so all applications must be sent directly to individual colleges. This can be expensive: the application fee (non-refundable) is $30–$90 for each university, and you may be charged for prospectuses and test applications. A College Day Fair is held in London when you can meet over 100 representatives from US universities.

Other locations in brief

The following information is taken from *Study Abroad*, compiled by the International Bureau of Education at UNESCO and by UNESCO's Division of Higher Education 2004–2005.

Australia

⊙ Expenses vary depending on course of study, institution and location.
⊙ Fees: A$7000–A$10,000 (eg Economics, Law); A$20,000 (eg Medicine, Science, Engineering).
⊙ Accommodation, travel, entertainment and board: A$7000–A$14,000.
⊙ Medical insurance: A$275 pa approx.

Russian Federation

One year's study on a contract basis: US$1500–US$7500 depending on subject and lodging arrangements. Foreign students can be eligible for monthly grant under intergovernmental agreements.

Bermuda

If you fancy somewhere warm and exotic like Bermuda, expect to pay around:

⊙ Tuition: Bermuda$3300
⊙ Accommodation/board: Bermuda$4000
⊙ Books: Bermuda$500.

Further information

Full information about fees, maintenance grants and loans

⊙ England: *A Guide to Financial Support for Higher Education Students in 2006/07* (which is the source for the loan statistics in this book), Department for Education and Skills (DfES) Publications Centre. (Braille and cassette editions also available.) Tel: 0800 731 9133 (general enquiries: 01325 392822). Fax: 0845 603 3360. Website: www.dfes.gov.uk/studentsupport.

⊙ Scotland: *Student Support in Scotland: A Guide for Undergraduate Students 2005/6*, available from any Scottish university or the Student Awards Agency for Scotland (SAAS), 3 Redheughs Rigg, South Gyle, Edinburgh EH12 9YT. Tel: 0131 476 8212. Email: saas.geu@scotland.gsi.gov.uk. Website: www.student-support-saas.gov.uk.

⊙ Northern Ireland: *Financial Support for Students in Higher Education 2005/6*. Student Support Branch, Department for Employment and Learning (Northern Ireland), Rathgael House, Balloo Road, Bangor, Co. Down BT19 7PR. Tel: 028 9025 7710. Website: www.delni.gov.uk/index.htm.

⊙ Wales: National Assembly for Wales, Higher Education Division 2, 3rd floor, Cathays Park, Cardiff CF10 3NQ. Tel: 029 2082 5831. Fax: 029 2082 5823. Website: www.learning.wales.gov.uk.

NHS

⊙ NHS Bursaries in England: NHS Student Grants Unit, 22 Plymouth Road, Blackpool FY3 7JS. Tel: 01253 655655. Courses helpline for England: 0845 606 0655. Website: www.nhscareers.nhs.uk/home.html.

⦿ NHS Bursaries in Wales: NHS Student Awards Unit, 2nd floor, Golate House, 101 St Mary's Street, Cardiff CF10 1DX. Tel: 029 2026 1495. Helpline 8045 606 0655.

⦿ NHS Bursaries in Scotland: Student Awards Agency for Scotland, 3 Redheughs Rigg, South Gyle, Edinburgh EH12 9HH. Tel: 0131 476 8227.

⦿ NHS Bursaries in Northern Ireland: Department of Health, Social Services and Public Safety, Human Resources Directorate, D1.4, Castle Buildings, Stormont, Belfast BT4 3SL. Tel: 028 9052 0699.

EU students

⦿ For information on tuition fees for European Union students, plus other information, contact: EU Customer Services Team, Room 38, Mowden Hall, Darlington, Co. Durham DL3 9BG. Tel: 0141 243 3570 (10am–4pm). Email: EU_Team@slc.co.uk. Website: www.studentfinancedirect.co.uk/EU.

⦿ UK Socrates-Erasmus. Address: Rothford, Giles Lane, Canterbury, Kent CT2 7LR. Tel: 01227 762712. Fax: 01227 762711. Email: info@erasmus.ac.uk. Website: www.erasmus.ac.uk.

⦿ Leonardo da Vinci: check with your university or college.

⦿ *Investing in the Future – Financial Support for EU Students,* from DfES Publications Department. Tel: 0845 602 2260.

Students from abroad studying in the UK

⦿ *Studying in the UK: Sources of Funding for International Students*, available free from UKCOSA. Download from www.ukcosa.org.uk. Student advice line: 020 7107 9922, open Monday to Friday 1pm–4pm.

⦿ *UCAS Instructions for Completion of the Application Form by International Students*. Free from UCAS with your application form.

⦿ Useful contact for funding enquiries: British Council Information Centre. Tel: 0161 957 7755. Ask for the Education Information Centre. Email: general.enquries@britishcouncil.org. Or call in at their London drop-in centre at 10 Spring Gardens, London SW1A 2BN, where you will find access to a website (www.educationuk.org) giving full information about courses. Or you can write to the British Council at Bridgewater House, 58 Whitworth Street, Manchester M1 6BB.

⦿ *A Guide to Studying and Living in Britain*: full of practical advice. Published by How to Books. Available from Trotman, tel: 0870 900 2665, or visit the website www.trotman.co.uk/bookshop.

Refugees and asylum seekers

Check out the following websites:

⦿ www.info-for-asylumseekers.org.uk

⦿ www.heran.org.uk

⦿ www.ukcosa.org.uk

⦿ www.refugeecouncil.org.uk.

Mature students

⦿ *Returning to Education: A practical Handbook for Adult Learners*. Published by How to Books. Available from Trotman, tel: 0870 900 2665 or visit www.trotman.co.uk/bookshop.

⦿ *Mature Students' Directory*, Published by Trotman. To order, tel: 0870 900 2665 or visit the website www.trotman.co.uk/bookshop.

Disabled students

⦿ Students' Welfare Officer at your university or college, students' union, local Citizens Advice Bureau.

⦿ Skill: National Bureau for Students with Disabilities. It runs a special information and advice service open Tuesday 11.30am–1.30pm and Thursday 1.30pm–3.30pm, tel: 0800 328 5050, and also publishes a number of useful leaflets (free to students) and books for the disabled. From Chapter House, 18–20 Crucifix Lane, London SE1 3JW. Or available on website. Minicom users: 0800 068 2422. Email: info@skill.org.uk. Website: www.skill.org.uk. Fax: 020 7450 0650.

⦿ Benefits Agency or JobCentre/JobCentrePlus: address should be in your local telephone directory.

⦿ Royal National Institute for the Blind, RNIB Education and Employment Service, 105 Judd St, London WC1H 9NE. Helpline open: Monday–Friday 9am–5pm. Tel: 0845 766 9999. Email: helpline@rnib.org.uk. Website: rnib.org.uk.

⦿ Royal National Institute for Deaf People, 19–23 Featherstone Street, London EC1Y 8SL. Tel: 0808 808 0123. Minicom: 0808 808 9000. Fax: 020 7296 8199. Email: informationline@rnid.org.uk. Website: www.rnid.org.uk.

⦿ *Bridging the Gap: A Guide to the Disabled Students' Allowances*, Students' Support Division 1, Room 215, Mowden Hall, Staindrop Road, Darlington DL3 9BG. Tel: 0800 731 9133. Textphone: 0800 328 8988. Fax: 0845 603 3360. Also available from www.dfes.gov.uk/studentsupport/formsandguides/index.shtml.

⦿ *The Disabled Student's Guide to University*, published by Trotman. To order, tel: 0870 900 2665 or visit www.trotman.co.uk/bookshop.

Students from the UK studying abroad

⦿ *Study Abroad*, UNESCO publication, available from the Stationery Office. New edition for 2004/5. TSO, PO Box 29, Norwich NR3 1GN. Tel: 020 7873 0011.

⦿ *Getting into American Universities*, published by Trotman. To order, tel: 0870 900 2665 or visit www.trotman.co.uk/bookshop.

⦿ *You Want to Study Where?! The pros and cons of studying abroad*, published by Trotman. To order, tel: 0870 900 2665 or visit www.trotman.co.uk/bookshop.

4

Paying your way

Work experience, working abroad, a year out, travel

Why do students work?

There are many reasons why students work, either before or during their study course. In this chapter we investigate some of those reasons and give advice on what sort of work you can expect to find; how to go about getting it; who to contact; and what to read. There is also some helpful information on the travel scene, insurance and holidaying abroad, plus anecdotes from students about their experiences. But when all is said and done, the main reason why you would work is to ...

Make money to fund your degree

If you have read the first two chapters in this book, you will realise that what you are likely to get to finance you through university just isn't enough. A large number of students work, most from sheer financial necessity, and their aim is to earn as much as possible. Around 39% work during term time – on average 15 hours a week, but many students worked a lot more, according to a NatWest survey. Of these, 41% said they had skipped lectures because of work.

⊙ 78% of students said they would not be able to afford uni if they didn't work.
⊙ 88% of A level students expect to have to roll up their sleeves and work 15 hours a week to get through uni.
⊙ Average earnings were £4000 pa.
⊙ 41% said they thought their studies could be adversely affected because they had skipped lectures to earn money.

(NatWest Student Money Matters Survey 2005.)

Work during term time

Of those who worked during term time the Students' Money Matters Survey found:

⊙ 43% worked weekdays
⊙ 43% worked at weekends
⊙ 53% worked in the evenings.

We didn't ask for their final degree grades!

Should you/can you work during term time?

Most universities and colleges allow students to work during term time; in fact, many universities have set up job shops, so you could say they are actively encouraging it. But most suggest a limit on the number of hours you work during term time – generally 15 hours a week, though some say 10–12 and others 16.

The university students' union is a great source of work, giving job opportunities in students' union shops and bars. How many students actually work during term time varies between universities. Many universities just don't know. However, the following universities suggest:

University	Percentage of students who work
Dundee, Bath	20%
London, South Bank	25%
Aberdeen, Glasgow, Sheffield, Surrey	30%
Edinburgh, Staffordshire	35%
Brighton	43%
Aston, Coventry, Lincoln, Oxford Brookes, Slade	50%
Middlesex, Portsmouth, Northampton, Sheffield Hallam	60%
Gloucestershire, Sussex	70%
Hertfordshire	80%
Huddersfield (top of the list)	90%

Going against the trend are Oxford and Cambridge, where many (but not all) colleges actively forbid or strongly discourage students from working during term time, except perhaps if they work in the student bar. Since the Oxbridge term is just eight weeks, and as one lecturer pointed out 'very intensive weeks at that', perhaps the colleges have a point. (For full figures and information on individual universities, see *The Student Book 2006*, published by Trotman.)

How many hours do students work?		
Hours worked	2005	2004
Up to 5 hours	9%	6%
6–10 hours	24%	21%
11–15 hours	21%	24%
16–20 hours	27%	28%
21–25 hours	9%	10%
26–30 hours	4%	3%
Over 30 hours	3%	5%
		(NatWest Student Money Matters Survey 2005)

The tutor's view

'When it comes to work, academic staff attitudes vary from the positive to the negative. Obviously they would like it if students didn't have to work, but are realistic, especially with the introduction of fees. If you want to encourage students from diverse financial backgrounds, then you have got to be prepared to let them work.'
Co-ordinator of Student WorkPlace, the University of Manchester job shop

The students' view

'The necessity of finding part-time work means the quality of your college work suffers.'
PGCE student, Bangor

'Get a job with a good employer – for money, experience, skills and references.'
Final year Sociology student, Kent

'Part-time work teaches you discipline and keeps you from being in the bar every night.'
3rd year Sociology student, De Montfort

What are university job shops?

Among the most important innovations in recent years are university job shops. They can be found in most universities throughout the UK and more are opening all the time. They all seem to operate on their own individual system but have one thing in common – to find work for students during term time and the holidays. Pay is never less than the minimum wage, which is currently £4.25 (£4.45 from October 2006) for 18–21-year-olds and £5.05 (£5.35 from October 2006) for those over 22.

However, our research showed that, on average, students were earning £5.69 per hour.

★ student
TOP*TEN* **jobs**

Sales assistant/cashier

Barman/-maid

Waiter/-ress

Administration assistant

Support worker

Receptionist

Student/university representative

Officer Training Corps

Fitness instructor/leisure centre assistant/sports coach

Cleaner

Close-up on three job shops

Job shops come under a variety of names. There is Joblink at Aberdeen, Student Employment Service at Edinburgh, WorkStation at University College London, CUBE at Coventry and PULSE at Liverpool. All seem to have different ways of working.

Cardiff University's **Unistaff Jobshop** was one of the first job shops established in the country. It offers both a student employment agency and a JobCentre-style service with a 'drop-in/phone-in and see what we have available' attitude. It also emails all available jobs to the students on its books. Many companies are taking advantage of this value-for-money, effective service, which is just as well. By the end of the last academic year Unistaff had 4000 students on its books and it looks as if this is going to be its busiest year ever – registrations are up again, with over 2000 new students registering in the first two months of the new term. Jobs vary from bog-standard bar and data entry work to the more off-beat, such as planting lettuces and dressing up as Bart Simpson!

Southampton's **Careers Advisory Service (CAS)** has a free online vacancy service called 'e-jobs'. Up to 50 new vacancies come in weekly and a large number of students use the service. Types of jobs include IT, admin support, clerical, secretarial, nursing care, driving and teaching. Asked if they would accept any kind of job, Becki Davies, who works in the employer liaison team at the CAS, said: 'We have a vacancy code of practice and don't carry commission-only or pyramid-selling vacancies.' Students who have registered apply for jobs directly. Employers can also access the system to advertise jobs. The service is open to all undergraduate and postgraduate students. Just log on to www.careers.soton.ac.uk and register for e-jobs via the 'news and events' tab on the home page. How are unsuitable vacancies kept off the site? Becki has her finger firmly on the delete key and commission-only jobs at the local casino were trashed pretty smartly.

Student WorkPlace is the specialist work experience unit of the University of Manchester Careers Service. It handles all types of student work, including part-time jobs, industrial placements, vacation work and voluntary positions. Students can search vacancies online or register to receive appropriate vacancies by email. Around

Rebecca's story

It's just the most fantastic feeling to be sitting in your room with £1000 in notes spread out across your bed, and you are waiting for the garage to turn up with your new car – a metallic, silver, 5-door Peugeot 205 K-reg. Suddenly all the hard work seems worth it.

I decided back in the summer of my second year that I wanted a car. But raising the cash to buy it was only part of the story; I also needed £500 for insurance, and was trying to manage without taking out a loan.

All the summer I worked in a sports shop and at nights and days off as a bouncer. A job made to measure for a 5ft pint size like me.

Back at uni I worked in another sports shop and five nights a week in the uni bar, often working until 3am.

My lecturers weren't too pleased with the hours I was working. But once I had made it, I could afford to cut back a bit. The trouble was, I became addicted to work.

Rebecca graduated with a 2:1 in Leadership in Sport from Reading University.

200 jobs are advertised each month. Manchester students can also find information on around 60 company sponsors and over 100 national and international work experience schemes. Recent jobs included bone-mass-density technician, northern soul DJ, dog walker, gig reviewer, juice artist, mystery diners, countryside ranger and TV/film extra.

Does your university have a job shop?

Check it out as soon as you arrive. Jobs go very quickly. Most students want or need to take jobs during the long summer vacations. Your university job shop or that of a university closer to home may be able to help you here.

Thrift tips

'Potatoes and more potatoes – mixed with cheese, with ham, with butter – at least you're full.'

3rd year Egyptian Archaeology student, UCL

'Forget the gym – walk. You'll be fit and save a fortune.'

1st year Korean Studies student, Sheffield

'Cover your plates with cling film and save on the washing up.'

3rd year Forensic Science student, Wolverhampton

Cathryn's story

As an English student at Sussex University, Cathryn was looking for a well-paid summer vacation job. But what she found was an amazing experience and not what you might expect. She became the carer for a paraplegic. When asked why she wanted the job she answered, 'the money'. And in student terms it was good money: £6 an hour for a 24/7 week, every other week. Surprisingly, that was the right answer. Jacob, the young paraplegic, was just 23 and had recently graduated from Sussex University. He wanted someone who saw caring for him as a job, not a mission. Disabled for two years, having jumped into the wrong end of a swimming pool, he was now paralysed from the shoulders down. There was no time in Jacob's life for self-pity. He had a full social life and was an active member of a Youth Group. So for Cathryn this meant a hectic three months of meetings, social events and driving up and down to London: she even went with him to a summer camp in Wales. By the end, Jacob was a friend rather than a job, and still is. Through him she has met a whole new circle of friends. She earned around £3500 over the summer and enjoyed every moment of it. She found the job through the Sussex University job shop which, she says, has some fantastic and unusual well-paid jobs on offer. If caring isn't your scene, how does hot air balloon instructor – in France – grab you?

Term-time working can be fun, as Jono, a third-year student studying Innovative Manufacturing and Technology at Loughborough University, discovered, when he joined the OTC.

Jono's story

It was 3am, dark, cold and the middle of winter; I was sleeping in a ditch. A hand grabbed my shoulder and shook me violently – it was my turn to go on sentry duty, there was three inches of snow on the ground and we were under fire ...

If you want to earn money and have some fun, join the OTC (it's a kind of cop-out TA for students). There are field weekends once every five weeks, when you are paid £80 to crawl around in the cold and wet from Friday evening to Sunday with a gun in your hand shooting at the enemy (blanks of course).

All too often you'll be sleeping out in the open. If you're lucky, you can sling a hammock between two trees and kip down, but that's luxury. Snow isn't as bad as rain. One weekend it tipped it down for 48 hours non-stop, and it doesn't matter how waterproof your gear is: after ten hours of throwing yourself on the ground and getting into trees, you are soaked to the bone. That's when you start wondering what on earth you are doing there.

But believe me, it is cracking fun. You feel you've achieved something. It's the camaraderie, the challenge, often the sheer absurdity of it all. There are some fantastic expeditions, like parachute jumping in Cyprus. There was just one drawback – I was on work experience at the time and missed it!

Pay for students in the OTC is currently £34.31 per day for Officer Cadets and £54.23 per day as a Second Lieutenant (TA).

What work are students doing and how did they find it?

Students seeking evening or weekend work during term time will probably find it easier in a large city than in a small town. London students should fare better than most – which is just as well, since they are among the most financially stretched.

You are most likely to find work in bars, restaurants or general catering, dispatch-riding (must have your own wheels and a fearless mentality!), pizza delivery, office or domestic cleaning, childminding, market research, modelling, offices (temporary), hotels, and of course shops and supermarkets.

Here are a few examples of what students are doing, discovered by *Students' Money Matters*:

Type of work	How found job	Pay per hour	University
Nightclub	Job centre	£5.50	Essex
After-school kids' club	Caretaker's office at uni	£5	Sussex
National Trust admin	Temp agency	£6.50	Lancaster
Work with disabled	Relation	£7.50	UWE
Interior design	Relation	£5.20	Kingston
FC turnstile operator	Advert in programme	£7.50	Southampton
Cinema cashier		£5.28	Lancaster
College cleaner	College	£5.70	Oxford
Basketball coach	Interview	£10	Wolverhampton
University Air Squadron		£4.20	Liverpool
Door supervisor	Rugby team	£8	Luton
Language teacher	Contacts	£12	Sussex
Painter/finisher		£4.85	Lancaster
Scientific assistant	Internet	£5.35	APU
Tea packer	Word of mouth	£4.40	Cambridge
Bilingual customer service	Friend	£6.80	Strathclyde
Party planner		£5	Hull
Games technician	Advert	£4.50	Wolverhampton
Fire evacuation steward	Friend	£5	Liverpool
Campus theatre	Friend	£5.50	Southampton
Fund raiser	Job exchange	£5.88	Hull
Theatre – front of house	Advert	£5.83	Cardiff
Band musician	Created band	£50 (for a set)	Oxford
Furniture restorer	Job before uni	£5	Paisley
Art gallery	Previous employer	£5	Brighton
Piano teacher		£6.80 approx	Robert Gordon
Estate agent	Friend	£10	City
Web wizard	Local council	£12	Leicester
DJ		£10	Stirling
Gym instructor	Gym member	£5.57	Wolverhampton
Ironing	Imagination	£5	De Montfort
Internet shopper	Job shop	£5.50–£11	Hertfordshire
Bouncer	Students' union	£4.50	St Andrews
Dog walker	Offered	£5	Leeds Met

> ### Advice note
>
> DON'T LEAVE IT TOO LATE!
> If you want to work over the Christmas holidays, start planning early, even before you go up to uni – competition is high.

Further information

Who to contact

⊙ University job shop
⊙ Employment agencies
⊙ Job centres
⊙ Local employers on spec.

What to read

⊙ Local newspaper job ads
⊙ *Summer Jobs Britain* (updated annually)
⊙ *Summer Jobs Abroad*.

Both these books are available from Vacation Work, 9 Park End Street, Oxford OX1 1HJ. Tel: 01865 241978. See also www.trotman.co.uk.

Work experience and internships

What counts as work experience?

'All experience is good and can count as work experience', according to Liz Rhodes of the National Council for Work Experience (NCWE). 'A placement in an industry where you are being considered for a career is of course excellent and a great way for you to find out if it's right for you, but even a job in the local restaurant, shop or office can help build key transferable skills – from dealing with people to prioritising and keeping a cool head in a crisis', she says. Make the most of the opportunities and experiences that come up. You'll be surprised just how much you have learnt and the challenges you've faced, and it could do wonders for your CV. Visit www.workexperience.org.uk for more advice on work experience, from different types of programmes, to how to go about setting up the placement.

What is really meant by work experience?

In terms of students, work experience is the opportunities offered by different organisations for students to gain specific experience of working in an area that will help them with their degree studies, or with entrance into a career. Of course it helps that students are paid to do this work so finding a placement during the vacations is a double whammy.

What is an internship?

Work experience by a different name. The word 'internship' came from the USA and was spread by multinational companies throughout Europe, where it is now widely used. In the States some internships are unpaid, so it is always worth checking. Sometimes the phrase 'vacation placement' is used.

Who provides work experience?

Many organisations that are unable to offer sponsorship or industrial placement do offer vacation work experience – banks, insurance companies, accountancy and law firms, for example.

Big companies such as Procter & Gamble, IBM, Deutsche Bank, PSA, Peugeot, Citroën etc take on a number of students for vacation work each year. Many of these companies offer placements abroad. Some of these placements are better than others. The NCWE holds an annual competition to find the company offering the best work placements. Overall winner this year was Northumberland candle maker, Best Kept Secrets. Cancer Research UK, BP and Toyota were also among the award-winners.

How do you find a vacation placement?

Companies advertise in your university careers advice centre; or try www.work-experience.org, or www. prospect.ac.uk. Expect a fairly intensive interview, as many companies think vacation work might lead to a more lasting relationship, eg full-time employment after you graduate, and are looking at you with this in mind.

You may also find openings in areas where sponsorship is out of the question and industrial placements are difficult to find, such as personnel, marketing or publishing. If you are considering the media, advertising or journalism you may well find securing paid work impossible. However, if you are prepared to work unpaid, just for the experience, then you might have better luck. Try some of the local radio stations, the many TV channels and TV production companies, local papers (especially the freebies) and the wide range of different magazines that are published. It will be a high-energy activity securing success, as you will need to write to individual editors giving details of how you could add value to their publication or programme. Ideally select ones you know something about.

Having stressed the difficulties of finding work, Aberystwyth reports:

'We had four placements with a local newspaper, one with a local radio station, and a local PR company regularly takes students and graduates under the CPW scheme [see page 112]. They received payment and these placements have led to graduate jobs in all three areas of work in the last few years.'

Work experience placements are not all one-sided: the employer gets something out of it, too – the chance to look at a possible new employee at close quarters and often to get a special project undertaken. But actually getting a work placement is incredibly competitive.

'Vacation placements are an excellent opportunity for students to learn first-hand what a particular career would involve. Choosing the right career and the right employer are important and often difficult decisions. There will be a whole range of options to consider and students will want to be as well informed as possible. Spending a couple of weeks with a prospective employer gives you a very good idea of what the work would involve and what kind of atmosphere you would be working in. Students should not assume, though, that taking part in a vacation scheme will be a short-cut to a job; equally, failing to get a placement with a particular firm will not count against you. After all, the number of vacation places available is limited. Students who have had a placement with us are treated the same as everybody else when it comes to applying for a training contract.'

Julia Clarke, partner with responsibility for graduate recruitment at international law firm Clifford Chance. Clifford Chance offers 90 vacation placements of between two and four weeks during the Easter or summer break, and currently pays £270 a week.

Facts and figures on work experience

⊙ Three-quarters of employers who recruit graduates offer work experience.

⊙ Six out of ten recruiters said that placement students were a prime source of graduate recruitment.

⊙ Manufacturing and production are the best areas to contact for a vacation placement.

(IRS Survey 2005)

Cash crisis note

• Placement opportunities are advertised on www.prospects.ac.uk.

Cash crisis note

- Around half a million students look for work placements in the summer. Competition is high. To avoid disappointment start looking as soon as you have your uni place. Work experience is becoming an important deciding factor on a student's CV, and an important aid to financial survival. Check out your uni job shop or the website www.prospects.ac.uk.

How will I find a placement?

Big employers

Large companies such as Procter & Gamble offer what they call summer internships to students on a worldwide scale. They see it as a fair means of assessing students' ability and hope eventually to recruit most of their graduates through their internship scheme. ICI is another major company that has a summer internship programme. It offers 6–12-week placements across Europe to undergraduates from all academic years who have demonstrated high achievement and are confident of getting a good degree. It looks for team players with good interpersonal skills and proven leadership ability. Your university careers office should have details of these and other programmes with major companies. Otherwise contact employers directly, or look on the net.

Small employers

Small companies can be contacted directly, or you could try Shell STEP. This UK-wide scheme is designed to encourage small- and medium-sized employers to take on undergraduates for an eight-week summer placement to carry out a specific project which will be of benefit to both the employer and the student. Students have the opportunity to use their existing skills and the chance to develop new ones while experiencing life in the workplace. Opportunities are open to second- and penultimate-year undergraduates of any degree discipline.

You'd earn a minimum of £185 per week. This is in the form of a 'training allowance' and is exempt from tax and National Insurance contributions. In 2005, 1110 projects were undertaken across the UK.

Money, of course, is important. (If you're hungry and you've only got 5p in your pocket, it is very important.) But so is getting the right job at the end of your degree course. The competition out there is very strong, even for top graduates, so you need to make your CV stand out. Taking part in a Shell STEP work placement in an area relevant to your future career aspirations is certainly one way to achieve this.

For details, visit the Shell STEP website, www.step.org.uk, where you'll find more information and an online application form for the summer programme, or contact your University Careers Advisory Service. While Shell STEP operates in England,

Scotland and Northern Ireland, Wales has its own scheme, Cymru Prosper Wales (CPW), which is similar to Shell STEP (tel: 01792 295246; www.cpw.org.uk), or contact your university careers advisers.

What four Shell STEP students achieved in 2005

Neil Koronka from Dunfermline, an Aero-Mechanical Engineering student at Strathclyde University, was placed at Alba Diagnostics, a brake manufacturer based in Glenrothes. He was tasked with redesigning a new, increased-capacity pressure brake bleeder. Neil saw the product design through market research stages right up to prototype development. The improvements Neil incorporated into the product could ultimately increase the company's turnover by over £250K.

George Hutchinson from Rosendale, who's studying Manufacturing Engineering at Cambridge, was placed at Weston EU Ltd, a manufacturing solutions company based in Colne. George was asked to examine the frequency checking of turbine blades manufactured for Rolls Royce aircraft engines. He produced work instructions for the process and other related procedures to meet with quality standards. He also undertook an investigation into the possibility of reworking blades that failed frequency tests. His findings will provide a significant reduction in costs and have resulted in the saving of £13,000 pa.

Laura Scully from Leicester is studying Psychology with Sociology at Leicester University. She undertook a project at St George's Nursery School, also based in Leicester, to design a marketing plan and create a new website. She conducted research to assess the company's position, designed and managed the implementation of the website and developed new brochure designs. The project objectives were met and as a result the company predicts that its turnover could increase to around £500,000.

David Hewett from Leamington Spa, a Mathematics student at Warwick, carried out a project at Tailor Made Systems based at Warwick Science Park. His task was to build a computer model to simulate MALMS, which is a mobile system that monitors the effectiveness of airfield ground lighting. David carried out a detailed study, exploring positioning factors and risk analysis, and producing statistical analysis to support his work, which will help them to develop this exciting product.

What Shell STEP 2005 students thought of their Shell STEP experience:

- 97% thought that their employability has improved as a result of participating in Shell STEP
- 97% said that they would recommend Shell STEP to a friend
- 93% said that the Shell STEP programme met or exceeded their expectations.

Ethnic minorities

The Windsor Fellowship Undergraduate Programme

The Windsor Fellowship is an educational charity that works in partnership with leading UK employers and educational institutions, and provides management development programmes targeted at black and minority ethnic (BME) undergraduates to help maximise their individual, social and academic talents. It includes residential seminars, voluntary work and work placements (minimum 6 weeks), which provide a real-life insight into employment with leading organisations. Sponsors include the Bank of England, John Lewis Partnership, British Library, Friends of the Earth and several government departments such as the Audit Commission, Home Office and the Department of Works and Pensions. Application forms and further information can be downloaded from www.windsorfellowship.org/leadership.

Oxford University

Oxford University Careers Service offers much support for those looking for work experience. Its website, launched in October 2002, has an extensive, searchable database with over 250 types of work experience opportunity advertised on it at any one time. Opportunities include summer internships, part-time work, careers-related courses, longer placements, volunteer work and overseas work. This is backed up by a well-resourced Information Room with further details about the organisations and opportunities concerned. A team of professional careers staff helps with students' work experience queries – ideal for those wanting tips to track down the more elusive work experience opportunities. The service also runs a Work Experience Fair each January, an introductory event called Get Started with Work Experience, for those beginning to look at work experience issues, and a Making the Most of Work Experience session for those about to embark on experiential opportunities. Oxford University students and graduates who completed their courses up to four years ago can access all these services by registering online, free, at www.careers.ox.ac.uk.

Further information

Who to contact for work experience

- ⊙ Local employers
- ⊙ Major employers
- ⊙ Course directors
- ⊙ College notice boards
- ⊙ Your university careers advisers
- ⊙ University job shops
- ⊙ STEP
- ⊙ Local employment agencies.

Surf the net

There are a number of websites that can help you find work experience. Here are just a few of the best:

- ⊙ Prospects, www.prospects.ac.uk, the graduate careers website, which has a work bank section.
- ⊙ National Centre for Work Experience (NCWE) – www.work-experience.org – which is based in the CSU, aims to support and develop quality work experience and encourage employers to offer more opportunities.

⦿ Best part-time jobs: hotrecruit.co.uk; or through UCAS: www.ucas.com.
⦿ Just Jobs for Students: www.justjobs4students.co.uk.

Making your work experience work for you

The supply of graduates continues to grow and fortunately the graduate labour market is buoyant. And looking ahead, employers expect their demand for graduates to increase.

The areas with most vacancies are likely to be accountancy, professional services firms, engineering, industrial companies, investment banks and the public sector. Almost a fifth of all vacancies are in buying, selling and retailing. London and the south-east of England are the graduate hot spots.

What are employers looking for?

Whatever the state of the employment market and whatever area of work interests you, getting that first foot in the door is incredibly competitive. All employers are seeking the best students, and with increasing numbers of graduates coming out of our universities the pool is getting larger and larger. It is not unusual to have 4000 applications chasing 100 places. Despite the number of graduates around, many companies surveyed said they were not able to find graduates with the skills they required to fill all their vacancies. Obviously companies can interview only a small proportion of prospective applicants. So – how do they seek out the best? What are their criteria? And what do you need to have on your CV, in addition to a good degree and possibly work experience, to make you stand out from the crowd and turn an application into an interview? We asked some major employers.

'We find that candidates who have some work experience, or who have taken the opportunity to broaden their horizons by working in the community or even travelling, have normally had a greater chance to develop and practise the sort of skills we are looking for.'
Graduate Resourcing, Royal Bank of Scotland

'Initiative and follow-through; leadership; thinking and problem-solving; communication; ability to work with others; creativity and innovation; and priority setting. We look for evidence of these skills, which together we'll be able to develop further to run the organisation of the future.'
Human Resources Manager, Recruitment, Procter & Gamble UK

'We are looking for the next generation of senior managers, the people who will drive our business forward in the future, so the kinds of qualities we are seeking – conceptual and analytical thinking, strong interpersonal skills, ability to influence and motivate others – can't all be demonstrated through a good academic record, important though it is. We want to know about other areas of achievement as well.'
Group Recruitment, ICI

Don't just sit back and think, 'I have a degree – everybody will want me', because the sad fact is they won't. The notion that students can walk into top jobs simply because they have a degree is a fallacy. Not everybody is a blue-chip high-flyer. So, if you want one of those top jobs then you have got to be proactive and start lining up the kind of skills and experiences that employers are looking for now – which is why getting the right work experience is so important.

Skill check

- Motivation and enthusiasm
- Team working
- Oral communication
- Flexibility and adaptability
- Initiative/proactive.

Fact check

- 84% of students we canvassed said they worked because they needed the money.
- 73% of employers we canvassed said they like the graduates they take on to have had previous work experience.

Job check

Always keep your future career in mind when you head for holiday and even term-time jobs. That's the advice of the National Centre for Work Experience. Skills learnt from time spent working can make a great contribution to your CV and help convince a future employer that you are better than the competition. Whatever and wherever the job – supermarket, pub, the SU – make the most of the opportunity to enhance your employability.

To help you, here is the NCWE check list:

- Set some personal objectives for the period of employment before starting a job: what do you want to get out of it, beyond the pay packet?
- Don't be afraid to ask questions and take notes when being briefed by your boss at the outset. Better to ask now and be clear than make mistakes later.
- Keep a note of challenges you overcome each day and any problem-solving required. This demonstrates initiative and prioritising skills.
- Grab any chance to take on more responsibility: undertaking new tasks is a sure way of developing new talents.
- Do the best job you possibly can for self-satisfaction and the possibility of being asked back for the next vacation – maybe even a permanent position in the future.
- Ask for feedback from your boss and the people you work with – there may be room for improvement – and note successes and achievements: these are what you need to put on your CV.
- Make suggestions – just because you're a holiday worker or work experience student doesn't mean you don't have good ideas, and your colleagues will always appreciate seeing things from a new perspective.

⊙ Keep a diary of your thoughts throughout the placement. This will help you to add your achievements to your CV and will show you how far you've come.

⊙ Ask for a reference from your boss; it will stand you in good stead for moving on to a permanent job.

⊙ Work hard, but take the time to get to know your colleagues and enjoy the work atmosphere. After all, you may be spending every day there for a while!

Advice note

'Dress for success' is the advice for jobseeking students in the 2005 Prospect Finalist publication. Whether attending an interview, recruitment fair or assessment day, creating a favourable impression is important. Getting the right look shows you understand the employer's business.

Stop press!

⊙ www.getalife.org.uk provides up-to-the-minute information on employment issues for students and graduates.

⊙ www.prospects.ac.uk/chat is a communications channel enabling students to put their careers questions to big-name recruiters – opens Tuesdays at 1pm and Wednesdays at 2pm.

⊙ Prospects also has a 24-hour chatroom, where job-seeking students and graduates who wake up in a cold sweat in the middle of the night need not be in anguish alone. See www.prospects.ac.uk/links/gradtalk.

⊙ Get the balance right. Work–life balance rates as the third most important factor (32%) when choosing a job, topped only by salary, and training and development opportunities (45% each) (MORI survey).

⊙ Work placements do the business. Three-quarters of employers who offer work placements recruit graduates from their work experience pool of talent (IRS Survey, November 2005).

Salary check

Graduate salaries are on the up.

⊙ Starting salaries for graduate positions are likely to be higher than ever this summer, with the median graduate salary predicted to be £23,000 (although the rise of 2.3% is the smallest increase in the last five years).

⊙ Vacancies are also expected to rise by 14.6% (AGR Recruitment Survey).

⊙ Investment banking commands the highest starting salaries at £35,000, with legal work at £29,000 and management consulting at £28,500 (AGR Recruitment Survey).

⊙ At the other end of the scale: the predicted median figure for sales is £17,500, general management £19,962 and purchasing and retail management at £20,000.

- While, unsurprisingly, the highest earnings are to be found in London, which has a mean salary of £25,000 – much higher than all other regions – the lowest median starting salary was in Wales: £18,700.
- Manufacturing engineering, sales, research and development, IT and investment banking are likely to see the greatest percentage increase in vacancies.
  (AGR Winter Survey 2006.)

What to read

- *Prospects Pocket Directory*: hundreds of jobs for students and graduates – from your university careers service.
- *Hobsons Directory*: careers service or public library. To order, tel: 0870 900 2665 or visit www.trotman.co.uk.

Industrial placements

The idea of the four-year sandwich course that includes an industrial placement was never envisaged as a financial lifesaver, but many students are finding that a year in industry, with a good salary, is helping them to clear their debts while they gain invaluable experience. But with more higher-education institutions developing more sandwich courses, finding good industrial placements is becoming increasingly difficult. This is felt mostly where courses are fairly new and the institutions haven't yet built up a good rapport with industrial concerns. When applying to universities, it is worth checking out the extent and quality of the industrial placements offered to students. There are essentially two sorts of sandwich courses: those where you take a year out – usually the third year – to work in industry; and courses in which you do 6 months at university and six months at work.

In the beginning, industrial placements were mainly for courses in Engineering, but increasingly courses in Business Studies, Retail, Computer Sciences and languages include an industrial placement year. Aberystwyth has taken this a step further with their YES scheme.

What is the YES scheme?

The University of Wales, Aberystwyth has pioneered an initiative to give any student in the university who is not already on a sandwich course the opportunity to take an industrial year out. The scheme is called YES (Year in Employment Scheme), and currently over 40 students at Aberystwyth are saying YES to the opportunity. They come from a range of disciplines: Arts, Economics and Social Sciences, Information Studies, Law and the sciences. You can choose a placement that is relevant to your degree subject, such as accounting, marketing, scientific research, events management or environmental conservation work, or use the time to experience work in an area that is totally new to you, such as human resources, retail management, journalism or production management.

You can even work abroad: YES students have recently worked in Europe, Australia, New Zealand, Africa and the USA. Students also work with major employers in the private, public and voluntary sectors such as IBM, KPMG, the Environment Agency, the National Trust and Voluntary Service Overseas. Salaries vary from around £8000 up to £18,000, although some voluntary placements may only pay expenses. With everybody now having to pay fees, earning money for a year during study is a definite bonus. Aberystwyth is adamant – with some justification – that the skills learnt during the year out have enhanced both degree performance and employment prospects. The latest figures it prints show that students who have undertaken work experience gain employment after graduation quicker than students who have not participated in any form of work experience. Joanne Bullock, YES Project Officer, believes 'YES provides an opportunity for students to develop their employability skills whilst earning money and having some fun!'

Kristina's story

Kristina, a student at Aberystwyth studying Marketing with Law, decided to take a year out under the YES Scheme. In this letter to the YES Officer she talks about her amazing experiences.

'Dear All

'Just thought it was about time I wrote and let you know how my YES placement is going. As you know, I'm working for IBM. I started early July and it's a year's contract, but they've already extended it until September which is great. I'm having such a fantastic time – it's definitely the best decision I think I've made!

'I work in their Marketing department – my official title is: EMEA Series Marketing and TopFlight Co-ordinator (very flash). My minor job role consists of doing admin things, such as reports/charts (yawn) – only three a month so I don't mind. But my major role is organising one of IBM's largest events called TopFlight.

'This involves bringing around 60 of IBM's major customers from all over the world (that's 60 per event, and there are two events per week) to the US, mainly Austin in Texas. These people are the multimillion-pound-spending customers – very rich and important – so it's definitely a challenge! I organise their invites/flights/transport/hotel; their days out at the conference; the speakers; the evening restaurants/venues; even down to choosing what we are eating and the material and colour of napkins. It's so much fun and when I'm out in Austin I also get treated like a VIP, because the suppliers know that I'm the one at the end of the day who will say, "You're not good enough and I'm not going to use this hotel again." When one hotel manager first met me, she nearly fell off her seat when she discovered I was only 21 – such power at such a young age! (chuckle)

'I've definitely found my niche and see my future in event organising. I only got this job because the previous job-holder (a full-timer) left and I stuck my hand up and said "I'll have a go!" I'm so lucky.

'All in all everything is going amazingly well!!

'Best wishes

Kristina'

Jono's story

Jono, now at Loughborough University studying Innovative Manufacturing and Technology, decided to take a year in industry before going to university. But it wasn't all plain sailing:

'I wanted a break from academic study; I also wanted some engineering experience, so I decided to take a gap year. It turned out to be the hardest year of my life. Rather than go off travelling the world like my friends – Mexico, Barbados, Kenya, oh the glamour, the excitement, the sun – I applied to the Year in Industry organisation, who found me an industrial placement in a company in deepest, darkest Lowestoft called Pilot Drilling Control. They make specialist equipment for the oil and gas drilling industry – clever stuff.

'I was working in the machine shop on mills and lathes, making things for oil and gas drilling and it did give me cracking experience. I really enjoyed what I was doing. What I didn't enjoy was the hours. I was working a 48-hour week including Saturday mornings. I was dead on my feet, getting up at 6am and not getting back home until 6.30pm when I'd crash out – my social life was zilch – and all for £6500 a year. What didn't help was the 55-minute drive to get there. After six months I was on my knees and thought of quitting, but I didn't. I stuck it out. And now I am glad I did. I learnt a lot and I came out of it feeling really good about myself.'

When is the best time to do a year in industry?

If you take your year in industry at 20 you are going to earn substantially more than you would at 18, so it could help pay off your debts – you will also know more about your topic so the experience can be more valuable. But if you take a year out before you start at university, the money you save will help to ease your finances once you start managing on student funding, and the experience will help with your studies.

Another point to consider: most universities charge fees during a year out in industry, and though these are much reduced you will probably have to pay around £600 (current figures). If your industrial placement is taken as a gap year either before or after university you won't have to pay this.

Could an industrial placement lead to sponsorship/employment?

Sometimes a year in industry is an integral part of a sponsorship scheme (see page 147 for full details). If it is not, a successful period of work experience can result in your employer offering to sponsor you for the rest or the whole of your degree. With three-quarters of employers that recruit new graduates providing work experience and around 89% turning to their sponsored students when filling vacancies, there is no doubt the student who has spent a successful placement with an employer is in a good position regarding future employment. An industrial placement provides the opportunity for you to get to know your employer and your employer to get to know you. It will help you to develop work-related skills that employers value.

The Year in Industry

If you are looking for paid work experience in industry, which could really help your future career and possibly lead to university sponsorship, The Year in Industry (YINI) are the people to contact. The organisation has extensive contacts with UK companies interested in taking on high-calibre students in the year between school/college and university, and also undergraduates during their course.

A Year in Industry enables students to have a real taste of industry, and experience challenging, interesting, paid work, often undertaking activities that assist in driving businesses forward.

Over 70% of Year in Industry students go on to achieve either a First or upper Second Class degree, well above the average. Many are offered sponsorship through university and/or paid summer vacation work. For some, it is an opportunity to confirm a career choice before starting a degree course; for others it's a means to save some money towards their university course. The organisation has placed more than 8000 gap-year students since 1987.

The Year in Industry is a national scheme providing a high-quality package for students with a wide range of organisations, mainly (though by no means exclusively) in engineering, science, computing and business. For a full list of participating companies for the current year, check out www.yini.org.uk.

Applications for placements should be made as soon as possible. The earlier students apply, the more opportunities are available. And the more flexible you are about where you will work, the greater the opportunity for a placement.

Salaries range from £8000 to £14,000 pa, depending on location. An administration fee of £25 is payable after application to and acceptance onto the scheme. For further information, contact: The Year in Industry, University of Southampton, Hampshire SO17 1BJ. Tel: 023 8059 2430. Fax: 023 8059 7570. Email: enquiries@yini.org.uk. Website: www.yini.org.uk.

What YINI students think:

'The past year has been a brilliant experience and very beneficial. It has given me the confidence to expand my skills, develop within the workplace and to choose my future career with greater accuracy.'
Claire Loram, Teign School, Devon (South West Water, Exeter)

'I developed invaluable CAD and computer skills. I have learnt about teamwork, company structure and project management. I now have a better understanding of civil engineering companies and projects.'
Stuart Penman, Royal Grammar School, Buckinghamshire (Babtie Group, Aylesbury)

Further information

Thinking about taking a sandwich course?

Then the internet is the place to look. There are a number of electronic resources that can help in the search for sandwich courses or other work placements:

- ⦿ Sandwich courses are listed as a course subject under 'S' on the Universities and Colleges Admissions Service (UCAS) site: www.ucas.com.
- ⦿ Course Discover is a useful package for finding sandwich courses, and the information can be accessed at most schools and local careers organisations.
- ⦿ ASET (Association for Sandwich Education and Training) is the national body for work-based learning practitioners, an educational charity that promotes best practice for work placements, as well as providing support and advice for all professionals who work in the field. Contact: ASET, 3 Westbrook Court, Sharrow Vale Road, Sheffield S11 8YZ. Tel/Fax: 0114 221 2902/3. Email: aset@aset.demon.co.uk. Website: www.asetonline.org.
- ⦿ The National Centre for Work Experience (NCWE) has useful information on a range of work experience opportunities. Website: www.work-experience.org. If you want advice on work experience they are the people to ask.
- ⦿ Around 119,400 students were thought to be on sandwich courses in 2004–2005 (HESA student returns).

Who to ask about placements

- ⦿ If you are not a sponsored student, contact your department at university. It will have a list of possible employers who might offer placements.
- ⦿ Contact employers directly – don't forget the smaller companies, which might have just one placement but don't advertise in case they get deluged.

What to read

- ⦿ *Engineering Opportunities for Students and Graduates*, published by Professional Engineering Publishing Ltd, available free from IMechE, c/o Marketing & Communications Department, 1 Birdcage Walk, London SW1H 9JJ. Tel: 020 7222 3337. Email: marketing@imeche.org.uk. Download from www.pepublishing.co.uk or www.engopps.com.
- ⦿ *Everything You Wanted to Know about Sponsorship, Placements and Graduate Opportunities*, regularly updated and published by Amoeba Publications. Available from Trotman, tel: 0870 900 2665, or visit www.trotman.co.uk/bookshop.

Gap year

Taking a gap year after A levels is becoming increasingly popular: around 30,000 students each year are thought to take a year out. After 13 solid years on the academic treadmill many young people just feel that they need a chance to recharge their batteries. Most universities will accept deferred entry; many institutions – such as

Oxford and Cambridge – actively encourage it. But don't assume that deferred entry is an automatic right. You must always ask, and if the course is popular, you may be refused.

Many young people use their gap year to gain a skill or experience in a specific organisation as well as to make money. Often this results in them having a ready-made job to walk into during vacations, once they have started their degree course. (See Jono's story on page 119.) Others just want fun and new experiences or the chance to do something to help others. Here we look at three very different kinds of gap year: to raise money, voluntary work and to travel.

A gap year to raise money

If your aim is to save money, your best bet is to work as close to home as possible, where bed and board are likely to be at a very advantageous rate – if not free – and to avoid travel costs. There are always plenty of jobs going in shops, restaurants and pubs. Go for the multiple outlets, such as Next, Tesco or a pub chain. You will then have street cred, and may be able to find a part-time term-time job in your university town. But since you have a whole year to work and a clutch of A levels to offer, you might be able to find a job with better pay and which stretches your ability more. But be realistic: you are not going to earn great bags of gold. A gap-year student could expect to earn at least the minimum wage, which is £4.25 per hour (£4.45 from October) for 18–21-year-olds and £5.05 (£5.35 from October) for those aged 22 and over. But you might be offered more. One student we interviewed was earning £7.50 ph. Save just a quarter of that and you will be thankful for it once you start at uni. The first term is very expensive. Being sensible – prudent even – doesn't have to be boring.

A gap year isn't only about earning money: many students see it as a chance to gain useful experience towards their career, to gain skills or to help others.

Fall in for a gap year challenge!

How does trekking and horse-riding in the Rocky Mountains, a sailing expedition in Norway and Bavaria, white-water rafting in Belize or going on exercises in and around Hong Kong grab you for a gap year experience? These are all things that gap year Commissioned Officers have spent their time doing on an Army gap year either before university, or as an Undergraduate Army Placement. Students are placed in a regiment and given real responsibility. It's no easy ride. It gives you the chance to discover what you are made of and what an Army career could be like. It will develop your personal skills, quicken your intellectual agility, broaden your horizons and provide you with a year crammed with interest, challenge and not a little fun, plus of course excellent pay. And there's no obligation to join. To find out more and how to apply, visit www.army.mod.uk/careers/officer/gapyear.html. Pay is around £11,000–£14,000.

What students did in their gap year

Anna spent her year working for a Life Assurance/Insurance company to fund her Politics and International Marketing course at Reading.

Joanne worked for a supermarket driving a fork-lift truck, but managed to get heavily into debt before she even started an Equine Science course at Aberystwyth.

Ruth travelled in Nicaragua for 6 months, but still managed to save £600 for uni working in a pub. She is studying Latin American Studies at Essex.

Lucky Ryan split his time between working in a ski resort and surfing in Australia before his Engineering course at Cambridge.

Christopher worked in a sausage shop where he not only became a proficient sales assistant, but also learned how to mix up a 'mean' sausage. It paid for driving lessons, got him on the road and gave him a £2000 bank balance when he started a course in Business Administration at the University of the West of England.

Alice had six part-time jobs for the first 4 months, then became matron at a boarding school. Finally she went Inter-Railing round Europe. She is now studying Music at Durham.

Kerry started her year working in Disneyland near Paris. She then worked at Eurocamp in Italy and Camp-America in Northern California. She didn't save a bean but had a great time. She went on to study Maths at Liverpool.

Johnny's year was spent playing cricket for Middlesex County. He is studying Computer Science at Kingston.

Alexis did a work placement at Time Magazine office in New York before taking up a place at Kingston University to study Journalism/Media and Cultural Studies.

Giles worked as an Associate Director on a film project, before studying Politics at Hull.

Lucy worked in a lab for nine months, and then on a ranch in the USA. She is now at Cambridge studying Veterinary Medicine.

Jordan went to China to study martial arts at a school near Si Ping City but saved remarkably little. He is now studying Chinese Language and History at Sheffield University.

Emily worked as a care assistant in a school for deaf children with special needs, as well as the chicken counter at Tesco, before going to Stirling University where she is studying Health Psychology.

Conni took a job as a classroom assistant in the dance and drama department of a school and sometimes helped out with PE – useful experience for her degree course in Dance and Sport at Wolverhampton University.

Joshua attended a school in Weert, a small town in the Netherlands, but earned nothing. He is now in his third year studying Linguistics at Cambridge.

Elizabeth taught in a primary school in Tanzania before making an overland trip from Dar es Salaam to Cape Town. She then worked in an office in the UK to save for her course in Modern Languages at Cambridge.

George decided to use his gap year to lay the foundations for his career, which was a lot of hard work and earned him nothing except invaluable experience:

George's year

' "Going, going, gone – the bungee jumper misses the water by a whisker." Is it news? It was my story and it was on air.'

George, who went on to study Politics at Bristol University, joined GWR, Bristol's local radio station, for a week's work experience when he left school. That became two weeks, then three, and finally the whole year. He became Overnight Reporter, which involved turning handouts from local organisations and PR companies into topical news stories.

'Local dog shows and sponsored activities: it was hardly world-shattering news. Each day I had five minutes of air time to fill. Sometimes I would go out on the streets and talk to people – then chop these interviews to eight-second sound bites. I had always wanted to be a journalist – this experience confirmed my ambitions.'

Unfortunately for George, the work was unpaid so his afternoons were spent working in Tesco.

Skills gained:

- Confidence
- Being able to meet deadlines
- Being concise – a whole story in half a minute
- Interviewing and talking to complete strangers
- Solving problems.

Further information

Who to contact

- The Army offers gap year opportunities through a Short Service Limited Commission scheme as well as undergraduate placement years. To find out more, contact the Army's Short Service Limited Commission scheme, the Schools Liaison Officer through your school careers staff, or try the local Army recruitment office – the address will be in the phone book. Tel: 08457 300111. Websites: www.army.mod.uk/careers/officer/gap_year.html (for full details on gap years) and www.armyjobs.co.uk (for general recruitment information).
- Banks, insurance companies, accountancy firms – many offer work experience; always worth a try.
- Shops, supermarkets, chain stores – try to find an organisation with a number of local outlets, and one that offers a training scheme.
- Teaching – you don't actually need any training to take up a temporary position as assistant teacher or matron in a preparatory school. As an assistant matron you could find yourself darning socks and getting the kids up in the morning. As an assistant teacher you'd probably be involved in organising sport and out-of-school activities, coaching and supervising prep and classes when staff were away. Current rates of pay are in line with the minimum wage with a small amount deducted if food, accommodation, etc are included. Term ends in July, so you would then have two months' travelling time. For gap year vacancies try

Gabbitas Educational Consultants, Carrington House, 126–130 Regent Street, London W1B 5EE. Tel: 020 7734 0161. Websites: www.gabbitas.co.uk and www.teacher-recruitment.co.uk.

A voluntary work gap year

How would you like to teach in Africa, India, Mexico or Paraguay, while having the experience of a lifetime? Go on an Art History Abroad course to Venice, Florence, Bologna? Work and travel in the USA? Work with the needy – the homeless, young offenders, children with special needs? Take a Trekforce or Greenforce expedition which offers the chance to help international conservation projects in such far-flung places as Belize and Kenya? Do you see yourself working to save endangered rainforests, wildlife or coral reefs, or perhaps developing some theatre techniques?

Year Out Group

Once you've made the gap year decision, the Year Out Group is a good starting point if you are seeking adventure or a great experience.

The Year Out Group is an association of more than 30 leading year-out organisations that was launched in 2000 to promote the concept and benefits of well-structured year-out programmes, to promote models of good practice and to help young people and their advisers in selecting suitable and worthwhile projects. All the organisations have agreed to adhere to a Code of Practice and appropriate operating guidelines. Projects last from four weeks to a year and are available in the UK or overseas. For many of them you will have to finance yourself (this is considered part of the challenge) – but others do pay quite well. It is wise to start your planning early and to do it in as much detail as possible. In a full gap year there is time to work to earn money as well as to work on a project that is worth while, exciting and which could change your life forever. Each year, Year Out Group produces a booklet called 'Year Out' that provides information on planning a well-structured gap year. The booklet is sent to all schools, colleges and careers offices each spring. To learn more about the members of Year Out Group and the opportunities they offer, read on. You can also contact them directly or via the Year Out Group website, www.yearoutgroup.org, from which you can also request a copy of the booklet.

So what's on offer?

- Africa & Asia Venture, which combines teaching and coaching sports, plus community projects, with adventure in Africa, India, Nepal or Mexico. Tel: 01380 729009; email: av@aventure.co.uk; website: www.aventure.co.uk
- African Conservation Experience – opportunities to work on game and nature reserves in southern Africa. Tel: 0870 241 5816; email: info@ConservationAfrica.net; website: www.ConservationAfrica.net
- Blue Venture – projects and expeditions that enhance global marine conservation and research. Tel: 020 8341 9819; email: enquiries@blueventures.org; website: www.blueventures.org
- Art History Abroad courses including a Grand Tour. Tel: 020 7582 8082; email: info@arthistoryabroad.com; website: www.arthistoryabroad.com

- BSES Expeditions. Six-week expeditions in a challenging environment, usually between July and September. Tel: 020 7591 3141; email: bses@rgs.org; website: www.bses.org.uk
- BUNAC work and travel programmes – USA, Canada, Australia, New Zealand. Tel: 020 7251 3472; email: enquiries@bunac.org.uk; website: www.bunac.org (see also BUNAC, page 133)
- Camp America – join the staff at a summer camp. Tel: 020 7581 7373; email: enquiries@campamerica.co.uk; website: www.campamerica.co.uk
- CESA language courses abroad. Tel: 01872 225300; email: info@cesalanguages.com; website: www.cesalanguages.com
- Changing Worlds offers volunteer and paid placements worldwide. Tel: 01883 340960; email: welcome@changingworlds.co.uk; website: www.changingworlds.co.uk
- Coral Cay Conservation – coral reef and rainforest conservation – in the Philippines, Honduras, Fiji, Malaysia, etc. Tel: 0870 750 0668; email: info@coralcay.org; website: www.coralcay.org
- CSV (Community Service Volunteers) never turn anyone away for placements of four months or more in the UK. Board and lodging is free and a small allowance is provided. Tel: 0800 374991; website: www.csv.org.uk
- Flying Fish – full range of courses to help you upgrade your watersport qualifications. Tel: 01983 280641; email: mail@flyingfishonline.com; website: www.flyingfishonline.com
- Frontier Conservation – conservation projects worldwide. Tel: 020 7613 2422; website: www.frontier.ac.uk
- GAP Activity Projects worldwide – assist in schools, hospitals, on conservation projects and outdoor projects in 34 countries. Tel: 0118 959 4914; fax: 0118 957 6634; email: volunteer@gap.org.uk; website: www.gap.org.uk
- Greenforce – join a conservation project and help scientific understanding. Tel: 0870 770 2646; website: www.greenforce.org
- i to i – work worldwide in media, health, building, teaching, conservation, community work. Tel: 0870 333 2332; fax: 0113 242 2171; email: info@i-to-i.com; website: www.i-to-i.com
- International Academy – winter sport instructor courses in Canada and elsewhere. Tel: 029 7828 2275; website: www.international-academy.com
- The Leap – volunteer work placements in Africa. Tel: 0870 240 4187; email: info@theleap.co.uk; website: www.theleap.co.uk
- Madventurer – volunteer projects as part of a team or as an individual in Africa and elsewhere. Tel: 0845 121 1996; email: team@madventurer.com; website: www.madventurer.com
- NonStopSki – winter sport instructor courses in Canada. Tel: 0870 241 8070; email: info@nonstopski.com; website: www.nonstopski.com
- Outreach International – volunteer projects with local communities mainly in Mexico but also Cambodia. Tel: 01458 274957; email: projects@outreachinternational.co.uk; website: www.outreachinternational.co.uk
- Peak Leaders – winter sport instructor courses and more in Canada and elsewhere. Tel: 01337 860879; email: info@peakleaders.co.uk; website: www.peakleaders.co.uk

- ⊙ Project Trust – worthwhile work in 25 different countries. Tel: 01879 230444; fax: 01879 230357; website: www.projecttrust.org.uk; apply online
- ⊙ Quest Overseas – projects and expeditions in South America and Africa. Tel: 020 8673 3313; fax: 020 8673 7623; email: emailus@questoverseas.com
- ⊙ Raleigh International – challenging community and environmental projects overseas. Tel: 020 7371 8585; fax: 020 7371 5116; email: info@raleigh.org.uk; website: www.raleighinternational.org
- ⊙ St James's & Lucie Clayton College – a range of courses to improve your IT, business and communication skills in readiness for university and the workplace. Tel: 020 7373 3852; email: information@sjlccollege.co.uk; website: www.sjlccollege.co.uk
- ⊙ Students Partnership Worldwide (SPW) – helping to improve the lives of young people in Africa and Asia. Tel: 020 7222 0138; fax: 020 7233 0008; email: spwuk@gn.apc.org; website: www.spw.org
- ⊙ Tante Marie School of Cooking – specially designed courses to simply survive or to enable you to work your way round the world. Tel: 01483 726957; email: info@tantemarie.co.uk; website: www.tantemarie.co.uk.
- ⊙ Teaching & Projects Abroad – Africa, Latin America, Asia, Eastern Europe. Tel: 01903 859911; fax: 01903 785779; email: info@teaching-abroad.co.uk; website: www.teaching-abroad.co.uk
- ⊙ Travellers – voluntary teaching, work experience and conservation projects on many continents. Tel: 01903 502595; email: info@travellersworldwide.com; website: www.travellersworldwide.com
- ⊙ Trekforce – expeditions into exciting parts of the world on international conservation projects. Tel: 020 7828 2275; fax: 020 7828 2276; email: info@trekforce.org.uk; website: www.trekforce.org.uk
- ⊙ VentureCo – expeditions offering language training, conservation and community projects in challenging environments. Tel: 01926 411122; email: mail@ventureco-worldwide.com; website: www.ventureco-worldwide.com
- ⊙ Wind Sand & Stars – expedition in the Sinai desert with the Bedouin people. Tel: 020 7359 7551; email: office@windsandstars.co.uk; website: www.windsandstars.co.uk
- ⊙ Year in Industry – places potential engineering graduates in leading industrial companies in the UK. Tel: 0161 275 4396; website: www.yini.org.uk
- ⊙ Year Out Drama – develop your theatre skills while working with professionals. Tel: 01789 266245; fax: 01789 267524; email: yearoutdrama@strat-avon.ac.uk; website: www.yearoutdrama.com
- ⊙ Year Out Group – the association that has brought together all the leading year-out organisations mentioned here. Tel: 07980 395789; email: info@yearoutgroup.org; website: www.yearoutgroup.org.

Voluntary work abroad in developing countries is not as easy to find as it once was, especially if you have no recognised skill, and many organisations seek people over 21. Some projects will pay maintenance costs, and sometimes give pocket money, but it is not unusual for volunteers to be asked to pay their own fares.

Conservation work is much easier to find, both in the UK and abroad. Most of it is completely voluntary and unpaid. You might even be asked to contribute to food and accommodation. You could become involved in projects for the National Trust, the Royal Society for the Protection of Birds, on the restoration of cathedrals, working with disabled people and underprivileged children, painting, decorating – it's amazing what some students turn their hands to.

While the financial returns on both voluntary and conservation work are likely to be zero, in terms of your CV it could be of considerable value. Employers are impressed by the altruistic and enterprising qualities needed for voluntary work.

You could also try:

Long-term volunteering

The National Trust

If you are looking to fill a gap year, change career or gain work experience, and have six months or more to spare, then you could join the National Trust's full-time volunteering programme. As a full-time volunteer you could get involved in many different activities at Trust properties throughout England, Wales and Northern Ireland. You could work alongside a warden or forester on countryside management, assist house staff with aspects of running and preserving historic buildings and help with gardening, archaeology, education and promotion. Training is provided and accommodation may be available; some placements are available through the New Deal scheme. There's no pay, but out-of-pocket expenses are covered. For an information pack contact the central volunteering team on 0870 609 5383, visit the National Trust website at www.nationaltrust.org.uk/volunteering or email volunteers@nationaltrust.org.uk.

You can also volunteer for National Trust Working Holidays. Fruit picking and costume conservation are just two of the more unusual opportunities on offer. The Trust runs more than 400 conservation Working Holidays a year throughout England, Wales and Northern Ireland for as little as £70 for a week's full board and lodging (from £37 for a weekend). They take place at beautiful Trust locations and are open to volunteers aged 16 upwards. For a current brochure write to Working Holidays, Sapphire House, Roundtree Way, Norwich NR7 8SQ, phone the brochure line on 0870 429 2429, email working.holidays@nationaltrust.org.uk or see their website: www.nationaltrust.org.uk/workingholidays.

Archaeological digs

It won't earn you a fortune – more likely nothing (subsistence pay is rarely given) – but it can be fascinating work. See the Special Section included in every issue of *British Archaeology*, published six times a year by the Council for British Archaeology, St Mary's House, 66 Bootham, York YO30 9BZ tel: 01904 671417. Supplement gives full details of current UK digs. Subscription to British Archaeology £29; special rate for students in full-time education £17. But the magazine should be available in public libraries and selected retail outlets. For full details of membership and details of digs in your area phone the Council. Alternatively, contact the County Archaeologist for your district. The Council will have his/her address too. For archaeological digs abroad phone the Institute of Archaeology on 020 7504 4750.

BTCV

BTCV runs around 500 conservation holidays worldwide throughout the year. Prices start at about £60 for a weekend in the UK. Projects include pond maintenance, tree planting, step building, hedge laying, scrub clearance, dry stone walling and community development. Contact BTCV at Conservation Centre, Balby Road, Doncaster DN4 0RH. Tel: 01302 572244; email: information@btcv.org.uk. You can browse and book online at www.btcv.org/shop.

In the case studies below, five students talk about their gap year and the skills they gained.

Simon's year

'Being stuck up a mountain with little food and having insects dug out of your feet is all part of the gap year experience,' says Simon, now studying History and Media Studies at Sheffield Hallam University. He joined the Students Partnership Worldwide Scheme and taught for a year in Tanzania.

'There were some 50 of us from different schools scattered throughout the country. We had two weeks' training and then off we went. We were there to teach English to 14–24-year-olds – it is a bit daunting, I can tell you, standing up in front of a class of 70 who don't speak much English when you are only just 18. The place was just like the pictures you see on TV: poor shack schools with no windows but a fantastic atmosphere and people interested to learn. I earned £25 a month, which soon disappeared when we all met up at weekends. I went because I felt I wanted to do something useful, and it sounded like a wonderful adventure – which it was.'

Skills gained:

- Standing on your own feet
- Coping with problems and making decisions
- Understanding a culture very different from your own
- Confidence
- Communicating and overcoming the language barrier.

Carla's year

'I wanted to do something worth while with my gap year. Living in a mud hut, helping to provide clean water, healthcare and friendship to remote tribes in the African bush was more than I could have imagined – an amazing experience,' says Carla, now a Journalism student at the University of Lincoln.

'I had joined a medical ship called the Anastasis which was sailing to Cotonou in Benin, West Africa. We were all volunteers – doctors, nurses, dentists, galley workers and crew. The ship was a floating hospital and we were equipped to provide operations such as for cataracts. We docked, the news of our arrival soon travelled and people came from far and wide. I visited prisons and orphanages and had never seen such poverty. I gave away almost everything I had. A group of us ventured into the bush to help the tribespeople with digging wells, health and hygiene. We travelled by bush taxi – 13 hot, sticky people plus baggage, babies and livestock jammed into one small vehicle. I lived on yams and mangoes, came to understand the meaning of African time – today could be tomorrow, soon could be in six hours, eventually could be never – and learned a minute's grunting was how you said hello. They were delightful people. I made many friends, but it was difficult to change their long-held beliefs, like that the cure for AIDS was sleeping with a virgin. It was an experience that changed the course of my life. I kept a journal and sent newsletters home. Family and friends said I should take up a career in writing. So here I am, doing a Journalism course and dreaming of becoming a travel journalist.'

Skills gained:

- Independence
- Coping – no matter how bad things got
- Appreciation of what poverty really is
- Learning the importance of helping others
- Developing the ability to write.

Tim's year

'Vietnam is a very challenging project and we think you could do it' – that was how the charity Tim had applied to first put the idea to him and it's how he ended up in the small provincial town of Thanh Hoa, 180 km north of Hanoi, working in the university teaching English for seven months.

They were right, it was a challenge. He had never taught before, and could not speak the language, but that didn't seem to matter. One week of coaching in Scotland and he was on his way. 'Yes, it was daunting,' says Tim. 'I was teaching students who were all older than me. I was nervous before every lesson, but I said, "Right, it's going to happen", and it did.'

Most weekends he would cycle out to visit his students' homes. 'People are very hospitable and as a teacher I was given a lot of respect. Of course the police kept an eye on me all the time. The only trouble I encountered was when I stayed a day longer than expected. I was rich, compared with most people, earning $50 a month – probably as much as the dean.'

Back home in Sussex, Tim's next job brought him right down to earth – literally. He worked on a farm picking and packing vegetables and being paid £6.50 an hour for an eight-hour day. From there he moved to a school for foreign language students aged 8–12. 'I acted as a kind of Mum, making sure they got to lessons on time in the morning and to bed in the evening, and earned £200 a week.'

Having realised the course he intended to take at Oxford was not for him, he embarked on a second gap year working first at Marks and Spencer and then with Field and Trek, a camping and climbing retailer, earning around £5 an hour. So how was it that after two years' working he arrived at university with a bank balance of just £21.56? Where did it all go? 'On the important things in life,' says Tim. 'Sailing and hillwalking.' Tim is now studying Archaeology and Anthropology at Cambridge.

Skills gained:

- Taking responsibility for yourself
- Dealing with people and their problems
- Maturity.

Hannah's year

'Meet your class – your biology lesson will last three hours.' This is how Hannah, then aged 18, started her teaching assignment in Botswana. She was on her own. No warning. No time for preparation. No time to think. Her students were aged 18–35 and eager to learn. She had studied Biology for A level, but she soon found teaching it was very different.

So started six incredible months living in a tiny village. She had a small room built in the bush with just one electric ring to cook on, and a separate toilet and shower even further into the bush, which she shared with hornets, baby snakes, spiders and a poisonous toad. 'You couldn't help but enjoy yourself. Botswana people are so friendly and generous – always giving. And the pace of life is incredibly relaxed. Their favourite phrase was "No worries".'

Hannah had decided she wanted to do something worth while as well as exciting during her gap year, so she started her search by looking at charities on the internet. A small organisation called Project Trust based on the Island of Coll in the Hebrides caught her eye and she applied. 'Just getting to Coll was a test of ingenuity,' says Hannah. 'Two missed connections, a night on a ferry and a £200 speedy taxi drive across Scotland, financed by Virgin trains, were just part of the adventure. After that, tests such as making a model of the Eiffel tower or giving an impromptu talk on a random topic seemed like nothing at all.' To go on the trip she had to raise £3500, which she did by organising raffles, contacting likely companies, even charging her friends to come to a big party.

After six months in Botswana, Hannah moved on to Johannesburg to work in a children's home. Johannesburg was a Mecca for gap-year students and time off was spent travelling round South Africa, often 16 of them at a time, which she found incredible fun. Hannah is now studying Law at Anglia Ruskin University.

Skills gained:

- Dealing with the unexpected
- Organising projects
- Speaking up when things aren't working out
- Handling difficult situations.

Abi's year

Abi is 18 and has a place at Roehampton University to study Drama, but decided to take a gap year: 'mainly because I just wanted a break from education and the chance to do something I had never done before'. It certainly looks as if she is going to do just that. We caught up with her at our publishers where she was desperately earning as much money as possible before she sets out on that great experience.

'I am off to Kenya with the Tearfund, a relief charity which helps people in 90 countries throughout the world. In Kenya I shall be working mostly with kids and young people and helping to run a nursery in the slums. We will be giving health education and helping with HIV/Aids. I also hope to test out my acting skills.'

Based on the outskirts of Nairobi, she will be living in a tiny flat – two bedrooms, one living room, a bathroom and kitchen – with six other girls. 'I just hope we all get on.'

She will earn nothing. 'In fact I will have to pay to go – £2500 – and I will need another £500 for pocket money while I am there. I'm saving like mad and my parents and church have promised to help.'

She is hoping to travel a bit while in Kenya. 'We get ten days' holiday and are planning to go on a safari and then go down to Mombasa.'

Skills gained:

'I'll tell you when I get back!'

Further information

What to read

- ⊙ *A Year Out in the UK or Overseas: Student Guidelines*, try www.yearoutgroup.org
- ⊙ *Taking a Year Off*, Margaret Flynn, published by Trotman. To order, tel: 0870 900 2665 or visit www.trotman.co.uk/bookshop
- ⊙ *A Year Off . . . A Year Off?*, published by Lifetime Careers. Available from Trotman, tel: 0870 900 2665 or visit www.trotman.co.uk/bookshop
- ⊙ *Opportunities in the Gap Year*, published by the Independent Schools Careers Organisation. Available from Trotman, tel: 0870 900 2665 or visit www.trotman.co.uk/bookshop
- ⊙ *The Gap Year Guidebook*, published by John Catt Educational Ltd. Available from Trotman, tel: 0870 900 2665 or visit www.trotman.co.uk/bookshop
- ⊙ *Before You Go: The ultimate guide to planning your gap year*, Tom Griffiths, published by Bloomsbury Publishing plc. Available from Trotman, tel: 0870 900 2665 or visit www.trotman.co.uk/bookshop
- ⊙ *Working Holidays Abroad* – try grape picking, yacht crewing, driving, tour guiding, beekeeping – there's information on 101,000 jobs in 70 different countries. Available from the Central Bureau, Seymour Mews House, Seymour Mews, London W1H 9PE
- ⊙ *Making the Most of Your Gap Year*, published by Trotman. To order, tel: 0870 900 2665 or visit www.trotman.co.uk/bookshop
- ⊙ *Taking a Gap Year*, Susan Griffith, published by Trotman. To order, tel: 0870 900 2665 or visit www.trotman.co.uk/bookshop.

A gap year for travel abroad

What employer is going to give you time off to travel the world? None. You will never, ever get a chance like this again. So if you have a yen to travel, make the most of your time, and budget wisely. Many gap-year students, especially those who take their gap year after their studies, do it to travel. Some work before they go and see it as a great holiday. Others work their way around from country to country.

When you start to investigate the student travel scene, you'll discover that there's plenty of help available. The path to the Far East, the kibbutz or Camp America is well worn. There is a plethora of publications and organisations, cheap travel firms, ticket concessions – even government advice – handed out to get you safely there and back. If that makes it all sound rather overplayed, pioneers can be accommodated. Backpacking and inter-railing are always journeys into the unknown. Things rarely turn out exactly as you had envisaged. That's the excitement. As for working your passage, most students do a wide range of jobs in a variety of countries before they get back home again. Skiing instructor, courier, au pair, grape picker, summer camp assistant – *Students' Money Matters* met them all.

Further information

Who to contact

◉ The Year Out Group (see page 125) has more than 30 organisations eagerly looking for willing students in order to help fulfill their travel dreams.

◉ AIESEC runs a Work Abroad Programme, which finds work placements for suitable students and recently qualified graduates with companies and other organisations throughout the world, offering work experience for a placement of two to 18 months. Typical placements are for marketing, business studies, IT, engineering, teaching and voluntary projects. It operates in over 85 countries and is represented at 25 universities throughout the UK. Check out its website, www.workabroad.org.uk, or contact AIESEC United Kingdom, 29–31 Cowper Street, London EC2A 4AT. Tel: 020 7549 1800.

◉ Au pair/nanny: try adverts in the *Lady* magazine and *The Times*; also see the *Au Pair and Nanny's Guide to Working Abroad*, published by Vacation Work, available from Trotman, Tel: 0870 900 2665; or visit www.trotman.co.uk/bookshop.

◉ BUNAC – to meet the cash crisis facing many students, BUNAC (British Universities North America Club) organise various paid work and volunteer programmes for students and young people interested in working in the USA, Canada, Ghana, New Zealand, South Africa, Australia, Costa Rica and Peru (see information on the Year Out Group on page 125). It offers financial help through its BUNAC loan plan for Work America and Work Canada schemes. Those working on the Summer Camp USA and KAMP programmes will find that their air fares are paid in addition to all food and accommodation. Every year, BUNAC awards three scholarships of up to £1000 each to help applicants cover the costs of taking part in a BUNAC work-abroad programme to the USA or Canada. To enter the Green Cheese Scholarships, all you need to do is submit a humorous piece of original, creative writing based on a travel-related topic. You're free to write about anything at all – whether it's a trip to the other side of the world or a journey you made closer to home. Entries should be no more than 1500 words. Contact your university/college or BUNAC, 16 Bowling Green Lane, London EC1R 0QH. Tel: 020 7251 3472. Fax: 020 7251 0215. Email: enquiries@bunac.org.uk. Website: www.bunac.org.

Try the internet: feed 'student gap year' into your favourite search engine and you'll have an amazing choice – Ultimate Gap Year, Mad Gap Years, 100s of Gap Year Ideas, Gap Years in 20 Countries and the Gap Year Directory – which tells you what to do, where to go, and has a range of special travel offers and much more besides.

Advice note

While hunting out an amazing adventure, bear in mind that one day you will need to impress a future employer, and what you decided to do now could give you the skills needed to secure a career. That trek through the jungle when a wild beasty slunk off with the rations might provide the ideal answer to the question, 'Have you ever been faced with a challenge when your swift actions saved the day?' Even losing your tickets need not be a complete disaster and dismissed as incompetence, but turned into a useful episode of resourcefulness. Get the picture – always keep your CV in mind.

What to read

All these titles are published by Vacation Work and are available from Trotman, tel: 0870 900 2665; or visit www.trotman.co.uk/bookshop.

- *Summer Jobs USA, Summer Jobs Abroad*

- *Live and Work in France, ... in Spain and Portugal, ... in Italy, ... in Germany, ... in Belgium, the Netherlands and Luxembourg* – a series of books giving details of temporary and permanent work in various countries. Prices vary

- *Working Your Way Around the World* – offers authoritative advice on how to find work as you travel, with hundreds of first-hand accounts. Find out how to become a barmaid, kiwi-fruit packer, ski guide or jackaroo

- *Working in Ski Resorts* – offers details on a variety of jobs from au pair to disc jockey and snow cleaner

- *Teaching English Abroad* – guide to short- and long-term opportunities for both the trained and untrained. Eastern Europe, Greece, Turkey, Japan – the choice is vast and varied

- *Directory of Jobs & Careers Abroad*

- *International Voluntary Work* – gives details of over 500 organisations that recruit all types of volunteers for projects in all parts of the world. It's the A–Z of voluntary work, published by Vacation Work and available from Trotman, tel: 0870 900 2665; or visit www.trotman.co.uk/bookshop.

If you can't afford the books suggested in this chapter, look in your local library. Nearly all the books mentioned here should be found in the reference section of your local public library, and if they are not your library might well order them for you. A group of you might think it worth while buying some of the publications mentioned.

'Students have the time and the opportunity to travel and experience the "ideal" of freedom. You won't get that chance again.'
Loughborough University student, back from Africa

Thrift tips

'It is much more economical to pay rent with bills included. It may look more expensive initially, but works out cheaper in the long run.'

3rd year Performing Arts student, Derby

'Work in a fast-food take-away and eat your favourite junk food for free.'

4th year English student, Cheltenham

'Choose flatmates the same size – it extends your wardrobe.'

1st year Animal Management student, Bradford

The student travel scene

It's all very well to whet your appetite for travel, but how are you going to manage to get to that exotic destination? This section looks briefly at the student travel scene.

As a student, can I get cheap travel abroad?

Yes: there are a number of travel organisations that operate special schemes for students. In fact you will find they are vying for the privilege to send you off on your travels, often dropping the price in the process. If you decide to take the cheapest, make sure it is a reputable organisation, with ABTA (Association of British Travel Agents) membership. It's better to be safe than stranded.

How do I go about getting cheap travel?

If you are already a student, your college Student Travel Office is the best place to start. There you'll find experts who will understand your particular needs and financial restraints, and are ready to give you advice. If you are taking a gap year, or your college has no travel office, then the biggest name in the student travel business these days is STA Travel.

STA Travel specialises in travel for young people. With over 65 branches in universities and on high streets throughout the UK, and 450 worldwide spanning Asia, Australia, Europe, New Zealand, South Africa and the USA, STA Travel is a life-saver if you are ever stranded. They will help send you to just about anywhere in the world and, if you have any problems en route, you can call their international help desk, available worldwide. It is their policy to employ only young and well-travelled consultants in their branches, many of them ex-students who can provide first-hand advice on everything from the initial planning of a trip to the best bars to drink in. *360°*, published by STA Travel, is free and packed full of handy hints, from the top five adrenaline activities down under to their fave festivals around the world.

Chris Connon of STA Travel says:

> 'Whether you want to coach rugby in Fiji, take an African safari, inter-rail around Europe or simply need a cheap flight home, STA Travel can help you get there. All our staff are well-travelled and love speaking about their holidays so can offer you first-hand advice. We've been in the business for over 25 years and have over 450 branches worldwide, so you'll have loads of support while you're on the road. Most of our tickets are flexible, so you can change your mind along the way ... and we are very, very passionate about travel.'

On-campus STA Travel offices are at: Aberystwyth University; Bath University; Belfast University; Birmingham University; Bradford University; Cardiff University; Durham University; University of Kent; University of London Union; Imperial College, London; King's College, London; Leeds University Union; Liverpool Guild of Students; London School of Economics; Queen Mary's & Westfield College; Loughborough University; Manchester University; Northumbria University; Nottingham Trent University; Reading University; Sheffield University and Warwick University. High street branches near universities include: Aberdeen, Belfast, Birmingham, Bournemouth, Bradford, Brighton, Bristol, Cambridge, Cardiff, Coventry, Dundee, Edinburgh, Exeter, Glasgow, Leeds, Liverpool, London, Manchester, Newcastle, Nottingham, Oxford, Preston, Sheffield and Southampton. National telesales: 0870 160 6070; website: www.statravel.co.uk.

The web is also a great source for cheap travel and excellent deals for students.

Advice note

Never pay full fare on bus, coach, train or plane. Take advantage of rail and coach cards, bucket shops selling bargain tickets, classified ads, chartered flights, stand-by fares, advance bookings and deals offered by student travel companies. Some of the budget airlines are giving the most fantastic deals.

What should I join before setting off?

There are five cards that all travel-hungry students should look into:

- **ISIC: £7.** The International Student Identity Card (ISIC) is your ticket to over 33,000 discounts in more than 100 countries worldwide. As the one and only internationally recognised form of student ID, ISIC entitles you to student savings all around the world on flights, buses, trains, ferries, shops, restaurants, accommodation, entertainment and cultural sites and museums! Plus you get free access to ISIConnect services, low-cost international calls, free email address, travel safe and voicemail. ISIC is available to any student who is studying for more than 15 hours a week, and you can get yours from any branch of STA Travel, tel: 0870 160 6070. Don't leave home without one.

- **IYTC Youth Card: £7.** If you are not a full-time student but are aged 25 or under, the International Youth Travel Card (IYTC) is for you. You'll save money on airline tickets, rail passes, accommodation, telecommunications, currency exchange, shopping and also on entrance to museums and other cultural sites in more than 50 countries. Plus you get free access to ISIConnect services, low-cost international calls, free email address, travel safe and voicemail. Available in any branch of STA Travel, tel: 0870 160 6070.

- **YHA: £10** (under 26). YHA (England and Wales) Ltd offers access to domestic and international youth hostels. Changes made to membership rules last year now mean that you don't even have to be a member to use their youth hostels in the UK. Non-members just pay a £3 a night supplement. However, you do need a membership card to use hostels in other countries. An annual card is now down to £10. A two-year card costs £16.50 and a three-year card £20.95. There are over 5000 Youth Hostels across 64 countries. They all have assured standards for hygiene and safety. An annual card for those over 26 costs £15.95, but couples can buy a joint annual card for £22.95. To join call 0870 770 8868 or visit www.yha.org.uk. Address: YHA England and Wales, Trevelyan House, Dimple Road, Matlock, Derbyshire DE4 3YH.

- **Young Person's Railcard: £20.** This entitles all young people aged 16–25 to a third off most rail fares in the UK. Did you know that it also covers the London all-zone One-Day Travel Card? See leaflet for travel restrictions and useful discounts. (Mature students of 26 and over in full-time education also included.)
- **Student Coachcard: £10.** This entitles all students aged 17 and over to a third off National Express and Scottish Citylink fares; also some continental and Irish services – check with your local coach station or Victoria Coach Station, London, or phone National Express Call Centre on 08705 808080.

Cards to carry checklist		
Young Person's Railcard	£20	
Coachcard	£10	
ISIC	£7	
IYTC under-26 card	£7	
YHA card	£10	

Inter-Rail or Euro Domino Pass?

What are they? What's the difference? Which is best?

They are both train travel passes designed to enable you to see as much of Europe as cheaply as possible.

- Have the ultimate flexibility to see Europe the way you want to – you can go where you like, when you like. Your Inter-Rail pass gives you unlimited travel on the extensive network that covers 28 European countries and one African country – Morocco. Travel from 12 days to one month on the railways of Europe from just £159. It is available to European citizens and anyone who has been resident here for six months. Available from STA Travel (0870 160 6070 or www.statravel.co.uk) and other travel agents.
- Euro Domino pass allows you to explore just one country in depth. It offers from three to eight days' unlimited rail travel within a one-month period, so just make your choice from a list of 28 countries. Prices start from £26 for a three-day Czech Republic pass. Contact STA Travel for more details (0870 160 6070 or www.statravel.co.uk).

Further information

Who else could I consult?

The National Tourist Office or Board. Many countries have a national tourist office or board in this country. Most are based in London. London telephone directories can usually be found in the reference section of your local library.

What to read

The *Rough Guide* series (published by Harrap) and the *Lonely Planet* series cover almost every country and provide a useful insight into an area. Cost varies according to the country covered; try your local library.

As a student, do I need insurance?

Our advice is yes, you generally do need insurance when travelling abroad. Some work camps and voluntary agencies arrange insurance for those taking part in projects. Check this out, and check what it covers. There are certain reciprocal arrangements for medical treatment in some EU countries. These also need to be checked out. (Bear in mind: this doesn't mean that all medical expenses will be covered, and your property won't be covered if it's stolen.) Get the Department for Work and Pensions leaflet SA 28/30.

How much will it cost? What should it cover?

Every trip and every traveller is different: STA Travel offers three different types of cover – Backpack, Standard and Premier – to help you find the most appropriate cover for your needs. Backpack is aimed at those travelling light and on a tight budget. Standard offers comprehensive cover at a competitive price, including bungee jumping, downhill skiing and white-water rafting (grades 1–3). Premier is the most extensive cover and includes some additional benefits such as hazardous sports and adventure activities – recommended if you're planning to travel to North America. Endsleigh, on the other hand, offers two options (see tables on the next page).

Endsleigh also offers cover for winter sports, activity travel and most other activities students wish to do.

Contact STA Travel on 0870 160 6070 or www.statravel.co.uk, or visit one of their branches. Or call Endsleigh Insurance on 0800 028 3571 to be connected to your local branch. Alternatively visit one of their 130 branches, many of which are on university campuses, or click on www.endsleigh.co.uk.

Thrift tips from Oxbridge

'Enter competitions you see. Sell things you don't need. Use tea bags twice'

Economics student

'Ebay.co.uk is fantastic for selling anything'

Veterinary Medicine student

'Get involved in student marketing, medical testing, police ID parades – means a little cash to make life easier'

Chemistry student

'Mystery Shopping! www.gapbuster.com: quick good money'

English and Drama student

Advice note

Find out about any rail passes offered by individual European countries. STA Travel should be able to help you out – 0870 160 6070 or www.statravel.co.uk.

STA Travel

Timeframe	Destinations	Backpack	Standard	Premier	Premier incl. USA
1–4 days	Europe	£8	£11	£13	
	Worldwide	£17	£25	£28	£33
10–12 days	Europe	£12	£17	£21	
	Worldwide	£26	£37	£42	£45
31 days	Europe	£18	£26	£31	
	Worldwide	£32	£46	£50	£59
3 months	Europe	£44	£63	£76	
	Worldwide	£69	£99	£109	£123
6 months	Europe	£71	£102	£123	
	Worldwide	£117	£168	£193	£223
12 months	Europe	£120	£194	£232	
	Worldwide	£207	£296	£340	£393

Endsleigh

	Without luggage cover		With luggage cover	
	Essential	Comprehensive	Essential	Comprehensive
Up to 8 days (Europe)	£12.00	£15.00	£15.00	£18.75
Up to 22 days (Europe)	£18.72	£23.42	£23.40	£29.27
Up to 1 month (Europe; Backpacker)	*£23.04	n/a	*£28.80	n/a
6 months (Europe)	£79.20	£102.96	£99.00	£128.70
6 months (Europe; Backpacker)	*£79.20	n/a	*£99.00	n/a
6 months worldwide	£139.39	£209.09	£174.24	£261.36
6 months worldwide (Backpacker)	*£118.74	n/a	*£148.43	n/a
6 months study abroad (Europe)	£63.11	£82.05	£84.15	£109.40
6 months study abroad (worldwide)	£111.08	£167.73	£148.10	£223.64
12 months study abroad (Europe)	£126.23	£164.09	£168.30	£218.79
12 months study abroad (worldwide)	£222.16	£335.45	£296.21	£447.27

17.5% discount online for all travel cover *except* where marked *
*10% discount online for travel cover

★ TOP*TEN* most popular first-degree courses

	Number of students studying subject
Business & Administrative Studies	57,505
Social Studies	42,370
Subjects allied to Medicine	41,690
(but not Medicine & Dentistry: 9030 students study these subjects)	
Creative Arts & Design	41,505
Biological Sciences	39,510
Engineering & Technology	27,845
Languages	26,310
Computer Sciences	24,740
Law	21,025
Historical & Philosophical Studies	20,125
Most exclusive: Veterinary Science	830

(Figures provided by HESA from 2004/2005 student returns)

5

Spotlight on sponsorship

A guide to getting sponsorship, and what to expect from it

The major topics covered in this chapter are:

Probably the best and most comprehensive way of raising extra finance to help you through higher education is sponsorship. It gives you money during term time and work during the vacations.

In this chapter we turn the spotlight on sponsorship, on the changes to the sponsorship market that have been taking place recently, and on some of the companies most likely to give it.

Sponsors and sponsorship

What is sponsorship?

You've heard of big companies sponsoring events such as the London Marathon, the FA Cup and cricket test matches. It means that they back the event with money. In the same way, an organisation could sponsor you through university.

Fast facts on sponsorship	
Who gives it?	Major companies
When?	For a full course
	After first year of study
	After industrial placement
	For final study year
To whom?	Degree and HND students
Most sponsored subject	Engineering
Most likely sponsors	*Manufacturing and production companies
What it's worth	*£1500 pa bursary (median figure)
	*£1086 per-month work periods (median figure 2004)
Other plus points	Work experience – industrial placement, additional skills
Will it secure a job?	Helpful, but no guarantee
*IRS Bulletin, November 2005	

Who gives sponsorship?

- ⊙ Employers – mainly large companies, banks, accountancy firms etc (see also the Power Academy, page 143).
- ⊙ The three Armed Forces (see page 154).
- ⊙ Professional bodies, eg the Institution of Mechanical Engineers (IMechE) (see page 165).
- ⊙ Universities on behalf of employers.

Sponsorship of university students has been going on for many years. It was originally started to attract more young people into engineering. Even today engineering is the major area where sponsorship can be found.

Why do companies give sponsorship?

We canvassed some 150 employers. The reasons most often given were: to have access to high-quality students before they graduate, with the hope of future employment; to assess students over a longer period as potential employees; to develop a student's skills and have an input into their training; and to publicise the company as a potential employer among other students. Or, in their own words:

'Opportunity to see trainees in work situations before graduation.'

'Input of fresh ideas into the company.'

'Gives students a chance to look at us and we to look at them before job offer made.'

How does sponsorship work?

There are no hard-and-fast rules – every company devises its own scheme. In principle it works like this.

As a sponsored student you would get training, work experience and financial help while at college to varying extents, depending on the company scheme. You might be asked to work for a whole year in the company either before or during your course; you might be expected to work only during the summer vacations.

In return, the sponsor gets the opportunity to develop close ties with 'a potentially good employee' and to influence your development. There is generally no commitment on either side to employment after the sponsorship. However, since the company has invested a considerable amount of money in you as a student it is unlikely not to offer you a job.

Check out the Power Academy

The Power Academy is an engineering scholarship fund launched in 2004 for students studying an IEE-accredited degree course at a partner university. It is backed by the IEE, four universities and sixteen companies in the power industry. There are 54 scholarships available in 2006 to students studying at the University of Strathclyde, University of Manchester, University of Southampton and Queen's University, Belfast, for the full length of their course.

The sponsorship offers:

- ⊙ £2000 annual bursary
- ⊙ Payment of university fees
- ⊙ £200 book allowance
- ⊙ summer vacation work
- ⊙ free membership of the IEE
- ⊙ Annual seminar for all PA-sponsored students.

Why such generosity? The Power Academy was set up because there is a shortage of good power graduates coming out of our universities, and the industry could be facing a crisis. It is anticipated that 25% of the power industry's current engineering workforce will retire over the next 15 years, and there are not enough good people around to fill the vacancies. So it looks as if there could be some good jobs available in the future.

The companies involved include CE Electric, Central Networks, EDF Energy, National Grid Transco, Scottish and Southern Energy, Scottish Power, United Utilities, Western Power Distribution, EA Technology, Siemens, ABB, Areva T&D, VA TECH T&D, Atkins Power, Jersey Electricity and Viridian.

To find out more, log on to www.iee.org/poweracademy. See also Greg's story on page 148.

What would sponsorship mean to me?

There are many types of sponsorship. Generally, a sponsorship will include a bursary given while you are studying, and paid work experience, which is usually at the going rate for somebody of your age. In financial terms, it would probably mean that you would be around £40–£60 a week better off than your contemporaries during term time, with guaranteed work for at least 8 weeks during the summer. But it's not just about money – the work experience and training are valuable assets, too.

The question of cash

Looking at it purely in cash terms:

⊙ **£1500* (median figure) annual bursary**

Given during academic study. For manufacturing and production students this could be higher. The Armed Forces give higher rates still, but they have a different kind of arrangement.

⊙ **Salary £1086* monthly (2004 median figure)**

This is what you could expect to earn when working for your sponsor. However, salaries are generally age-related, so a third-year student would earn appreciably more than a pre-degree student. A meaningful average is therefore difficult to provide. As starting salaries for graduates have risen by 3% this figure may also have increased.

(*IRS Employee Bulletin, November 2005.)

Employers' additional costs

From the employer's point of view the costs don't stop there. Generally a sponsorship includes training, which may well mean several weeks at their training centre. Some companies provide a personal tutor for students. There are also courses and meetings to arrange work experience. All this takes time, and time costs money. Every time somebody stops to tell you how to do something, it's work time lost to the employer.

It's a fact!

⊙ Three-quarters of employers that recruit new graduates provide work experience.

⊙ One in four employers provide sponsorship.

⊙ Four in ten manufacturing and production companies provide sponsorship.

⊙ 89% of employers who provide sponsorships turn to their sponsored students when seeking to fill vacancies.

Will my sponsorship bursary affect what I get as my financial support package?

Any scholarship or sponsorship you receive should not be included when calculating fees you must pay – if any – and how much loan you can have. Money earned during vacations is also not included. So for a normal sponsorship the answer is probably no.

Application for sponsorship

How do I get sponsored?

1 You apply to a company that offers sponsorships. These are generally offered to students doing specific subjects.
2 You are offered sponsorship after a period of work experience.
3 Your university has contacts with employers.

What subjects are most likely to attract sponsorship?

Engineering outstrips any other subject, with the largest number of sponsorships being found in the manufacturing and production sector. However, there are good opportunities for civil engineers in the construction industry.

Many employers look for subjects with a close link to their own business activities. Good examples would be Food Science, Quantity Surveying and Polymer Technology. So if you feel you are studying a degree relevant to a company's business it is worth a try.

Any discipline: a few organisations, especially in the financial sector, will sponsor people on any degree course, but you have to have an interest in finance.

When could I get sponsorship?

- After A levels or BTEC for a full degree or HND course.
- After a gap year spent with a company, between A levels and higher education.
- After your first year of study.
- After a successful period of work experience or an industrial placement year.
- For your final year of study.

While sponsorships are still given to A level students for their full three to four years of academic study, more and more companies are choosing to sponsor students later in their degree course, when a commitment to the subject has been established. Work placements and sponsorships are now considered to be one of the best graduate recruitment tools by large employers. A recent IRS survey suggested that around 70% of sponsored students take up employment with their sponsor on graduating.

The University Schools Liaison Officer of IMechE says:

> ‘The sponsorship market has changed over the last few years.
> Companies have certainly cut back on numbers and many offer
> only a final-year sponsorship, but I think it has reached its
> trough. Many of the smaller organisations that only want one or
> two sponsorship students are now going straight to the
> universities of their choice and asking for who they want. This is
> largely to avoid having to deal with the thousands of
> applications which advertising in our publication would
> engender. There are some good sponsorships around which are
> well worth going after.’

What to expect when applying for sponsorship

The application form

These are more likely to be online than paper forms these days and you need to think
carefully when filling them in, because you only get one chance. Mess it up, and your
application will go no further.

Employers are – quite naturally – looking for the brightest and best students to
sponsor; they want to have the pick of the potential high-flyers at an early stage.
When many students first apply for sponsorship they have only their GCSE results,
possibly some AS level results and a headteacher's report to show what they are
capable of. This can be tough on those who wake up academically after GCSE or who
really excel only in their one chosen subject. But good employers are more aware than
you might expect; selection is not on academic qualifications alone. Sponsors are
looking for signs of those additional qualities needed to succeed in your chosen
career: leadership potential, the ability to grasp ideas quickly and to work in a team.
They want ambitious, innovative, get-up-and-go people who can think for themselves
and get things done. So if your GCSE grades slipped a bit – or, as one student we
interviewed put it, 'you look like Mr Average on paper' – think through what else you
have been doing. Playing in the football or hockey team; helping out at the local club;
hiking across Europe; getting a pop group together – it could help to redress the
balance. Remember: the application form is the first weeding-out process, and you are
up against stiff competition. This is no time for false modesty – you've got to sell
yourself for all you're worth.

The interview

Interviews vary enormously. Some companies give a full-scale assessment with
psychometric testing, tricky questioning and watching how you respond to certain
situations. Others are much more laid-back and go for a straight interview. Whatever
the process, if you are an A level student it will probably be something quite new to
you. Don't worry. The company will be fully aware of this and will not ask you to do

something you are not capable of. Remember, too, that your competitors will be in much the same position.

Still, don't expect an easy time at an interview.

How I got my sponsorship

Alex is 18 and a first-year student at Manchester University. This is her story:

'Out of the blue a letter arrived from Manchester University saying Procter & Gamble were offering sponsorships and would I like to apply? Would I! I had applied to Manchester University to study Chemical Engineering with Chemistry; I had a provisional place, but A levels were still several months away. If I was interested, I had to apply direct to P&G – online.

'Having filled in my application form, I was then asked to complete a "personality" test, again online.

'Next I went to Manchester to take yet another test, this time "critical thinking". This was in two parts – an English section and a lateral thinking section. I was told it was the same test given to graduates wanting to join the company. It was not exactly difficult, but certainly challenging. I think if you didn't have an engineer's mind you might struggle. We were told the results right away.

'Two weeks later I was back in Manchester for an interview. I was very nervous and a bit scared. By now I had learnt this was a new sponsorship programme being set up and that there were just two or possibly three sponsorships available – 25 students had applied. My chances of success were slim.

'I had never done anything like this before. It was a one-to-one interview with the head of the sponsorship programme. Most of the questions were based on how you would cope in difficult situations and leading a team – and they wanted examples. Fortunately I had been on the Duke of Edinburgh's Award Scheme, so I had plenty of examples of leadership. But it was tough. You had to think on your feet, and concentrate hard.'

Alex was successful, and so were two other students at Manchester University.

A few weeks after starting her course, Mike Dean, who runs the sponsorship programme, arrived in Manchester to take all three sponsored students out for dinner so they could meet. They are now close friends. Alex's advice on getting sponsorship? 'Do your homework; research the company you are applying to.'

What Alex receives:

- Bursary of £1500 pa (she has used this to cover her fees and books)
- Ten weeks' guaranteed work experience during the summer. Pay: £1650 a month
- Entrée to the P&G staff shop where all P&G products are sold at cost price – 'Anyone fancy a Pringle?'

Work experience

Students gain amazing experience during placements, but make sure it is the right experience for you. It is important not to be so mesmerised by the bursary money that you don't consider what the company offering sponsorship does and whether it can provide experience that will help your career. The downside to a sponsorship is that during your degree all your work experience will be in one company and, because of this, it can shape the direction of your future career. When you go for your interview ask about the experience and training you can expect and the skills you will acquire.

Greg's sponsorship

'The most amazing piece of luck' is how Greg Metcalf would describe getting sponsorship for his degree. Greg is currently in the final year of a degree in Electrical Engineering and Electronics at Manchester University. For the last two years of his degree he has been sponsored by National Grid, which controls most of the UK electricity transmission system. This is how it happened:

'It was towards the end of my second year at university. It was like any other day; I was sitting in a lecture when Eddie Welch, the Industrial Liaison Manager, burst in. "Would anybody be interested in attending an interview at National Grid with the chance of a sponsorship?" Eleven hands shot up. Eleven applied. Eleven were accepted.'

'I knew what National Grid was, but not as somewhere you could knock on the door and say "give us the money". The sponsorship was organised under a new programme called the Power Academy, set up by the IEE (see page 143). All we had to do was send off our CVs and then attend an interview – not hard; it was with two newish graduates.

'They wanted us to work during the summer vacation and would then give us a bursary for the following year. It was very late in the year when all this happened and unfortunately I had already arranged work experience for that summer vacation at an oil refinery, but they gave me the bursary for the next year anyway – that meant £2000 plus my fees paid, plus a £200 book allowance. I can tell you that certainly alleviated the financial situation at home; my parents were more than chuffed.

'I actually spent the money on updating my wheels – nothing flash – a 1993 Vauxhall Cavalier, which was better than the banger I already had. This was not a luxury – my car is my pastime – my hobby – my relaxation.

'Last summer I worked at National Grid – what a fantastic experience. I joined their Asset Policy Group. I had to write a National Grid technical report on the environmental lifecycle of the different types of switching gear they used. This covered raw materials, manufacturing, commissioning, use, and then decommissioning. I had never done anything like this before. It was a real-world experience, the type of thing you would do in a genuine job. I felt I had done a worthy piece of work which they were happy with. In fact, it is being published right now. That will look good on my CV.

'I was working in Warwick and living in a huge student house with 23 other students. During that eight weeks I earned £2200 (based on a salary of £15,600). In such an environment, it is not surprising I didn't save that much, but I did have a great time.'

Greg has now applied to National Grid for a job, along with five other companies.

What Greg received:

Year 3	
Bursary	£2000
Fees	£1150
Book/software allowance	£200 (he did not use all this)
Membership of the IEE	
Earnings, summer 2005 (8 weeks)	£2,200
Year 4	
Bursary	£2000
Fees	£1175
Book/software allowance	£200 (used it all)
Membership of the IEE	

Thrift tips

'Get a bike.'

1st year Social and Political Sciences student, Cambridge

'Work on Friday and Saturday evenings so you don't drink.'

4th year Computer Science student, Paisley

'Make one of your BT Friends and Family numbers your internet server and save 20% on every call.'

2nd year Physics student, Durham

Terms and conditions

How much time do I have to spend with my sponsor?

Some sponsors demand you spend a year working with them either during your course or for a gap year before university. Others give you the choice. Most stipulate summer vacation work of six to eight weeks. Students often ask for more and may do Easter vacation work as well. Engineering firms are generally more demanding and the sponsorship is more likely to be geared to a sandwich course, so you could be looking at a full year in industry plus two summer vacation placements.

Planned vacation work

Some companies will hold special vacation-planning sessions. These are usually during the Easter vacation and can last anything up to a week. During these sessions you would plan with your sponsor how you want to spend your summer vacation time.

Comment: sponsors occasionally allow their sponsored students to gain experience in other companies during vacations, as they feel that it will help to broaden their mind and knowledge. But most are loath to do so, for obvious reasons.

Am I obliged to join my sponsor after graduating? Are they obliged to employ me?

No, you are not obliged to join your sponsoring company after graduating, unless it says so in your contract. Equally, they are not obliged to offer you a job. But there is no doubt that companies are taking a tougher stand these days, and seeking value for money from their sponsorships. For example:

⦿ Some companies will stop your bursary payment for the final year if you don't agree to join them after graduating.

⦿ A few companies demand reimbursement of their sponsorship money if you don't join them. You would have been informed of this before you agreed to a sponsorship.

⊙ Some companies only give sponsorship for the final year after a job offer has been accepted.

Comment: The Armed Forces are slightly different from other employers; they have always included service as part of their sponsorship schemes.

Fact file

43.4% of employers recruit from students who undertake work experience with them. 72% of employers offer work experience/sponsorship as part of their recruitment strategy.

(IRS survey, November 2004)

Can my sponsor terminate my sponsorship?

Sponsorship is a legal contract. Look at the terms carefully. Most agreements will have a clause that allows the employer to withdraw if your academic performance is unsatisfactory. There may be other clauses you should watch out for.

What exactly is meant by academic performance?

If you fail the odd exam, you're probably all right, but if your end-of-year results are so bad that you have to repeat the year, you may find that your sponsor is no longer interested.

Other aspects to consider

How do I choose a sponsor?

'Be practical – go for the cash' was one student's advice on selecting a sponsor. Certainly cash is something to bear in mind, but there are many other factors to consider:

⊙ Compare salaries for work experience and bursaries: the plus on one might rule out the minus on the other.

⊙ Check out the training (engineers: is the training accredited by the appropriate institution?) and the experience – is it a well-organised programme of development or are you just another pair of hands?

Advice note

⊙ Make sure any literature you are reading on sponsorship is up to date – school and college careers libraries are notorious for displaying last year's information.

⊙ Look at your contract in detail and, above all, check the small print.

⊙ Question your sponsor; they will respect you for that.

- Talk to students on the scheme; find out about projects undertaken; how many sponsored students joined the company as graduates?
- Where would you be located? Do they provide accommodation if away from home? Are there opportunities to gain experience abroad?
- Finally, ask yourself: is this the kind of company where you would want to make your career?

When should I apply for sponsorship?

- **Full degree course sponsorship**: some companies offer sponsorship for your full degree course. Applications for these schemes should be made early in your final school year, and at least by the time you send in your UCAS form.
- **Second-year degree course sponsorship**: some sponsors like to see commitment to their course among students before offering sponsorship. Applications should be made early in your first year at university. Ask your department head for likely sponsors.
- **Final-year degree course sponsorship**: increasingly, employers are offering sponsorship to students for just the final year of their degree course. Often this will be offered after a successful industrial placement year or summer vacation period. Employers offering sponsorship at this stage will expect students to agree to join them after graduation.

Jono's sponsorship

I went to Loughborough to study Mechanical Engineering, but a week after getting there I was asked if I would like to be a guinea-pig. They were starting up a completely new course called Innovative Manufacturing and Technology. If I took the course I would get sponsorship – a bursary of £500 a year for the first two years and then £1000 for the next two years. It wasn't the money that decided me: the course is really interesting; I liked the idea of doing something so new. There are only three students on the course. Another feature of the course is that the sponsorship comes from a mix of companies, so you receive a wide range of work experience and work in a number of different companies such as Perkins, Bentley, IMI Morgan, Caterpillar – all good names.

What's the competition for sponsorship?

Phenomenal. All sponsors say that applications outstrip sponsorships available, and it is getting worse – so get in early. The earlier you apply, the better. Applications for full course sponsorship should have been made by the time you send in your UCAS form.

What is a sponsor looking for?

A straw poll of sponsors suggested that sponsors favour students with:

- Good A level grades
- Maturity
- Potential
- Ambition

⊙ Evident team skills

⊙ Sense of humour

⊙ Hard-working attitude

⊙ Ability to get a good second-class degree

⊙ Interest in their degree topic

⊙ Ability to assimilate information and learn quickly

⊙ Spark that sets you apart from the rest

⊙ Business awareness

⊙ Interpersonal skills.

Fact check

⊙ Median starting salary paid to graduates in 2004 was £21,000 pa. Anticipated figure for 2005 is £22,000 (AGR Graduate Recruitment Survey 2005).

⊙ 16% of employers said they paid graduate starting salaries of £25,000–£30,000 and another 6% paid over £30,000 in 2004 (AGR Graduate Recruitment Survey 2005).

⊙ 306,365 first-degree students – a record number – graduated from higher education institutions in the UK (HESA release 2005).

⊙ 25% of employers said that sponsorship schemes were too costly to justify their use to their organisations (IRS Survey, November 2005).

⊙ Typical sponsors are large firms with 1000–9000 employees.

⊙ Approximately 119,405 students in the UK are enrolled on sandwich courses (HESA 2004–2005).

Which comes first – UCAS or sponsorship?

They both come at once, which makes for complications. However, both sides are aware of this, so a system has been worked out.

First you should discover whether a sponsor you are interested in requires you to gain a place on a particular course – if so, you should name that course on your UCAS form.

However, it could happen that an employer you had not originally been very interested in offers you a sponsorship with the proviso that you gain a place on a course not named in your selection on your application form. While UCAS does not generally allow students to make alterations to their original application, in the case of sponsorship they usually relax this rule.

What about deferred entry?

Another complication is whether you want deferred entry or not. If you get sponsorship, your sponsor may require you to do a pre-degree year in industry, but at application time you may not know this. If in doubt, apply for the current year. It is always easier to ask a university to defer your entry rather than bring it forward. On some courses, especially popular courses such as Law, deferment may be more difficult to arrange.

Will my university find me sponsorship?

If you are accepted on to a course either conditionally or unconditionally, it is always a good idea to ask the course director if they know of any sponsoring companies. Often they will have a list. Some students will find that they are automatically offered sponsors to apply to, and on some courses that are actually sponsored by employers, the sponsors are involved in the selection procedure. College prospectuses may give you some guidance. A number of universities advertise sponsored courses in *Engineering Opportunities for Students and Graduates* – for details see 'What to read' at the end of this chapter.

Not all sponsors advertise

If you look down the list of sponsors in most sponsorship books, you will be surprised how many large companies appear not to offer sponsorship or work experience, yet in fact they do. Many companies just don't have to bother to advertise – the requests flood in anyway. Others will have special relationships with selected schools or universities. So, just because a company doesn't advertise sponsorship, that shouldn't stop you from asking.

Don't forget the smaller companies

If you're thinking in terms of your CV, it must be admitted that a well-known name will carry more weight than a smaller company. But with a smaller, little-known company there is less competition. Perhaps more important, you are likely to be treated as an individual. You may well be the only sponsored student they have and can develop your own training and experience package. Of course, if they have no experience of sponsored students, they may not know what you are capable of and what experience you should be receiving. So you could find you have to stand up for yourself.

Is it best to apply to local companies?

It is always best to apply to a company that interests you. Nevertheless, some companies do prefer to take on local people. From their point of view, there is no accommodation problem when it comes to work experience, and statistics show that many students want to return to their own home town to work when they complete their studies. So the company is more likely to keep the sponsored student as an employee.

Will sponsorship be good for my CV?

Yes – but with reservations; 73% of the companies we asked said sponsorship was a plus point. The others felt that it made little difference. A careers adviser at Bath University said that, while sponsorship on your CV shows that you have been 'selected', it was the work experience that would be seen as the important element on a CV.

Of course, employers will probably ask why you didn't join the company that sponsored you, so you will need to have a well-phrased answer. Most employers realise that a decision made at the age of 18 may not look so right when you are 22. It's always worth remembering that your would-be new employer may write to your sponsor for a reference, so it's important to leave your sponsoring company on good terms.

Should I try the Armed Forces?

The three Armed Forces offer very generous sponsorships, which can cover fees and full living costs. But their Cadetship and Bursary schemes are not open-ended. There is a service commitment involved and those taking them up should think very carefully about what they are getting involved in. Full details are available from:

- Army Officer Entry, Freepost LON15 445, Bristol BS38 7UE. Tel: 08457 300111. Websites: www.army.mod.uk/servingsoldier/condofserv/mm/index.html (for students looking for support while at university); www.army.mod.uk/careers/officer (for students looking for an army career); www.armyjobs.co.uk (for army jobs).
- Royal Air Force, Officer Careers, Freepost 4335, Bristol BS1 3YX. Tel: 0845 605 6555; website: www.rafcareers.com.
- The Royal Navy and Royal Marines Careers Service, Dept BR211, FREEPOST GL672, Cirencester GL7 1BR. Tel: 0845 607 5555; website: www.royalnavy.mod.uk.

Will I pay tax on my bursary?

You do not have to pay tax on a bursary. But if your annual earned income is above the tax threshold of £5035 you would have to pay tax. So a year's placement is probably not tax-free.

Advice note

Been unlucky in securing sponsorship? Try the back-door entry. When you're looking for a summer vacation job, seek out companies that you feel could be interested in sponsoring your particular skills. You may be lucky, and there's no harm in asking.

Can I get sponsorship once I've started my degree?

Yes. As we said under the 'When should I apply for sponsorship?' section, more and more companies are giving sponsorship just for the final year or from the second year of a course. These sponsorships often develop from a successful period of work experience during the summer vacations, or through an industrial placement during a sandwich course.

Should sponsorship determine which course I choose?

In theory, no. First you should decide on the course that best suits you. You're going to spend at least three solid years – and possibly more – studying, so make sure you're going to enjoy it, otherwise the results could be at best disappointing and at worst disastrous.

I'm a sponsored student, but find I don't like the course I'm studying. What can I do?

This happens. You choose a course in something that you may never have studied before, and after a term or so you discover that you and the subject just don't get along together. A sponsorship is not a life sentence, and neither is a degree course. Talk first to your college tutor. It may be just one aspect of the course you don't like. Then talk to your sponsor. You will probably be able to change your degree course, but it may be more difficult – or impossible – for your sponsor to put you on an appropriate sponsorship scheme. Don't despair. Whatever you do, be frank about your change of heart – and the sooner the better, before too much time and money are wasted.

To sum up
What do I gain from being sponsored?

- Money – probably an annual bursary plus good rates of pay when working.
- Training – most sponsorships will involve some form of training.
- Meaningful work experience.
- Guaranteed employment for the summer in an area that will assist you with your studies.
- Chance of future employment – but no guarantee.
- Help with final-year project work – possibly.
- Opportunity to gain first-hand knowledge of the working environment where you might possibly start your career.
- Understanding of what it means to work in industry.
- Chance to gain new skills.
- Plus-point to put in your CV.

What do I lose?

- ⊙ Your holiday time is not your own. So, for example, you would not be able to spend the whole summer abroad going Inter-Railing.
- ⊙ You have the chance to see only one industry/company during work experience.
- ⊙ You make a career choice at 18 that may not be what you want at 21.
- ⊙ You may be obliged to work for a company whether you want to or not, because of a payback clause.
- ⊙ You may be asked to work in locations that are not very appealing and possibly a long way from home.

Further information

Who to contact

- ⊙ The Year in Industry (see page 127).
- ⊙ Local employers that interest you – many employers prefer to sponsor local students.
- ⊙ Don't forget the smaller companies. Some may never have thought of offering work experience before, so it can be a matter of making yourself sound a good bet.
- ⊙ Your course director.
- ⊙ Your university or college may well have a list of sponsors who are interested in sponsoring students on your particular course. Some universities advertise in the books below.
- ⊙ Black and Asian high-flyers – try the Windsor Fellowship Undergraduate personal and professional development programmes, which include summer work placements and community work. Application forms and further information can be downloaded from www.windsorfellowship.org/leadership.

What to read

- ⊙ *Everything You Wanted to Know about Sponsorship, Placements and Graduate Opportunities*, regularly updated and published by Amoeba Publications. Available from Trotman, tel: 0870 900 2665, or visit www.trotman.co.uk/bookshop.
- ⊙ *Engineering Opportunities for Students and Graduates*, published by the Institution of Mechanical Engineers on behalf of the engineering profession. It lists sponsors and universities with sponsored courses, companies offering industrial placements and internships and is available free from IMechE c/o Marketing & Communications Department, 1 Birdcage Walk, London SW1H 9JJ. Tel: 020 7222 3337, email: education@imeche.org.uk.
- ⊙ *University Scholarships, Awards and Bursaries* by Brian Heap, published by Trotman. To order, tel: 0870 900 2665 or visit www.trotman.co.uk/bookshop.

★ TOPTEN *social spenders*

	Weekly spend
2nd year Sports Coaching, Wolverhampton	£200
1st year Pharmacology with Human Physiology, Wolverhampton	£200
3rd year Geography and Education, Wolverhampton	£80
1st year Computer Games Design, Wolverhampton	£80
2nd year Film Studies, Wolverhampton	£70
1st year Nursing, Wolverhampton	£65
3rd year Zoology, Southampton	£60
2nd year Physical Education, Wolverhampton	£55
1st year Criminology, Lancaster	£50
1st year Product Design, Robert Gordon	£40

6

Other sources to tap

Scholarships, charitable awards, trusts, competitions

The topics covered in this chapter are:

In this chapter we investigate all the other legitimate sources of finance you could tap to raise extra cash, and how to set about approaching them. They include trusts, charitable awards, scholarships, bursaries (from sources other than from your local authority or university, such as professional institutions) and competitions.

Other sources of finance: a reality or a vain hope?

You are right to be a little sceptical. If there were a prodigious number of organisations all eager to hand out money to students, you wouldn't have seen so many student demonstrations called to highlight their financial plight. But there are a surprising number of educational charities, trust funds and foundations, professional bodies, and benevolent funds available in this country offering financial help to students. This may take the form of a scholarship or charitable award. One directory of grant-making trusts we consulted listed over 1500 organisations under the broad heading of Education. But before you get too excited and think you've found the route to a crock of gold, be aware that when you start sifting through the many restrictions which trusts generally have to abide by, you soon realise there are relatively few – if any – that could meet your exact needs.

What is a scholarship?

Scholarships differ from sponsorships in that they provide money while you study, but without the industrial training. They can, of course, be for a specific purpose like travel, to fund some special area of research or possibly to study abroad. They are usually, though not always, given by an institution – this could be your university, a professional institute or a charitable trust – rather than by individual companies.

Competition is keen. Awards can be made on grounds of academic achievement or need. Whatever the criteria, they are not going to come your way without considerable effort and often disappointment, so be prepared. Nobody gives money away easily.

How does a scholarship differ from a bursary?

It doesn't, really. Look up 'scholarship' in the dictionary and you'll find the definition is: 'award of money towards education'. Look up 'bursary' and it says, 'scholarship or grant awarded to students'. Sometimes a bursary is awarded if you meet certain criteria – for example, bursaries are given to low-income students under the new top-up fee funding arrangements (see Chapter 2) and to nurses/midwives undertaking training (see Chapter 3). To win a scholarship there is more likely to be an element of achievement (for example academic, musical or sporting).

Fast facts on alternative sources of finance	
Who gives bursaries and scholarships?	Charitable trusts, universities and colleges, professional bodies and institutions
How much?	From £12 to £4000 and everything in between
What is the success rate?	Low

What is a charitable award?

The difference between a scholarship and a charitable award is, again, very indistinct, and you could say there is no difference at all, as charitable awards can often be scholarships. Charitable awards are always paid out by a charitable organisation, which must abide by the terms and conditions of the original endowment. So however good and reasonable your case may be, if the money has to be paid out to a student from Gloucester studying Chemistry, it is no good being an Arts student from Leeds. To claim an award, both you and your financial predicament must fit the charity's help profile.

What kind of awards are available?

Often the payments are small – to buy books or equipment – but they can be quite substantial and cover fees or maintenance. So it could be from a few hundred pounds to a few thousand. They can be one-off payments, or given each year for the duration of your course.

Who gives scholarships and charitable awards?

Universities, schools, trust funds, professional institutions.

Finding out about scholarships and charitable awards

Can my school help me?

Yes, most schools will have a list of local charities that offer help to students. The fact that you have been to the school could be a condition of receiving a grant. Also try your primary school. It is a good idea to find out if such scholarships, grants and charitable awards are available before you send off your UCAS application, as these sometimes stipulate a certain higher education establishment.

Can my local authority help?

Your local authority should have details of any local charities offering help to students in higher education. Try also:

⊙ The Welsh Assembly, which offers bursaries to Welsh-born students attending Welsh universities.

⊙ The Carnegie Trust for the Universities of Scotland, which provides financial assistance to students of Scottish birth or who have at least one parent born in Scotland or who have completed at least two years' secondary education in Scotland, and who want to attend Scottish universities to study for a first degree. They also offer vacation scholarships to enable undergraduates to undertake a research project during the long vacation. Scholarships are also given to graduates from Scottish universities with a first-class Honours degree for three years' postgraduate research at a university in the UK, more usually in Scotland. Contact Carnegie Trust for the Universities of Scotland, Cameron House, Abbey Park Place, Dunfermline, Fife KY12 7PZ. Tel: 0138 362 2148. Email: jgray@carnegie-trust.org. Website: www.carnegie-trust.org.

⊙ The Students' Award Agency for Scotland maintains a Register of Educational Endowments on Scottish trusts, many of which are local and open only to Scottish-born students wanting to attend Scottish universities and colleges. The Agency will search the Register on behalf of any student who submits an enquiry form. Forms are available from the Students' Award Branch, Gyleview House, 3 Redheughs Rigg, Edinburgh EH12 9HH. Tel: 0131 476 8212. Email: saas.geu@scotland.gsi.gov.uk. Or you can contact them through their website: www.saas.gov.uk.

⊙ See also 'What to read', page 172, for directories and registers on trusts.

Check out your parents' employers!

Or at least get your parents to. A surprising number of companies and large employers have special trusts set up to help with the education of their employees' or past employees' children. Typical examples:

⊙ The Miners' Welfare National Education Fund for dependants of those working in the coal mining industry.

⊙ The National Police Fund, which helps the children of people who are serving in or have served in the police force.

⊙ The Royal Medical Benevolent Fund, which helps the children of medical graduates, and the Dain Fund Charities Committee (contact the BMA), which helps the children of registered members of the medical profession.

⊙ The Royal Pinner School Foundation, which helps the children of sales representatives.

Do universities and colleges give scholarships?

Some higher education institutions are endowed by generous benefactors and can award scholarships and bursaries to selected students who meet the required criteria. Usually an institution will have a very mixed bag of awards, which bears very little relation to its academic strengths and interests. Most establishments don't give many awards, and competition in the past has been keen. But with the advent of top-up fees, universities are having to provide bursaries for students to offset the high cost of university education (see page 42). Many of the university scholarships on offer have a subject or location condition attached, which does considerably limit those eligible to apply.

University Scholarships, Awards and Bursaries (by Brian Heap, published by Trotman), supplies full information on the new bursaries universities are giving, especially to students from low-income families, and lists over 100 institutions offering scholarships or awards. These are largely for people studying specific subjects, or are travel awards. Subjects vary from the more usual (Engineering, History, Geography, Languages, Law and the sciences) to the distinctly unusual, such as Cultural Criticism Studies, Paper Science, Rural Studies, Retail Studies, Leisure, Town Planning, Textiles – and a whole lot in between.

A growing number of sports scholarships and bursaries are now available, covering areas such as rugby, cricket, netball and even golf. A sports scholarship is a boon for any student who plays in a national team and needs to take time out and coaching to train for an international/world cup series. You can be studying any subject to get a sports scholarship.

A number of universities and colleges give music or choral awards. Many of these are old foundations, and may include a commitment to take part in services in the college chapel or local church or cathedral. Then there are awards with geographical restrictions. For example, students at Bangor University might get an award of £100 if they live in Criccieth or, better still, £500 if they were born in the counties of Anglesey, Conwy or Gwynedd; and Exeter students whose parents have resided in Honiton, Devon for the last 15 years could be in line for £100 pa.

Your university may also give travel awards to undertake special projects during the vacation, for certain subjects. Ask your university for details of possible awards (see also *University Scholarships, Awards and Bursaries*, by Brian Heap).

Are there awards for foreign students?

Yes. Overseas students are eligible to apply for many of the awards offered by universities. In some universities there are awards specifically for foreign students. For example, Engineering and Applied Science at Aston (£1500–£3000), Law scholarships at City University (£1250) and the South East Asia scholarships for undergraduates or postgraduates at Stirling (up to £2000). For further information contact the British Council or British Embassy in your own country, the British Council here in the UK (www.britishcouncil.org) or the university where you will be studying.

How much would a college scholarship be worth?

Awards vary tremendously: some are given annually for the length of the course, others are a one-off payment. The highest award we found was £4000 while the lowest was £12 – this is because the foundation was made in the nineteenth century, when £12 was a lot of money, and its status cannot be changed.

Thrift tips

'*Student tutoring for GCSEs and A levels. Hourly rate £10.*'

1st year Sociology student, Manchester Metropolitan

'*Borrow from your parents: they are interest-free loans.*'

3rd year Applied Psychology student, Liverpool John Moores

'*Get the free overdraft and put it in a high-interest account, bond or ISA.*'

Business Studies student, Staffordshire

How would I go about getting a college scholarship?

Scholarship distribution methods differ from institution to institution and, of course, the terms of the foundation. Aberystwyth, for example, holds formal examinations during January each year. These can be taken at the student's own school or college. It gives 40 entry scholarships worth between £450 and £1150 a year. Entries need to be in by 15 December and scholars receive unconditional offers in March of the year of entry, together with the promise of university accommodation for the whole of their course. Up to 120 merit awards of £300 and an unconditional offer are also given to candidates who do well in the examinations but who narrowly fail to gain a scholarship. Music bursaries (£400) are also available. To be eligible, candidates must have obtained a Grade 8 music qualification in an orchestral instrument. Selection is by interview and closing date is mid-May.

The ancient Scottish universities all offer a range of bursaries. Those at Glasgow are awarded once students have begun their courses. However, at Aberdeen, Edinburgh and St Andrews, bursaries are available to entrants. Traditionally awards were made on the basis of exam performance, but at Aberdeen and Edinburgh, in particular, the bursary schemes have developed to include a significant number of awards, which take into account applicants' financial and personal circumstances. Application forms are available from the universities concerned; increasingly, bursary information and application forms can be found on university websites. Most of these scholarships are worth £1000 for each year of degree study (in total, £4000 for a Scottish Honours degree or £5000 for a degree in Clinical Medicine), with some 35 awards available for entry in September 2005, including 10 Alumni Annual Fund Bursaries and 20 Merit Bursaries. Competition is fierce. Last year there was a one-in-four chance of receiving an award.

First look in the college prospectus – it should either list the awards given, or give you an address to write to for details. This should be done early in the autumn term of your final school year and before or about the time you are filling in your UCAS form. Obviously at this stage you do not know which university you are likely to go to, and any exam can be held early in the academic year, before you have made your final decision.

Professional institutions

Do professional institutions give scholarships?

Some do, some don't. The engineering institutions are among the most generous. Awards are made to students studying accredited degree courses.

⦿ IEE, Michael Faraday House, Six Hills Way, Stevenage, Hertfordshire SG1 2AY. Email: scholarships@iee.org. Through its scholarships and awards the IEE promotes engineering as a career, rewards achievement and assists with postgraduate research. In 2006, the IEE will award 76 scholarships of £1000 pa for the duration of an IEE-accredited MEng degree course, including 50 IEE FUSE (Funding Undergraduates to Study Engineering) Scholarships, available for high-ability students in need of financial assistance. There are also eight grants of £1000 (one year only) available for final-year undergraduate students. There are

13 postgraduate scholarships ranging from £1250 to £10,000 pa, including the prestigious Leslie H Paddle Fellowship, and 11 travel awards ranging from £500 to £1000. See also sponsorship through the Power Academy on page 143.

◉Institution of Civil Engineers, One Great George Street, Westminster, London SW1P 3AA. Tel: 020 7665 2193; email: questawards@ice.org.uk; website: www.ice.org.uk/quest. The Queen's Jubilee Scholarship Trust (QUEST) awards over 60 scholarships each year to undergraduate students embarking

How I got a Whitworth Scholarship

Paul Tuohy is in his final year of a 4-year-sandwich degree in Mechatronic Engineering. He left school at 16 with a clutch of 11 GCSEs. He went on to study for his A levels, but illness meant that he would have to repeat a year and he decided to begin a Modern Apprenticeship instead. Having scored excellent marks for a BTEC ONC and HNC through day-release, he decided he wanted to continue studying. This is his story.

'I liked to learn something new, I had the study bug; so when the personnel officer at the company where I was working said the firm would sponsor me if I wanted to take a degree part-time, I jumped at the chance. However, there was one proviso: I needed the permission of my boss, the Chief Engineer. It seemed like just a formality, but to my horror he said categorically 'No!'. I could not believe it. Nor could anyone else. A few months later I left the company.

'To be honest, he probably did me a favour. I decided to study for a degree anyway, but to do it full time. It was to be a BEng (Hons) in Mechatronics with Industrial Experience. Fortunately I lived in Manchester and the course being offered at Manchester University was much better than the part-time course I had considered. Even though I had no A levels, the university said they would give me a chance. 'You may struggle with the maths,' they said and they were right, but other topics came more easily and I was prepared to work hard.

'I was used to having plenty of money to spend – I'd been on a salary of over £20,000 – and wondered how I would cope as a student. I had some money saved. I took out a student loan. My parents said I could live at home free while I studied and I bought a bicycle to save on travel fares.

'In my first semester my results averaged 76%. In my second semester I did even better, and with an average of 81% was awarded the Mechatronic Student of the Year Prize. It was then that our Industrial Liaison Manager, Eddie Welch, suggested I should apply for a Sir Joseph Whitworth Scholarship given by the Institution of Mechanical Engineers (IMechE).

'There were around 40 applicants that year and only ten scholarships to be awarded. Having filled in an application form, I attended an interview with a panel of some five lecturers and engineers down at the IMechE in London. It was tough. Two days later they phoned to say I had been awarded a scholarship valued at £3000 a year. That certainly helped with my finances.

'Last year I spent a year in industry at Rolls Royce. I am now back at uni and have received another award under the Whitworth Scholarship scheme – this time £4000.

'If I continue to do well, I should become a Whitworth Scholar, which means I can put BEng WhSch. after my name when I graduate.

'I have been offered the chance to return to Rolls Royce at the end of my degree, but as I said, I've got the study bug, and I am now thinking of doing a PhD.'

on ICE-accredited courses aiming to achieve Chartered, Incorporated or Technician Membership of ICE. The awards are up to the value of £1500 per year for the duration of the course, to a maximum total value of £6000 for one undergraduate course of study. Most QUEST awards are now provided in partnership with top engineering and construction companies that provide summer work placements and possible graduate employment. Students are also provided with mentors, who can give them a head start on the path to becoming professionally qualified.

⊙Institution of Mechanical Engineers, Prizes and Awards Department, ASK House, Northgate Avenue, Bury St Edmunds, Suffolk IP32 6BB. Tel: 01284 717887 or 717882. The Institution gives 35 undergraduate scholarship awards of £1000 pa for a maximum of four years (students must be or become an affiliated member of the Institution and have a place on an IMechE-accredited degree course); 20 awards of up to £750 for students studying or taking a work placement overseas; three awards of up to £1000 for overseas voluntary or project work; ten hardship awards of up to £1000 for students on IMechE-accredited degree courses; around 20 postgraduate awards of up to £1000 for advanced study, research programmes, hardship or overseas projects, with additional funds available for original research in the science or practice of mechanical engineering. They also give up to ten Whitworth Scholarships for undergraduate degree-level courses (including MEng and MSc) valued at £4000 pa (full-time study) and £2500 pa (part-time study). These scholarships are for outstanding engineers under the age of 31, who have served at least a two-year 'hands-on' engineering apprenticeship before commencing their undergraduate studies. Applicants must be British, Commonwealth or European Union citizens normally resident in the UK for at least 3 years prior to commencing their degree-level course.

⊙Institute of Marine Engineering, Science and Technology (IMarEST), 80 Coleman Street, London EC2R 5BJ. Tel: 020 7382 2600. Up to seven scholarships of £1000 are awarded each year to undergraduate students attending approved accredited courses leading to registration for Chartered status – (Chartered Engineer (CEng), Chartered Marine Scientist (CMarSci) or Chartered Marine Technologist (CMarTech) – who demonstrate a commitment to maritime engineering, marine science or marine technology by spending at least two years in the industry or in study. The Institute also offers awards to postgraduates through the Stanley Gray Fellowship scheme.

⊙Institute of Physics, 76 Portland Place, London W1B 1NT; tel: 020 7470 4800; email: physics@iop.org; website: www.iop.org. The Institute is offering 300 bursaries a year to encourage more students to study physics, especially those who would not traditionally choose the subject. Each student would normally receive £1000 pa for the duration of their course. (There may be variations in some universities.) These are not scholarships and aren't aimed at high-flyers. Universities will select the students who receive bursaries according to certain criteria such as financial hardship, students from schools with poor records for university attendance, mature students with families etc. Academic performance will only be used as a criterion when the number of deserving candidates outstrips the number of awards available. Bursaries will also be given to part-time students on a pro rata basis. To find out more talk to the university where you are to study.

Charities and trusts

Which charities and trusts give help to students?

You may be surprised to learn that it would take a book several times the size of this one to list them all. For example, the *Educational Grants Directory* (see booklist at end of this chapter) lists more than 1200 charities that between them give away more than £40 million a year – and this is by no means an exhaustive list.

But before you get too excited, most charities have restrictions on how much they can give away, to whom and for what reasons. Also, most charities and trusts will only consider you after you have exhausted all the more conventional avenues such as loans and Access funds.

Trusts and charities fall largely into four major groups:

⊙ **Need** – charities for the disabled fall into this group. Well-known names such as the Royal National Institute for the Blind (RNIB) and the Royal Association in Aid of Deaf People would come into this category, along with less familiar organisations such as the Shaftesbury Society and Scope.

⊙ **Subject** – into this category fall charities that will give help to students studying certain subjects. For example, the Company of Actuaries Charitable Trust Fund helps those studying to be actuaries; the Chartered Surveyors Company Charitable Trust and Mr Sidney A Smith's Fund help those studying Surveying; the Honourable Society of Gray's Inn is just one of a number of charities helping those studying Law; and there are quite a few charitable organisations set up to help those studying Medicine – for example the Charity of Miss Alice Gertrude Hewitt, which helps some 40 students aged under 25.

⊙ **Parents' occupation** – this can be a great source of additional income. If one of your parents is an airline pilot, artist, banker, barrister, in the clergy, coalminer, gardener, in the precious metals industry – you name it, there could be some help. Some trusts stipulate that your parent should be dead, but not all.

⊙ **Geographical location** – where you live can really make a difference. Take, for example, the lucky students living in the parishes of Patrington and Rimswell in East Yorkshire, in Oadby in the Midlands or in Yeovil in Somerset – they could be in line for help towards books, fees, living expenses or travel abroad. There are literally hundreds of these trusts covering many areas of the country. It has to be said that pay-outs can be small – under £100 – but they can be substantially more – say £1000.

'My income was extremely low, so I applied for as many bursaries (in and outside college) as possible. The effort paid off: I got a bursary from college for around £2000 and another from a company trust of £1000.'
1st year Law student, Cambridge

What sort of help do trusts give?

Help with fees, maintenance, books, equipment, travel either to and from your college or abroad, special sports activities, childminding and special projects. They all vary in what they will offer, and to whom.

Advice note

Before making an application to a charity, it is important to be clear in your own mind exactly what kind of student they are likely to help, and what kind of financial assistance you are after, otherwise you could be wasting both your time and theirs.

Is there anybody who could advise me on applying to charitable trusts?

EGAS, which stands for the Education Grants Advisory Service, is an independent organisation that will advise education students (over 16) on organisations to contact. You will need to fill in their questionnaire and they will then dip into their extensive database of charities and trusts and see which are the most likely bodies to help you. The criteria for eligibility is set by the individual trusts and charities or by the people who bequeathed the legacy, not EGAS, and these are extremely diverse. Trusts can seldom help in an immediate financial crisis. The longer you have to raise the funds, the more likely you are to succeed. To find out more and carry out your own search of trusts, the quickest route is to visit the EGAS website: www.egas-online.org.uk/ fwa/trustsearch.htm. Otherwise you can phone the EGAS helpline on 020 7254 6251, open Tuesday, Wednesday and Thursday 2–4pm. Or write to EGAS, 501–505 Kingsland Road, London E8 4AU, including a large stamped addressed envelope if requesting a questionnaire.

Can EGAS help overseas students and those wanting to study abroad?

It is very difficult to find trusts willing to fund overseas students who are already studying in the UK, and EGAS cannot assist students wishing to study outside the UK. However, there are trusts that give funding for travel, and these should be contacted directly. See the booklist at the end of this chapter for help if you would like to winkle them out.

What are my chances of hitting the jackpot?

Your chances are slim, though the odds are certainly better than the likelihood of winning the national lottery. Competition is fierce. EGAS receives well over 20,000 enquiries a year.

EGAS does not itself provide support but it is part of the Family Welfare Association (FWA), which does offer support to students from disadvantaged backgrounds. The FWA gives grants of around £175,000 per year to HE and FE students. However, any funding it does offer is usually small, around £150, for something specific like books, equipment or travel. It handles about 100 grant applications a month and most grants are given to help students in their final year. Typical examples of why money might be given:

⊙ For books or equipment
⊙ If a parent is suddenly made redundant and can't continue to finance your college course fees
⊙ To a student who has been paying their way through part-time work but feels they need to give it up for that final two-month push.

The EGAS website also includes a Guide to Student Funding, which has information on HE and FE funding throughout the UK, and the implications of student funding on benefits.

Last word

Be realistic when contacting EGAS. Don't expect miracles – they can rarely be worked.

When should I contact a trust?

Most trusts have an application deadline. This is usually given along with the general information in the trusts and grants directories. Check out each entry carefully; they are all different. Trusts are not the answer for a fast financial fix. Like all bodies, they tend to move exceedingly slowly. Your case will be scrutinised along with many others, so it could be months before you get an answer.

Could I get through higher education funded only by a charitable trust?

It could be done, but don't depend on it. Many charities won't consider you until you have tried all the usual channels available to students, and they do tend to give help towards the end of a course, rather than at the beginning.

If I get help from a charity, will it affect my loan and fees?

It shouldn't. Charitable awards, scholarships and sponsorships are not generally taken into consideration when calculating your fees and loan package.

Can I apply to more than one charity?

Yes, but blanket saturation is not advisable. Limit your applications to organisations that are really likely to give you funds.

How do I go about applying to a charity?

There are no set rules. What one charitable trust wants, another doesn't. Here is a general procedure to follow:

1 Put together a list of suitable charities by consulting either EGAS or the directories in the library.
2 Find out exactly what each charity is offering and whether you meet their criteria. Check if there is a final entry date for applications.
3 Write a brief note to selected charities, explaining your need and asking for an application form.
4 Fill in the application form. Make sure answers are clear, concise and truthful. You may be questioned on them later. Bear the trust's criteria in mind.
5 Photocopy the completed form before you send it back.
6 Wait patiently. These things can take many weeks to process.

Do students actually get help?

'As an Engineering student I needed a computer, but couldn't afford one. Were there any charities that could help? I searched around, and discovered the Earl's Colne Educational Trust, which assisted students living within ten miles of Earl's Colne in Essex. I lived in Halstead, just within the limits – it was worth a try. I wrote to them explaining my needs; they sent me a form; I filled it in; I waited; I went for an interview. The result: £500 – easy money. It cost just two sides of A4!'
Jonathan, when studying Electronic Engineering at Loughborough University

Competitions

Are they worth it?

The world is full of competition addicts. There are magazines devoted solely to the topic, steering readers to the next give-away bonanza. Whole families eat crazy diets just to get the labels off the right tins and jars. People do win – holidays in exotic places, new cars, toasters, DVD players, washing machines and cuddly toys. It's always worth having a go, if it only means the cost of a stamp and perhaps writing a catchy slogan. However, competitions cannot be seen as a serious means of raising finance. A little icing on the cake is the best you can hope for, and even that is a long shot.

But don't dismiss them altogether. If it's a competition aimed specifically at students, it very often involves writing an essay. Students, being the overworked (or lazy?) people as they are, tend to give them a miss, so the number of entries can be low. All the more reason to give it a try.

Some years ago the chartered accountancy firm KPMG ran such a competition, and seven lucky undergraduates won the chance to work for six weeks for the firm in such exotic places as São Paulo, Toronto, Cologne, Melbourne, Sydney, Harare and Tai Pei, earn a good salary and to travel. Not bad for a few hours' work on a 1500-word essay.

On similar lines, every year BUNAC (the British Universities North America Club) awards three scholarships of up to £1000 each to help applicants cover the costs of taking part in a BUNAC work-abroad programme to the USA or Canada. They're called the Green Cheese Scholarships, and all you need do to enter is write a humorous essay based on a travel-related topic. It can be about anywhere: an exotic trip to the other side of the world, or something less adventurous. Entries should be no more than 1500 words. For further details see www.bunac.org.

If it's a competition set by your university with prizes for excellence, in a subject area you know well, you're in with a real chance, and winning could be a useful addition to your CV.

Take for example the Student Skills competition run at the University of Wales, Aberystwyth. This is a unique event that sets out to help students recognise the employability skills they are developing whilst at university. The final runs alongside the university Careers Information Fair, and teams from most departments get involved. Each team designs and runs a stand at the fair. They also make a group presentation, which is assessed by a panel of national judges. The prize for the winning team is £1000. There are two other prizes of £500 each for the best stand and presentation. All students who take part will receive a £20 book token and will gain from the experience – the exposure to employers – and have a lot of fun. Each team is twinned with an employer; this is to help them identify what skills employers are looking for. International Politics was twinned with Reuters of London and spent four days with the company; Environment Science went to visit the Environmental Consultancy RPS Group; and Law went to Wragge and Co., a large law firm.

Win €1000

Or around £685 in our money. All you have to do is write a 900-word essay about your industrial placement and you could win 1000 euros. Last year's winner was Jonathan James Walton, studying Computer Science with a year in industry at the University of Kent, who wrote about his placement at AMS Ltd/BAE Systems. Next time round it could be you. The competition is run by ASET, the Association for Sandwich Education and Training.

On the other hand, you might find it more fun, though not so lucrative, to enter ASET's bloggers competition, called Student Stars. For this you have to produce a 'blog' at various stages during your placement year. Successful blogs will be put into the ASET website and in their newsletter and could win you £200. To find out more about both competitions, log onto the ASET website: www.asetonline.org, email asset@demon.co.uk or phone 0114 221 2902/3.

Best of luck!

Who won the *Students' Money Matters* £300?

Any student who took part in the *Students' Money Matters* survey this year was automatically included in our £300 prize draw. This year's winner is Sarah Remmer, a second-year student studying Sociology at the University of Bath. Congratulations, Sarah! With an anticipated debt of £19,500 when she leaves university, she is certainly a deserving case. But she has decided to use the money rather than save it: 'I will use some of it to take my friends for an evening out. Not the usual pubs we frequent giving cheap deals, but champagne and cocktails somewhere glitzy. The rest I shall use for driving lessons.' Sarah already has a scooter to get around locally, but this isn't much use for the five-hour journey up to her parents' home in Yorkshire.

> 'I was asleep in front of the telly when the phone call came. So I couldn't quite take in that I had won £300. At first I thought it was one of these dodgy offers. I had filled in the questionnaire because I wanted to get the point across that the loan should be linked to the cost of living in the area where you study and not just in London.'

A point many students would agree with, and which we have taken on board.

Lotteries

Then, of course, there's the lottery. Not strictly a competition, but an option. This book is not in the business of advocating gambling, and at £1 a go, or at least £104 a year depending on how addictive it becomes, is it worth it? The odds on winning the jackpot are 14 million to one, and if you did win, what would happen to your studies?

Finally, students have been writing in with news of competitions on the web and in the media. Here are a couple of their stories:

> 'Enter internet competitions using uni computers, since the web is free. I did and won a round-the-world trip, a TV, a video, a computer and £1000 in cash.'
> 3rd year Economics student at York University

> 'Whatever the prize, have a go. You can always sell it. I won a scooter worth £1000 in a radio competition. It was a life-saver. I sold it immediately, and was able to solve my financial problems, which were dire. Now I have a student loan, of course, but no overdraft.'
> 2nd year student, Lancaster

Cash crisis note

- Try www.prizefinder.com, or type 'competitions' into your search engine. This will give you information on all the competitions that are available on the web at the moment – best of luck.

- The litmus test with any competition has to be: 'Is it worth it?' Look at the hassle involved, the cost, the time factor, the number of cans of baked beans or cat food you have got to eat your way through and, above all, the odds – and then make your decision. The drawback with any competition is that the winner takes all, and the also-rans get nothing. Still, it doesn't hurt to keep your eyes open.

Further information
Where to look

- ⊙ On your college noticeboard
- ⊙ In the careers office
- ⊙ National newspapers
- ⊙ Student newspapers
- ⊙ The web.

Who to contact

- ⊙ EGAS helpline: tel: 020 7254 6251;
  website: www.egas-online.org.uk/fwa/trustsearch.htm
- ⊙ Scholarship Search UK: www.scholarship-search.org.uk.

What to read

- ⊙ The *Grants Register* lists over 3500 awards. Published by Macmillan. Tel: 01256 329242. Email: macdir@macmillan.co.uk. Very expensive (£155) – try your local library.
- ⊙ *Directory of Grant-Making Trusts*, published by the Charities Aid Foundation. Available from Trotman, tel: 0870 900 2665, or visit www.trotman.co.uk/bookshop.
- ⊙ *Educational Grants Directory*, published by the Directory of Social Change. Available from Trotman, tel: 0870 900 2665, or visit www.trotman.co.uk/bookshop.
- ⊙ *University Scholarships, Awards and Bursaries*, Brian Heap, published by Trotman. To order, tel: 0870 900 2665 or visit www.trotman.co.uk/bookshop.

★ TOP*TEN* **most voluble students**

	Weekly spend on telephone
1st year Religious/Childhood Studies, Wolverhampton	£60
2nd year HND Engineering, Wolverhampton	£50
1st year Nursing, Wolverhampton	£44
3rd year Business and Accounting, Wolverhampton	£36
3rd year History, UWE	£30
3rd year Property and Business, Westminster	£30
3rd year Management, UCE	£25
3rd year Accounting and Finance, Wolverhampton	£25
2nd year Politics and History, Wolverhampton	£25
3rd year Business Management, Coventry	£20

7

Postgraduate study

Where to find funding

The main topics covered in this chapter are:

The number of postgraduate students in the UK keeps increasing. In the last ten years the number of students on postgraduate courses has almost doubled. How are they managing to pay for their studies? Has funding kept pace with the demand? In this chapter we look at the main sources of finance for postgraduates.

Is it worth taking a postgraduate qualification?

Yes, if it's a subject you are particularly interested in or if it is a vocational course, and certainly if you are seeking a post in academia or a research-based organisation. But further qualifications are not going to guarantee you a better-paid job.

News update

An online postgraduate applications system that enables postgraduate students in the UK and overseas to apply electronically to HE institutions has been developed. Access is via www.prospects.ac.uk, which hosts the national postgraduate database, or through a participating institution's website.

> ## How many postgraduates are there?
>
> There are 532,630 students on postgraduate courses in the UK (HESA figures 2004/05).

> ## Fact file: bigger earners
>
> Postgraduate degree-holders earn more than their graduate counterparts, with males earning up to 20% more and females 34% more, according to the Higher Education Statistics Agency (HESA) and based on 2003 statistics.
>
> However, the AGR Winter Graduate Salary review 2006 reports that about 8% of employers offer higher salaries to those with a PhD – and around 12.9% of employers more for a non-MBA Master's. Of those who are offering more, a premium of £1000 extra is given for a Master's degree and £1,750 extra for a PhD.

How much will it cost?

Tuition fees

UK residents and EU nationals:

- ⊙ Average fee 2005–2006: £3168 pa
- ⊙ Average fee part-time: £1584 pa
- ⊙ Certain courses may be higher – eg Legal Practice course at £5200–£8500
- ⊙ Less for Graduate Diploma in Law/CPE courses, at £1125–£6000
- ⊙ MBA general range: £9500–£14,000 (£11,000 average, but could be double that at top schools).

Students from abroad – average for 2005–2006	Taught	Research
Arts/classroom	£8,300	£8,200
Science/laboratory	£9,900	£10,300
Clinical	£20,100	£20,400

Maintenance

The results of our research given in Chapter 1 will give you some idea of how much it is going to cost you to live. The International Student Centre estimated that the minimum a student from abroad needs to live in London was £800 a month. We think £1000 would be more realistic. Leeds University suggests on its website (www.leeds.ac.uk/welfare) that students living there will need £6130–£7345, depending on accommodation, just for essential living expenses . The NUS suggests £9318 would be needed if living in London and £7935 everywhere else, and that is just for a 39-week academic year. And, remember, none of these figures include fees.

Cash crisis note

- London is a LOT more expensive than you think (eg just a day pass on the tube is a fiver and that's only for the two central zones!), and landlords can ask for up to two months' rent as a deposit.

Sources of funding

Will I get funding?

Don't bank on it. Competition for funding for postgraduates is phenomenal. There is no all-embracing funding system as for first degrees, and students generally have to search around to get help. It is much easier to get a place on a course than it is to get the money to pay for it. Many postgraduates have to finance themselves with loans etc, which is probably why part-time study for postgraduates is increasing in popularity. If you are offered funding, make sure it covers both tuition fees and maintenance.

What are the possible sources of funding?

1 **Government funding** from research councils – these are by far the largest sources of funding in the UK. Some 7000 new awards are made each year. Each 'awarding body' funds different courses and there is no overlap, so it is important to identify the appropriate body for your needs (see page 179; for Scotland and Northern Ireland see also pages 184 and 185).

2 **Erasmus** (often known as Socrates-Erasmus) is a programme developed by the European Commission to provide funds for the mobility of students and staff in universities throughout the EU member states and the countries of the European Free Trade Association (EFTA). See page 94 for full details and information on Erasmus and other similar programmes, such as the Leonardo da Vinci scheme.

3 **Employers** will occasionally sponsor employees through courses, especially MBAs.

4 **Companies** may sponsor students on a research project. This could be as the result of a work experience association during a first degree, or in co-operation with one of the research councils.

5 **Trusts and charities** are more likely to award small amounts of money rather than full financial support, but certainly worth considering (see Chapter 6). Your Local Authority Awards Officer would have details of any local charities. Otherwise contact EGAS (see page 167 for details) or look in the published charities and grant-making trusts' directories and registers. Apply early: processing can be inordinately slow.

6 **Local authorities**. Except in the case of teacher training, local authorities are not required by law to fund postgraduates. Funding is discretionary, is given mainly for vocational courses that lead to certificates or diplomas, is means-tested and is subject to differing criteria between authorities. Likely subjects are Accountancy, Journalism, Law, Music, secretarial work, youth work and Computing. If you are tapping your local authority it is essential to apply early as their funds are limited, and you'll need to present a good case for yourself. But because there are no set rules for funding, it is always worth a try.

7 **Universities' own postgraduate studentship awards**. Many institutions have a small number of studentships available for specific courses. Aberystwyth, for example, gives around 12 awards each year to UK/EU PhDs for research degrees. Awards generally cover fees and maintenance. Closing dates vary. For the Aberystwyth competition it's 1 March. Check your university of choice for details.

8 **University departments**. They may have nothing, and probably won't advertise. But if they particularly want you, or there's something they are interested in doing, they may have sources they can tap. You could find that they stipulate you have to take on some tutorial work or assist the department. Tip from Aberystwyth: 'We say to graduates it's always worth a try; all it needs is the right phone call just at the right time.'

9 **Research Assistantships** are salaried posts in academic departments, which provide the opportunity to study for a higher degree. Salaries vary and opportunities can become available throughout the year. Watch the relevant press for adverts – the *Guardian, The Times, New Scientist, Nature* etc.

10 **Loans from banks** – see later in this chapter.

Can I get a student loan?

Only if you are taking a Postgraduate Certificate in Education (PGCE). Even though it's generally only a one-year course, you will be classed as a first- rather than a final-year student, so you can take out the maximum loan offered and you won't have to pay fees. (See page 186 for full details of special funding arrangements for PGCE.) Or you could try a bank loan (see page 192).

Cash crisis note

- From a student who knows:

  'You always need double the money you think you need when you are moving to a new location to study. There are always hidden costs.'

Award-making bodies

These are the main sources of government funding for postgraduates. There are some nine major award-making bodies in the UK. Each one operates independently and the awards they offer are all slightly different, as are their regulations. The information given here should therefore be seen as a general guide to what you could expect to get. All the award-making bodies issue information about their own awards, which can be gained by writing to them or phoning them (addresses are given later in this chapter) or by looking on the internet. The areas of study covered by individual research councils can change, so make sure any information you get is up to date.

What kind of government award could I get?

Basically there are four kinds of awards for postgraduate students:

- **Research Studentships**, which are generally a three-year award leading to a doctorate (PhD or DPhil).
- **Collaborative Research Studentships**, when the research project is part-funded by an outside industrial organisation and may well give the student some experience outside the academic environment. The collaborating company generally gives the student extra cash on top of the studentship award. The awarding body may also give an additional award on top of the basic studentship. This is certainly so with CASE awards (Co-operative Awards in Science and Engineering).
- **Advanced Course Studentships**, which are given for taught courses which must be of at least six months' duration, but are generally for one or possibly two years, often leading to a Master's (MSc, MA) or other qualification.
- **Bursaries**, which are allocated by the Central Social Care Council for courses in social work; the amounts offered are much lower.

Not all awarding bodies give all types of award. And some give additional awards and fellowships.

Is the award means-tested?

Only bursaries for training in social work are means-tested.

What could an award cover?

- Payment of approved fees to the institution
- Maintenance allowance
- Dependants' and other allowances
- Assistance with additional travel and subsistence expenses for something like fieldwork.

Do I have to get a 2:1 to take a postgraduate course?

Each course will set its own requirements. If you are thinking of specialising in your degree subject, a First or 2:1 is probably what you will need. For a vocational course, you'll need to show real commitment and interest in the subject. If, however, you are seeking funding from a government funding council, they will generally demand:

- A First or upper-second class Honours degree, or a lower second with a further qualification such as an MA for a Research Studentship
- At least a lower-second Honours degree for a taught/one-year course. (This does not apply to social work courses.)

How do I go about getting funding?

Start with your university careers office. Most are on the ball when it comes to tapping the meagre resources available to postgraduates. They may even publish a special leaflet on sources of funding for postgraduate study. Many of the publications listed at the end of this chapter, which we suggest you consult, should also be in the university careers library. Talk also to the tutors in your department, especially if you want to undertake a research degree, as they will know what projects are likely to gain funding. Consult university prospectuses.

When should I approach the award-making bodies?

If you want general information on their award scheme – any time. It is important to read thoroughly the individual information produced by the different award-making bodies, as closing dates, methods of application and what is on offer will vary. In most cases, application for awards is done through the institution you hope to join. Check information for procedure.

How do I apply for funding?

In the case of most research councils (BBSRC, EPSRC, ESRC, MRC, NERC, PPARC), funding to students is funnelled through university departments and courses. They select the students for their courses/projects and submit their names to the awarding body. Application forms are obtained from the department for your intended studies, and

---

A fresh approach to flexible work

Need to earn while you study? This could be the answer.

FreshMinds is an award-winning research and recruitment company that allows businesses to tap into the skills of the best 'Minds' on a flexible basis. These Minds are top graduates, postgraduates and business analysts drawn from leading universities, business schools and companies in the UK and Europe.

If you're in between periods of study or looking for a job, FreshMinds can provide high-level research work on a flexible basis. Their research and analysis supports decision-making in many of the UK's biggest and best companies. It ranges from information and data gathering to more complex analysis, including market research, company profiling and competitor benchmarking. You could be working on a project in their London office or on short-term placements with their clients that may last anything from three days to six months.

Only Minds who have a First or 2:1 degree (or equivalent) from a top university are considered for projects, placements or recruitment. To find out about the types of projects available and the selection process, log on to www.freshminds.co.uk or phone 020 7692 4300.

must be returned to them well in advance of 31 July when the department will submit it to the appropriate awarding council.

In the case of the Arts and Humanities Research Council (AHRC), awards are allocated by competition. Having secured an offer of a place on a course, students apply for an award through their referees and the institution at which they will be studying. Applications must be with the appropriate awarding body by the beginning of May, so make sure your application is with your course 'organisers' long before then.

Will it make a difference where I choose to study?

Yes. Not all courses or departments attract funding. It is important to find out the situation when you apply. And just because a course is eligible for studentships, and you have a place on that course, it still doesn't mean you will necessarily get one. It is very competitive. And remember, if you don't get funding it could mean you have to pay not only your own maintenance but also your course fees. In that case, a university close to your own home might be the answer, or studying part-time (day release, evening courses or distance learning).

When and how can I find out what projects have funding?

From April onwards your university should have a list of university departments that have been given funding by the awarding bodies. Under the scheme, universities are committed to attracting the very best students for the awards, so must advertise for candidates outside as well as within their own university. Typical media: *New Scientist*, *Nature*, the *Guardian* or university magazines, depending on the topic.

If you want a list of which courses and projects throughout the country have received funding, contact the appropriate awarding body after 1 April. Information may also be on their websites.

Can I approach more than one awarding body?

No. There is no overlap between the awarding research councils: they each have their designated topics they fund. So it is important to identify which body to apply to, as you can only apply to one. In the case of the Arts and Humanities Research Council there does appear to be some overlap between its three different arms. However, a course that attracts bursaries from one will not generally gain funding from other state sources.

The award-making bodies

Subjects given for each body have been selected to give a broad view of topics covered, and are by no means exhaustive. Candidates should check with the appropriate organisation, or on the appropriate website.

Arts and Humanities Research Council (AHRC)

The AHRC was established on 1 April 2005, and replaced the Arts and Humanities Research Board. The decision to create a Council rather than a Board underlines the importance of high-quality research in the arts and humanities for the cultural, creative and economic life of the nation.

Awards are available for Master's courses and doctoral study across eight subject panels as follows:

- Classics, Ancient History and Archaeology
- English Language and Literature
- Medieval and Modern History
- Modern Languages and Linguistics
- Librarianship, Information and Museum Studies
- Music and Performing Arts
- Philosophy, Religious Studies and Law
- Visual Arts and Media: practice, history, theory.

Research Master's Preparation Scheme

Type of award: Support for students undertaking Master's courses that focus on advanced study and research training, which provides a foundation for further research at doctoral level. Awards will normally be for one year's full-time study or two years' part-time study.

Amount: Studying in London: £10,600
Elsewhere: £8600
Part-time study: £275
Tuition fees: £3168 full-time/£1584 part-time

Professional Preparation Master's Scheme

Type of award: Support for Master's or postgraduate diploma courses that focus on developing high-level skills and competencies for professional practice. Awards will normally be for one year's full-time study and two years' part-time study.

Amount: Studying in London: £10,000
Elsewhere: £8000
Part-time study: £275
Tuition fees: £3168 full-time/£1584 part-time

Doctoral Scheme

Type of award: Support for up to three years of full-time study or up to five years' part-time study leading to a doctoral degree.

Amount: Studying in London: £14,300
Elsewhere: £12,300
Part-time study: £275
Tuition fees: £3168 full-time/£1584 part-time

Address: Postgraduate Awards Division
Arts and Humanities Research Council
Whitefriars, Lewins Mead, Bristol BS1 2AE
Tel: 0117 987 6543
Fax: 0117 987 6544
Email: pgenquiries@ahrc.ac.uk
Website: www.ahrc.ac.uk

Biotechnology and Biological Sciences Research Council (BBSRC)

Subject areas: Biological Sciences and associated technologies (Agriculture and Food Sciences, Animal Sciences, Biochemistry and Cell Biology, Biomolecular Sciences, Engineering and Biological Systems, Genes and Development Biology, Plant and Microbial Sciences)

Type of award: Research Studentship
Master's Studentship

Amount: Study in London: £14,300
Elsewhere: £12,300
(Doctoral Training Account minimum stipend can be higher)
For students with a recognised veterinary degree: £18,980
(CASE awards (Co-operative Awards in Science and Engineering) –
additional minimum £2500 by collaborator) PhD students whose projects fall in designated priority areas may receive a stipend enhancement of £2000 pa

Address: Biotechnology and Biological Sciences Research Council
Polaris House, North Star Avenue, Swindon SN2 1UH
Tel: 01793 413200
Email: postgrad.studentship@bbsrc.ac.uk
Website: www.bbsrc.ac.uk

Economic and Social Research Council (ESRC)

Subject areas: Area Studies, Economics, Economic and Social History, Education, Human Geography, Linguistics, Management and Business Studies (Accounting, Finance, Industrial Relations and other specialist management courses), Planning, Politics and International Relations, Science Technology and Innovation Studies, Psychology, Social Anthropology, Social Policy, Socio-Legal Studies, Sociology, Statistics, Research Methods and Computing as applied to the social sciences

Type of award: Annual Studentship Competition (1+3 & +3)
1+3 Quota awards
Joint NERC/ESRC PhD
ODPM Research Studentship
ODPM 1 year Master's
Welsh Assembly Research Studentships
CASE Studentships

Centre Linked Studentships
Joint ESRC/MRC Studentship

		Standard studentship	CASE
Amount:	Studying in London	£14,300 pa	£16,300 pa
	Elsewhere	£12,300 pa	£14,300 pa

Address: Economic and Social Research Council, Research, Training & Development Directorate,
Polaris House, North Star Avenue, Swindon SN2 1UJ
Tel: 01793 413150
Email: ptd@esrc.ac.uk
Website: www.esrc.ac.uk

Engineering and Physical Sciences Research Council (EPSRC)

Subject areas: Engineering, Chemistry, Mathematics, Physics, Information and Computer Technologies, Materials Science and the Life Sciences Interface

Types of support: EPSRC supports all of its postgraduate training through packages of funding provided to the universities. It is the responsibility of the university to assess student eligibility for and select students to receive funding. Prospective students should contact universities or departments directly.

Funding is provided for: Standard Research Studentships, Industrial CASE Studentships, CASE for New Academic Appointees, Engineering Doctorate (EngD), Master's degrees (MSc and MRes)

Amount: Amounts may vary depending on university but EPSRC requires that PhD students receive a stipend of at least the national minimum rate
PhD Students: £12,300
Research engineers at Engineering Doctorate Centres: £13,800

Address: Engineering and Physical Sciences Research Council
Polaris House, North Star Avenue, Swindon SN2 1ET
Tel: 01793 444000.
Website: www.epsrc.ac.uk

General Social Care Council (GSCC)

Subject area: Social Work

Type of award: Bursary for approved postgraduate qualification in Social Work for students normally resident in England who meet required eligibility and residency criteria.

Amount: The bursary provides a non-income-assessed grant of up to £2,900 depending on individual circumstance, the reimbursement of certain practice learning opportunity-related expenses and tuition fee support up to capped* amount. It also includes an income-assessed grant of up to £3745 and income-assessed allowances of various values to assist with certain costs.

*Fee support for 2006–2007 still to be announced. For full details plus eligibility criteria and application process download application pack, or phone/email the GSCC

Address: General Social Care Council Bursaries Office
            Goldings House, 2 Hay's Lane, London SE1 2HB
            Tel: Bursaries Customer Service Team on 020 7397 5835
            Email: bursaries@gscc.org.uk
            Website: www.gscc.org.uk

Medical Research Council (MRC)

Subject areas: Medicine (including tropical), areas of biology including Molecules and Cells, Inheritance, Reproduction and Child Health, Infections and Immunity (including HIV and AIDS), Cancer, Imaging, Neurobiology, Cognitive Science, Clinical Neurosciences and Mental Health, Health Services Research, Clinical Psychology, Epidemiology, Medical Statistics, Quantitative Biology

Types of support: MRC supports much of its postgraduate training through packages of funding provided to the universities as Doctoral Training Accounts. Prospective students should contact universities or heads of departments directly to see if there is funding available.

Funding is provided for: Research PhDs, Research Master's (MRes), Collaborative PhDs
            Advanced Course Master's Studentships
            Capacity Building Area (Priority Area) Studentships
            Industrial Collaborative Studentships

Amount: May vary depending on university but a PhD student should receive a minimum stipend of:
            Study in London   £14,350
            Elsewhere   £12,300

Address: Melanie Meek
            Medical Research Council
            20 Park Crescent, London W1N 4AL
            Tel: 020 7670 5408
            Email: students@headoffice.mrc.ac.uk
            Website: www.mrc.ac.uk

Natural Environment Research Council (NERC)

Subject areas: Geology, Organic Pollution, Geophysics, Physical Oceanography, Marine Ecology, Hydrology, Freshwater Ecology, Terrestrial Ecology,

Soil Sciences, Earth Observation and associated science, Atmospheric Chemistry, Science-based Archaeology

Type of award: PhD (3-year Research Studentship) can be straight research award or a CASE award (Co-operative Award in Science and Engineering), or an Industrial CASE Award
MSc (1-year Advanced Course Studentship)

Amount: PhD Stipend: £12,300 pa
Advanced Course Stipend: £7880
Conference allowance: £150
London weighting: £2000 for PhD and MSc students
(CASE award – minimum of £1000 pa by collaborator)

Address: Natural Environment Research Council
Polaris House, North Star Avenue, Swindon SN2 1EU
Tel: 01793 411500
Website: www.nerc.ac.uk

Particle Physics and Astronomy Research Council (PPARC)

Subject areas: Particle Physics, Astronomy, Astrophysics, Solar System Science

Type of award: Research Studentship – 179 allocated
Co-operative Award in Science and Engineering (CASE) – 10 allocated

Amount: Studying in London   £14,000 pa (£15,000 for CASE students)
Elsewhere   £12,000 pa (£13,000 for CASE students)
(CASE award – additional £600 pa given by PPARC plus minimum of £2760 pa by collaborating company)
(2006–2007 figures likely to rise in line with inflation)

Address: Particle Physics and Astronomy Research Council
Polaris House, North Star Avenue, Swindon SN2 1ET
Tel: 01793 442000
Email: studentships@pparc.ac.uk
Website: www.pparc.ac.uk

See box on page 192 for a quick reference guide to postgraduate awards.

Scotland

Graduates seeking funding for science-based subjects are eligible for studentship awards from most of the research councils mentioned here. Funding for postgraduate vocational courses mostly at diploma level (usually for one year) may be available through the Postgraduate Student Allowance Scheme (PSAS). Not all postgraduate courses are supported. The PSAS also provides funding for students taking PGCE or PGDipCE. Funding is means-tested. Contact SAAS on 0845 111 1711 for general enquiries.

Northern Ireland

- ⊙ Postgraduate students can compete for funding from the award-making bodies already listed.
- ⊙ The Department for Employment and Learning (DEL) offers two types of award: for research (MPhil, DPhil, PhD) and for approved courses of advanced study (Master's) in fields of humanities, science and technology and the social sciences. Awards are not means-tested.
- ⊙ For studentships to pursue postgraduate study In Northern Ireland (at either Queen's University Belfast or the University of Ulster) apply to the university for an application form. The offer of a place does not mean that funding will be provided.
- ⊙ The Northern Ireland Department of Agriculture and Rural Development provides funds for study (in Northern Ireland) in Agriculture including Horticulture, and related sciences such as Agricultural Economics, Engineering, Science and Food Science (closing date: last Friday in February).
- ⊙ Medicine – see the Medical Research Council's details for Great Britain.
- ⊙ The basic rate of maintenance grant for 2006–2007 is £12,300. Additional allowances may also be paid for dependants and students with special needs.
- ⊙ CAST awards: Co-operative Awards in Science and Technology support research projects at Northern Ireland universities for one or three years in collaboration with industry. Maintenance grant of £12,300 pa is supplemented by a payment from the collaborating body of at least 40% of grant figure.
- ⊙ Johns Hopkins Fellowship Award – a one-year Fellowship Award covering fees only for the Johns Hopkins University's School of Advanced International Studies in Bologna.
- ⊙ One student funded by DEL to take a one-year course in Administration, Economics and Law at the College of Europe, Bruges.

Booklet on awards available from: Department for Employment and Learning Student Support Branch, Adelaide House, Adelaide Street, Belfast BT2 8FD. Tel: 028 9025 7707. Website: www.delni.gov.uk.

Channel Islands/Isle of Man

Apply directly to appropriate education department.

I want to study abroad – can I get funding?

There are a number of routes you can take:

- ⊙ If you are thinking of undertaking postgraduate studies at the European Union Institute (EUI) in Florence, the College of Europe in Bruges or Warsaw, or the Bologna Centre in Bologna you may be eligible for an award from the DfES in England, the Student Awards Agency for Scotland or the Department of Education and Learning in Northern Ireland.

- Socrates-Erasmus, generally known as Erasmus (the European Community Action Scheme for the Mobility of University Students), and Leonardo da Vinci, which covers vocational training (see page 94).
- The UNESCO publication *Study Abroad* has 2574 entries and provides information on courses and international scholarships and financial assistance available in countries and territories worldwide. It should be available at your local library or careers office or can be purchased from the Stationery Office. (See booklist at the end of this chapter.)

Hot tips on funding from an Edinburgh postgraduate

- Many departments provide opportunities for undergraduate teaching and demonstrating. Pay varies – it may only be a few pounds a term (ie £500 a year) or could amount to several thousand.

- Work as a Research Assistant. Many staff secure a funding award that they must spend on their project, which includes assistants.

- Don't aim to fund tuition and living costs by taking a job. It is possible for Master's students to maintain a part-time job – and many do. But it is rare for a full-time PhD student to do so: a PhD is a job in itself. A few hours' work a week can ease the financial burden and provide useful respite from academic work – but only that.

- Try raising funding for individual experiments. Start with your department and funding sources for your individual subject. Success is more likely with experimental degrees than bog standards like French Literature.

- Don't underestimate the time your PhD will take. Practically all PhDs overrun. It can easily take four or more years to complete. Research Council funding lasts for three years only and they won't pick you for the fourth year. Budget for this. There is a good chance there'll be good money coming in once you qualify. In the meantime have a contingency plan – it would be dreadful to give up on the last lap.

- Money, or perhaps one should say lack of it, is a major stress factor for many postgraduates. Excellent students quit because they can't afford to be a student any longer. Unrealistic budgeting undoes many: whilst rent and food are generally factored in, things such as holidays, contents insurance etc are not. These all add up.

What help can I get if I want to train as a teacher?

England

Up to £225 a week just to train. A new package of incentives is available for students beginning a postgraduate course of initial teacher training (ITT) in September 2006. This includes:

- Training bursary of £9000 (non-repayable) for students training to teach secondary shortage subjects (which include Design and Technology, English (with Drama), ICT, Maths, Modern Foreign Languages, Music, RE, Science).
- Training bursary of £6000 for all eligible primary and other secondary postgraduate students.

- A non-means-tested loan to cover the cost of fees – up to £3000.
- A non-means-tested non-repayable grant of £1200 given to all students.
- An additional means-tested grant of £1500, which is non-repayable.
- Student loan based on the full-year allowance for students – up to £6170 in London and £4405 elsewhere, 25% of which is means-tested.
- 'Golden hello' paid to secondary-shortage-subject teachers on completion of their induction year: £5000 to those teaching Maths and Science; £2500 to all other secondary-shortage-subject teachers.

The training bursary will be given in nine monthly instalments (18 monthly instalments if you are studying part-time). It is not means-tested and is not a loan. Tax and National Insurance will have to be paid on any golden hello.

Wales

The actual package for Welsh postgraduates beginning a teacher training course in 2006, whether they live and study in Wales or study in the rest of the UK, works out so that you receive exactly the same funding as your English counterparts; but because the fees are lower if you study in Wales it is given in a different way. The major difference between Welsh students studying in Wales and in England is the training grant, which is lower in Wales because the fees are lower.

Domicile and training in Wales

- Training grant of £7200 (non-repayable) for students training to teach secondary shortage subjects. (Shortage subjects include: Design and Technology, English (with Drama), ICT, Maths, Modern Foreign Languages, Music, RE, Science and Welsh.)
- Training bursary of £4200 for all primary and other secondary students.
- Loan to cover deferred fixed fees of £1200.
- A non-means-tested element of maintenance grant – £1200 given to all students.
- A further means-tested grant of £1500, non-repayable, is available.
- From 2007–2008 a non-means-tested student loan based on the full-year allowance for students up to £4405, 25% of which is means-tested.
- Non-repayable fee grant will be given to offset rise in fees to £3000.
- 'Golden hello' paid to secondary-shortage-subject teachers on completion of their induction year: £5000 to those teaching Maths and Science; £2500 to all other secondary-shortage-subject teachers.
- There is also the Welsh Medium Incentive Supplement, under which students studying to teach any subject in Welsh but feeling their language skills are not up to the job can apply for a bursary of £1200 pa in addition to any other award held.
- Finally, if you really are strapped for cash, there are the Financial Contingency Funds that provide small hardship grants for those who face unexpected difficulties. To find out more about teacher training in Wales, phone 0845 600 0992 or visit www.useyourheadteach.gov.uk.

Welsh, but studying in another part of the UK

⊙ Training bursary of £9000 (non-repayable) for students training to teach secondary shortage subjects (which include: Design and Technology, English (with Drama), ICT, Maths, Modern Foreign Languages, Music, RE and Science).

⊙ Training bursary of £6000 for all primary PGCE students and other secondary PGCE students.

⊙ A non-means-tested loan to cover the cost of fees – up to £3000.

⊙ A non-means-tested non-repayable grant of £1200 given to all PGCE students.

⊙ A further means-tested grant of £1500, again non-repayable, is also available.

⊙ Student loan based on the full-year allowance for students, up to £6170 in London and £4405 elsewhere, 25% of which is means-tested.

⊙ 'Golden hello' paid to secondary-shortage-subject teachers on completion of their induction year: £5000 to those teaching Maths and Science; £2500 to all other secondary-shortage-subject teachers.

Teaching in Scotland

Sorry, but there is no training bursary or secondary-shortage-subject scheme in Scotland. The problem is not training teachers but getting them to go to some of the more rural or more difficult areas of Scotland. So this year (2006–2007) they are introducing for the first time a kind of a 'golden hello' scheme. If you tick the box to say you will teach anywhere in Scotland during your induction year, then you will be given what's called a 'preference waiver' payment of £6000. This is given in three instalments – £3000 in your first August pay packet , another £1500 in January and a further £1500 in April. If you are sent to one of the Scottish islands you may also qualify for the Distant Islands Allowance, which would give you an additional £1536 pa. So far the 'preference waiver' scheme is only scheduled for this year, but if the programme is successful, it could be extended. To find out more, phone 0845 345 4745, or visit www.scotland.gov.uk/education/teaching, or www.infoscotland.com/teaching.

Teaching in Northern Ireland

While students will receive the same general funding as undergraduates in Northern Ireland (see Chapter 3), no additional incentives are available. However, if you train in England or Wales you will receive the incentive package being offered to students there. See previous paragraphs headed England and Wales.

Is there any help if I want to go into Medicine?

There is a special deal for graduates domiciled in England and Wales who are on the four-year accelerated medical course for graduates.

From year two:

⊙ Your fees will be paid

⊙ You are eligible for an NHS bursary

From year one:

◉ You can apply for student loans for fees and maintenance.

Extra funding

Are there any other funds I can apply for?

There may be. But not all councils and funding bodies give them and these are under review.

Child Tax Credit

Available to students with dependent children and paid by the Inland Revenue. The amount you get will depend on circumstances. Call 0845 300 3900 (Northern Ireland 0845 603 2000) 8am to 8pm for more details, or visit www.inlandrevenue.gov.uk and check out how much you could get.

Access to Learning Fund

Usually given as a grant to students with higher-than-expected costs and according to need; part-time students can apply if studying at least 50% of full-time course. Contact your university.

Help for the disabled

The Disabled Students' Allowance for postgraduate study offers up to £5780 pa for full- or part-time students on a course that requires first-degree entry. See *Bridging the Gap*, free from the DfES publications department.

Are funding arrangements the same for all parts of the UK?

No. For residents in Scotland, Northern Ireland, the Channel Islands and the Isle of Man, funding arrangements are slightly different.

Advice note

Seeking a career in the legal profession? Check out *Graduate Prospects Law Directory*. With some 80 employers advertising 2000 training contracts, the publication also includes valuable insights into the broad spectrum of potential career paths. Website: www.prospects.ac.uk.

I want to study Law – what help is there?

With full-time course fees for the Graduate Diploma in Law (GDL)/Common Professional Examination (CPE) about £1125–£6,000, and the Legal Practice Course (LPC) running at an average of £5200–£8500 (but we have heard £10,000 mentioned), most students are going to need some help:

1 **Sponsorship/training contract**. This is the best route financially. A firm providing a training contract/sponsorship would pay for your fees at law school for one or two years, give a maintenance allowance and possibly vacation work. But sponsorship is competitive and even the best students can find it difficult to get. There is an increasing number of good people around to choose from. Those who do secure sponsorship would normally expect to complete their training contract with that firm. Occasionally a longer commitment to employment is demanded. Clifford Chance, a leading international law firm, recruits 120 trainee lawyers each year. The firm will cover the cost of tuition fees for its future trainees on the GDL and LPC and will provide a maintenance grant during this period. For sponsorship information see the CSU publication *Prospects Legal*, available from your university.

2 **Vacation Placement Programmes**. A number of firms run these programmes for second-year undergraduates (or final-year if you are a non-lawyer), when they will size you up for a training contract. To get accepted for a placement programme is in itself an achievement, but it is certainly no guarantee of success.

3 **Law Society Bursary Scheme**. Available for students taking GDL and LPC. It is very limited, competitive and includes hardship criteria – but worth trying. The bursary is made up from a variety of funds and grant-making trusts which have been grouped together under an umbrella scheme. Application forms available from February to April – closing date 30 April in the year you hope to start your course. More information and application form available from the Law Society's Information Services hotline – 01527 504433 (open 8.30am to 5pm Monday–Friday) or info.services@lawsociety.org.uk. See also www.lawsociety.org.uk.

4 **Law Society Diversity Access Scheme**. This aims to provide support to those with talent who will have to overcome particular obstacles to qualify as a solicitor. These could relate to social, educational, financial or family circumstances or to disability. For further details see www.lawsociety.org.uk.

5 **Local authority grants**. Local authorities are not obliged to fund GDL or LPC students, and rarely do, but they do have discretionary funds available for a wide

Advice note

⊙ A recent Graduate Prospects report showed that further study is the main route into a legal career. Of the 6610 law graduates surveyed from the 2002 cohort, almost half (46.6%) went on to postgraduate courses or training for certificates and diplomas such as the Legal Practice Course or Bar Vocational Course.

⊙ If you haven't already got a training contract, getting through law school isn't necessarily a passport to a position in a law firm.

range of courses and, providing you meet their criteria for awards, you could strike lucky. There are no hard-and-fast rules, as every local authority has its own policy. Your local authority may well issue a leaflet giving information on study areas eligible for financial support. Enquire at your local education authority. Failing that, contact the Law Society (website above).

6 **Loans**. If all other lines of attack have failed there is always a loan (see below).

Laura's story

Laura is studying at the College of Law (London).

'Most of the top law firms recruit for training contracts two years in advance, ie in the third year of uni or at the beginning of the GDL. This can lead to the bizarre situation I found myself in where you get a job in a law firm before you have even started studying law!

'Competition for places at the top firms is extremely stiff: applicants are all expected to have at least a 2:1 degree, As and Bs at A level and a lot more besides – they must have something extra to make them stand out.

'Despite maintenance grants and the funding of law college fees by law firms, it is quite usual for students to finish law college with up to £30,000 of debt. Many take professional-studies loans of up to £20,000 because the maintenance grant usually only covers rent in London and little else! It can be quite stressful to be in so much debt, but I think most people view it as an investment – in themselves. The debt repayments can be quite crippling when you are a trainee, but are less significant on qualification as there is usually a big pay rise when you qualify. The debt is manageable, but it may not be great if you suddenly decide after law college or the training contract that law is not for you!

'For the top law firms, the recruitment process is long and laborious, involving long and testing application forms. If your application is successful, there are usually up to three interview stages, which include verbal reasoning tests, a team exercise, a written exercise and interviews with partners.

'The careers department in my college was fantastic and gave one-on-one advice and guidance about firms, how to tailor application forms to present yourself in the best way, and they also provide mock interviews and feedback from other students.'

What about other professional qualifications?

Accountants, engineers, actuaries – all usually join firms that specialise in that kind of work. The firm will pay for your training and pay you while you are being trained.

I want to study in the United States

It's not cheap. Tuition for one nine-month academic year in state universities ranges from $4000 to $13,000 and in private universities from $8000 to $35,000. On top of that you will have living expenses, which vary tremendously from $7000 to $20,000. Don't automatically rule out the more costly courses, as the university may offer financial help through:

⊙ scholarships or fellowships
⊙ teaching/research assistantships
⊙ a loan.

Awards from bi-national exchange programmes, foundations or corporations etc may also be available. See the appendix in the Fulbright Commission guide to *Postgraduate Study in the US*, available from the Fulbright Commission (details on page 97), or log on to www.fulbright.co.uk.

Quick check				
Awards		In London	Elsewhere	Any location
BBSRC		£14,300	£12,300	
ESRC		£14,300	£12,300	
MRC		£14,350	£12,300	
PPARC		£14,000	£12,000	
AHRC	Research Master's	£10,600	£8600	
	Professional Master's	£10,000	£8000	
	Doctoral Award	£14,300	£12,300	
EPSRC	PhD studies			£12,000
	Engineering Doctorate			£13,000
NERC	PhD studies			£12,000
	Advanced course			£7880
GSCC				Up to £2900 depending on where based

Loans

OK, so nobody is going to fund me – can I get a loan?

Yes, but not the student loan. There are four excellent alternative schemes.

1. The Career Development Loan

Available only to those taking vocational training of up to two years. You can borrow up to £8000 and not less than £300. The loan is designed to cover course fees (only 80% given if you are in full employment) plus books, materials and living expenses where applicable. The loan is provided by the banks (Barclays, Co-operative, the Royal Bank of Scotland) and can be for a full-time, part-time or distance-learning course. Interest on the loan is paid by the government while you are studying and for one month after your course has finished (or up to six months if you are unemployed when repayment should start). Phone 0800 585505 for a free booklet on Career Development Loans; line open seven days a week 8am–10pm.

Cash crisis note

- Career Development Loans: though you can only get a CDL for two years, if your course is longer, it may be possible to take out a loan just for the final two years.

2. The Business School Loan Scheme

If you want to take an MBA, the Association of MBAs (AMBA) should be able to help. It runs a special scheme to assist graduates and other suitable applicants to study for a Master's degree in Business Administration. The scheme is run in conjunction with NatWest bank. To take advantage of the scheme you need to have a Bachelor's degree or other suitable professional qualification, a minimum of two years' relevant work experience or five years' experience in industry or commerce, and to have secured yourself a place on an MBA course at a business school that is on the Association's approved list. Maximum loan for full-time students is two-thirds of present or last gross salary, plus tuition fees for each year of study. Preferential interest rates are given during the course. Repayment starts three months after completion of your course and you have up to seven years to pay it off. See www.mbaworld.com.

3. Law School Loans

Assisted by the Law Society, a number of major banks run a special scheme to help students fund law school courses. The loan, which currently stands at up to £25,000, is given at very favourable rates. For more details and an application form contact the banks directly.

International business school ranking

Where the top UK schools come in the world's top 100:

London Business School	4
University of Oxford: Said	26
Warwick Business School	32
University of Cambridge: Judge	34
Manchester Business School	37
City University: Cass	42
Cranfield School of Management	63
Lancaster University Management School	69
Imperial College London: Tanaka	75
University of Durham Business School	82

4. Postgraduate Loan

What loans do banks offer to postgraduates?		
Bank	Course area	Amount offered
Barclays	Professional Study Loan (Medicine, Dentistry, Optometry, Veterinary Science)	£15,000
	Law studies	£25,000
	Career Development Loan (for vocational training lasting at least one week) MBA Loan	£300 min; £8000 max
Co-operative	Career Development Loan	£300 min; £8000 max
HSBC	Professional Studies Loan	Can apply for the following: ⊙ Course fees and living expenses up to a total maximum of £25,000. ⊙ Additional funding available in one year to cover large purchases like a car; still within the maximum total of £25,000.
	Medical, Dental, Veterinary	Undergraduate Medical, Dental and Veterinary students can apply for funding from their fourth year of £5000 and a further £5000 in each subsequent year of study up to a maximum of £25,000. Available to UK residents only.
Lloyds TSB	Further Education Loan	Up to £10,000. No repayments for 48 months, after which repayment can be spread over 5 years. Optional 4-month repayment holiday.
NatWest	Professional Trainee Loan: for Barrister, Solicitor, Doctor, Dentist, Pharmacist, Vet, Chiropractor, Optometrist, Osteopath, Chiropodist/Podiatrist, Physiotherapist NatWest College of Law Loan	Up to £20,000 for full-time students (full-time trainee solicitors and barristers can borrow up to £25,000. Part-time trainee solicitors and barristers can borrow up to the cost of course fees). No repayments during study and 6 months after.
	MBA Loan	Up to £25,000 for full-time students (part-time students can borrow up to the cost of course fees). No repayment whilst studying and for 4–9 months after, over a max of 10 years from date of loan. Tranche drawdown option available. Amount and repayment timings vary.
Royal Bank of Scotland	Law student Loan (GDL/LPC full-time or part-time)	Up to £15,000 repayable over 7 years (conversion courses limited to £5000)
	Healthcare, Chiropractic, Dentistry, Veterinary, Osteopathy	Up to £15,000 repayable over 7 years
	Career Development Loan	£300 to £8000
	Graduate Loan (any purpose) Interest-free Graduate Repayment Loan	£1000 to £15,000 for those who have graduated in last 3 years and who have full-time job or job offer.
		The interest-free limits available are up to: £2000 in the first year after graduation, £1500 in the second year and £1000 in the third year. Whole sum must be repaid 3 years from graduation.

Cash crisis note

- If you have just graduated and already have a loan to pay off, think twice before getting even further into debt.

Advice note

Want to know more about the cost and routes to funding for postgraduates? Log on to www.prospects.ac.uk and access Funding for Further Study. The guide is designed to cater to the needs of the myriad of people who might consider participating in further study. Information on how to secure employer sponsorship makes it as relevant to those returning to study as those going straight from university; and it also offers specific advice for both international students and those with disabilities.

Overseas students

What help is there for students coming to the UK from abroad?

There are scholarships specifically for overseas students, but these are few, so apply early.

The Overseas Research Students Award Scheme (ORSAS) was set up to attract high-quality international postgraduate students to the UK to undertake research. The scheme is administered by individual universities on behalf of the Department for Education and Skills. Awards provide funding to pay the difference, in most cases, between the fees charged by academic institutions to international students for tuition and those charged to home/EU students. Awards do not cover maintenance or travel expenses. For full information visit www.orsas.ac.uk, which includes information on eligibility, the application process and the universities taking part in the scheme. If you cannot find the information you need, email orsa@hefce.ac.uk or the university where you intend to study.

The best source for finance is your own home government. Failing that, try the British government through the British Council, the Foreign and Commonwealth Office or the Overseas Development Agency schemes.

International Students House provides accommodation bursaries for postgraduates from developing countries who are studying in London, including students from all non-EU central and eastern European countries. Students should already have won a scholarship to cover fees. Last year some 40 bursaries were given. It also administers the Mary Trevelyan Fund, a hardship fund which will give up to £500 to London-based final-year postgraduates and undergraduates from developing countries who are facing financial difficulties. Last year this scheme was undersubscribed. Contact: Chris Hutty, International Students House, 229 Great Portland Street, London W1W 5PN. Tel: 020 7631 8369. (See *Sources of Funding for International Students* in booklist for foreign students studying in the UK.)

There are also the Commonwealth Scholarship Plan, the UN and other international organisations. Some universities give awards and scholarships specially to students from abroad – but each university needs to be contacted individually. Some charitable trusts also cater for foreign students. EGAS (see details on page 167) might be able to help you winkle them out, or check for yourself in appropriate directories (see below). EU students can compete for UK postgraduate awards already listed in this chapter, but on a fees basis only.

As a student from abroad, what is it really going to cost?

⊙ **Fees** – there is no set rate of fees for postgraduate courses. In the past there has been a recommended minimum, but each institution can charge what it wants. Fees for overseas students are generally substantially more than those for home students. EU nationals are generally eligible for home UK student rates. Science courses are usually more expensive than those for the arts. For average overseas postgraduate fees in 2005–2006 see page 174.

⊙ **Living expenses** – our research in Chapter 1 will give you some idea of what things in Britain are likely to cost.

Further information

Who to contact/What to read

⊙ *Postgraduate Study and Research*, graduate careers information booklet updated regularly. Free from your careers service or £3.30 from CSU Ltd, Prospects House, Booth Street East, Manchester M13 9EP. Tel: 0161 277 5271.

⊙ *Prospects Postgrad Magazine*, options for further study and research, from CSU Ltd. Issued once a term.

⊙ Prospects website – it's massive: www.prospects.ac.uk.

For trainee teachers

⊙ In England – Teaching Information Line: 0845 6000 991; websites: www.tda.gov.uk, www.teach.gov.uk, www.dfes.gov.uk.

⊙ In Wales – Teaching Information Line: 0845 600 0991 (English); 0845 600 0992 (Welsh language); websites: www.teach.gov.uk (available in English and Welsh); www.studentfinancewales.co.uk for information about student fees; www.teachertrainingwales.org for information on ITT courses in Wales.

⊙ In Scotland – tel: 0845 345 4745; websites: www.scotland.gov.uk/education/teaching, www.infoscotland.com/teaching.

⊙ In Northern Ireland – apply to your Educational and Library Board (ELB).

For law students

⊙ *Focus on Law*, the most comprehensive information about firms offering sponsorship, available from university or careers services or by direct mail from CSU Ltd, Prospects House, Booth Street, Manchester M13 9EP. Tel: 0161 277 5271.

⊙ *Lawyer 2B* is a dedicated magazine for law students and those considering a career in or around the legal profession. A sister publication of the *Lawyer*, it provides news, comment, features and careers advice in an informal yet informative style. *Lawyer 2B* is released five times a year and is available free from most UK law schools.

⊙ For vacation placements or mini-pupillages look at the Prospects website: www.prospects.csu.ac.uk.

⊙ For general information see www.lawsociety.org.uk. Click on Student Guide.

For study abroad

⊙ *Awards for Postgraduate Study at Commonwealth Universities* and *Commonwealth Universities Yearbook* (information on over 700 universities worldwide). Tel: 020 7380 6700. Website: www.acu.ac.uk.

⊙ *Study Abroad*, international scholarships, international courses – UNESCO, HMSO, PO Box 276, London SW8 5DT.

⊙ *Scholarships and Funding for Study and Research in Germany*, German Academic Exchange Service, 17 Bloomsbury Square, London WC1A 2LP. Tel: 020 7235 1736.

⊙ *Beginners' Guide to Postgraduate Study in the USA*. Information on applying, tuition fees, etc. Educational Advisory Service, Fulbright Commission, Fulbright House, 62 Doughty Street, London WC1N 2JZ. Tel: 020 7404 6994. Include an A4 SAE with 40p stamp. Email: education@fulbright.co.uk. Website: www.fulbright.co.uk.

⊙ Try the UK Embassy or High Commission of the country where you are interested in studying: they may well have guides on awards and assistance offered.

For foreign students studying in the UK

⊙ *Sources of Funding for International Students*, free from the British Council Information Centre, Bridgewater House, 58 Whitworth Street, Manchester M1 6BB. Tel: 0161 957 7755. Email www.generalenquiries@britishcouncil.org.

⊙ *The International Student's A–Z: A guide to studying and living in England, Wales or Scotland* (3 editions). Published annually by International Students House, 229 Great Portland Street, London W1W 5PN. Tel: 020 7631 8369.

★
TOP*TEN* book-buying students

	Termly spend
3rd year Music, Wolverhampton	£500
4th year Law, Wolverhampton	£400
2nd year Biomedical Sciences, Southampton	£300
1st year Computing, Wolverhampton	£300
1st year Sport Science, Coventry	£250
Joint 6th place goes to students from a range of universities, and all years, studying Law, Linguistics, Environmental Management, Genetics and Molecular Biology, Mathematical Business Analysis	All £200

8

Making the money go round

Banking and budgeting

The main topics covered in this chapter are:

In this final chapter, we try to give you some advice on how to manage your money, with the help of students, Leeds University Welfare Service and a bank student adviser who has first-hand knowledge of some of the financial difficulties students get themselves into, and how best to help them.

Problems and predicaments

'My rent is over £55 a week. There's gas and electricity and telephone on top of that; I'm not making ends meet.'

'I've got an overdraft of £3000, the bank is charging interest; if I've got an overdraft how can I pay the interest charges?'

'I thought: "£1400, wow!" at the beginning of the term and blew the lot in the first few weeks. I haven't even the money for my train fare home.'

'I'm a Geography student and have to go on a compulsory trip. Where on earth am I going to find £120?'

'I know now that I shouldn't have bought the car and spent all that money on booze, but ...'

A bank student adviser's view

A student loan of over £4000! It certainly sounds a lot, but is it really? If all you are receiving is the standard funding for students then you haven't got wealth beyond your dreams, just the absolute minimum for survival. Bear that in mind right from the start and every time temptation looms, then you shouldn't go far wrong. There will always be those who like to live on the edge – spend now and cope with debt and disaster later. Most students who get into debt are genuinely surprised at how easily the money 'just slipped through' their bank account. Debt has a way of just creeping up on you if you let it. So be warned.

Budgeting – what it is and how you do it

The principles are incredibly simple. Putting them into practice is, for many people, incredibly hard. It is a matter of working out what your income and expenses are and making sure the latter doesn't exceed the former. It may sound rather boring, but it's a lot better than being in debt. The students quoted earlier obviously didn't budget.

Student advice

'Take out a certain amount of money each week and keep it in a glass jar; then you can see it going down.'
2nd year English Language student, Lancaster University

'Save coppers and small change; you'll be surprised how much you save – providing, that is, you don't cheat.'
1st year student, Birmingham

Where to keep your money – bank, building society, under the mattress?

Before you can start budgeting you need to choose somewhere to keep your money. We would recommend either a bank or a building society. They are generally quite keen to attract students' accounts because they see students as potential high-earners. Earlier in this book there are details of the different freebies the banks offer to entice students to join them (see page 67). These are worth studying, but shouldn't be the deciding factor. More important is to choose a bank or building society that is located close to your home or place of study. While these days you can use the cash-dispensing machines in most branches of most banks and building societies, they haven't yet invented a machine that can give advice.

Cash crisis note

- Beware the private-enterprise cash machines; they generally charge for withdrawals, sometimes as much as £2. Not a good deal if you are only drawing out £10. Most banks' cash machines are free to users whether you are a customer of that bank or not. The machine will always tell you if it is making a charge, so always check.

What type of account?

There are a number of different types of account. At the bank you'll need to open what's called a current account so you can draw money out at any time. Many banks offer accounts specially designed for students, so it's worth checking with them. Some current accounts give interest. It is not as much as a savings account, but every little helps. Check your bank for interest rates.

A building society current account is very similar to a bank account. They, too, give instant access to your money, and also pay interest on any money in your account. How much depends on the going rate and your building society.

Look for 'free banking' – this means that you don't pay charges when in credit or within your interest-free overdraft.

Caution

- ⊙ Don't keep your cheque guarantee card and chequebook together. If they're stolen, somebody could clean out your account.

- ⊙ Keep your Personal Identification Number (PIN) secret. Never write it down or tell it to anyone else.

- ⊙ Cheques take three days to clear from an account. So don't go on a mad spending spree if you find you have more money in your account than you thought. The read-out on the cash machine may not be up to date.

Shop around

If you are looking for a bank account, Leeds University advises students to shop around and compare the banks and what they can offer you in terms of overdrafts etc. If you want an overdraft, the simplest way to compare charges is to ask for the EAR – Effective Annual Rate. This is a standardised way of expressing the total cost of borrowing if you were continually overdrawn for a year. It is, they advise, also worth while asking the following questions:

⊙ How much interest will I earn if I am in credit?

⊙ Do I get a free overdraft facility? If so, how much?

⊙ If I want to arrange a larger overdraft, will I be charged an arrangement fee?

⊙ What will the interest rate be on my overdraft?
⊙ If I am overdrawn without consent, how much will I be charged for:
  ⊙ the unauthorised balance
  ⊙ the bounced cheques?

What will you get when you open an account?

When you open an account you may receive some or all of these services and facilities:

⊙ Chequebook, which you can use to pay big bills and for large purchases.

⊙ Cheque guarantee card, which could be for up to £100. Some banks limit it to £50 for students. This states that the bank will guarantee your cheque up to the amount shown on the card and so the shop where you are making your purchase will let you take the goods away there and then.

⊙ Cash card, which enables you to withdraw cash from a cash machine, and may offer additional payment functions.

⊙ PIN – this is your own Personal Identification Number, which you will need to remember and use when getting money from the cash dispenser.

⊙ Debit card (SOLO, Switch or Delta) which will automatically debit your account for goods bought when passed through a terminal at the point of sale.

⊙ The three-in-one card. Most banks and building societies combine the facilities mentioned above into multifunctional cards which act as cheque guarantee cards, give access to cash machines and can be used as debit cards so you can purchase goods and services without writing a cheque.

⊙ Account number, which you will need for any correspondence with your bank.

⊙ Paying-in book containing paying-in slips, probably with your branch name printed on them, which you can use when paying in cheques and money. Just fill in the slip and pass it to your bank. Most banks provide pre-printed envelopes, which you can pick up in your branch and then post through a letter box in the banking hall. You can also pay cheques in through some cash machines.

⊙ Statements sent to you at regular intervals (we would advise you to ask for it monthly). The statement will give details of the money going in and out of your account – an essential part of budgeting properly.

⊙ PC and internet banking.

⊙ 24-hour telephone banking which allows you to keep in touch with your student account and credit card account day and night.

⊙ Student Contents Insurance.

Your income – how much?

It's all very well to have an official piggy bank in which to keep your money, but where is the money going to come from and how much is it likely to be? If you have read the rest of this book, you should by now have some idea how much you are likely to have as a student. If you look at our budgeting plan, we have listed some of the likely sources. With a little ingenuity you may have discovered others.

A step-by-step budgeting plan

1 Take a piece of paper and divide into three columns (see page 195). On the left-hand side write down your likely income sources and how much they will provide, for example:

⊙ grant

⊙ parental contribution

⊙ student loan

⊙ money from Access to Learning Fund

⊙ money earned from holiday job

⊙ money earned from term-time job

⊙ sponsorship.

2 The trouble with budgeting, especially for students, is that money generally comes in at one time, often in large chunks at the beginning of a term, and your outgoings at another. When you work you will probably find it easiest to budget on a monthly basis, but as a student you will probably have to do it either termly or yearly depending on how the money comes in.

3 In the middle column write down your fixed expenses – things that you have to pay out – like rent, gas, electricity, telephone, food etc. Don't forget to include fares. Now total them up.

4 Subtract your fixed expenses from your income and you will see just how much you have, or haven't, got left over to spend. Draw a line under the list in your right-hand column and now list your incidental expenses – things like socialising, clothes, the cinema, hobbies, birthdays etc. This is your 'do without' column: the area where you can juggle your expenses to make ends meet.

5 Apportion what's left over to the things listed in this final column, making sure you've got at least something left over for emergencies. Do the figures add up?

6 Seems simple enough and logical on paper. But of course it doesn't work quite as easily as that. There's always the unexpected. You can't get a job. Your car needs a new battery. People use more gas than expected. Did you really talk for that long on the phone?

7 Having worked out your budget, use the final column on your budget sheet to fill in exactly how much your bills do come to. In this way you can keep a check on your outgoings and how accurate your predictions were, and do something before the money runs out.

If you are having difficulty putting together a budget, look at the student examples at the end of Chapter 1, page 26.

Hot tip from a burnt student

'There are so many hidden costs at uni – expenses pop up all the time. It's impossible to budget at the beginning of term, which makes financial management a nightmare – sports levies, balls, tours, travel, books – and that's just for starters.'

2nd year Music student, Durham

Income		Outgoings		
			Predicted	Actual
Grant	£	Fees	£	£
Bursary	£	Rent/college board	£	£
Parental contribution	£	Gas	£	£
Fee loan	£	Electricity	£	£
Student loan	£	Telephone	£	£
Sponsorship	£	Launderette/cleaning	£	£
Job	£	Food	£	£
Access to Learning Fund	£	Fares while in college	£	£
Other	£	Fares to college	£	£
		Car expenses	£	£
		Books/equipment	£	£
		Compulsory trips	£	£
		TV licence	£	£
		Student rail/bus card	£	£
Total:	£	Total:	£	£
		Socialising	£	£
		Hobbies	£	£
		Entertainment	£	£
		Clothes	£	£
		Presents	£	£
		Holidays	£	£

What is a standing order?

Regular payments such as rent can be paid automatically from your bank account through a standing order. You just tell the bank how much to pay out and to whom, and they will do the rest. The system is ideal for people who are bad at getting round to paying their bills. Forget to pay the electricity and you'll soon know. Standing orders are not so easy to organise when you are in shared accommodation with everyone chipping in to pay the bill.

What is Direct Debit?

With a Direct Debit set up on your account, the bill is again paid automatically, but it works in a different way. The bank of the organisation you are paying the money to will collect the money direct from your account. This is an ideal way of paying when the amount being paid out is likely to change.

Cards and the catches

Credit cards

These are an easy way to pay for things but can also be an easy way to get into debt. When you have a card such as Mastercard, Visa or Barclaycard, you are given a credit limit. This means you can make purchases up to that sum. Each month you receive a statement of how much you owe. If you pay back the whole lot immediately there are no interest charges. If you don't, you will pay interest on the balance. There is usually an annual charge for credit cards. You can use your card in the UK and abroad at most shops and many restaurants. They are a way of getting short-term credit but are an expensive way of borrowing long term. On the plus side they are a way to spread payments or ease temporary cashflow problems.

Store cards

Many stores, such as Marks & Spencer, offer credit cards that operate in much the same way as described above, but can only be used in that particular store or chain of stores. Although most stores will check your credit rating before issuing you with a card, they are still too easy to come by – get a stack of them and you could find you're seriously in debt. A store card is quite different from a store loyalty card – the type issued by Boots, Tesco and many other organisations. These give you points for everything you buy in that store, which you can save up and use to purchase products. A good thing to have if you are a regular customer.

Debit cards

You've probably seen the Switch/Maestro card in action, as most stores and garages have the system installed. By simply passing your debit card through a Switch/Maestro terminal, the price of the purchase you are making is automatically deducted from your account. What could be easier? Details of the transaction will show up on your next statement. Some stores will offer you 'cash-back' on a debit card, which could save you a trip to the bank.

Safety check

Most banks and building societies will not send plastic cards or Personal Identification Numbers to customers living in halls of residence or multi-occupancy lodgings, because they could go astray or sit in the hallway for days unclaimed. All too easy to steal. You may have to collect them from a branch nearby.

Cash crisis note

- While most big stores and pubs will not charge for giving cash-back, some of the smaller stores may. Always check.

What if the money runs out?

Help, I'm in debt!

Don't panic, but don't sweep the matter under the carpet and try to ignore it, because it won't go away. In fact it will just get worse. Get in touch with the Student Welfare Officer at your university, the student adviser at your local university branch or your bank manager. Or all three. Through experience they will be able to give the best advice and help. Impoverished and imprudent students are not a new phenomenon.

'I needed £200 to put down as my deposit for renting a house next year, but I hadn't got it, so I went round to my bank and they extended my overdraft.'
1st year Urban Planning Studies student, Sheffield

Caution
Don't borrow from a lot of places. If you've got an overdraft and a student loan, that's probably enough.

Getting an overdraft

The bank is the student's friend – or it should be. The interest-free overdraft facilities that most banks offer students (see page 68 for how much) are considered by many students to be an essential part of their income – helping to fill that financial black hole between loan payments. The *Students' Money Matters* Survey showed that 71% of students had overdrafts. Overdraft facilities vary enormously, as do the amounts you can borrow – up to £1250 in your first year. **But don't take it as a right**. Always ask your bank first if it will grant you this facility and whether you have to apply for it each year. Otherwise you will be in trouble and could be charged interest. If you think you are likely to go over the interest-free overdraft rate – and many students do – check out the consequences – charges can be high. And remember, whatever you borrow has to be paid back eventually.

If you find yourself overdrawn, get on the phone or call in immediately to your bank. Many of the clearing banks have campus branches or at least a branch in the town geared to dealing with students. They'll probably be sympathetic and come up with a helpful solution.

A planned overdraft

'I'm going for an interview and need something to wear.'

This is not an unusual request from students in their final year – jeans and a scruffy T-shirt rarely make a good impression. Banks are very good at coming up with a plan to help you out with an obvious or specific need. After all, an interview success could mean you'll clear your overdraft that much more quickly.

An overdraft is often the cheapest way of borrowing, but there are charges and interest rates, which need to be checked out. The advantage of an overdraft is that you don't have to pay it back in fixed amounts, though the bank has the right to ask for its money back at any time.

Borrowing on credit

'Haven't got the money at the moment so I'll buy it on Mastercard.'

Easily done, but be warned – though Mastercard/Visa is excellent as a payment card, credit can cause problems. If you don't pay off your bill by the date given on your statement, you will have to pay interest and, compared with other sources of borrowing, this is very high. Unlike your friendly bank, credit card companies are not the sort of people you can negotiate with, and are very likely to sue. Don't see them as another source of income.

Thrift tips

Leeds University Union Welfare Service suggests these ways of managing your money:

- ⊙ Get value for money – use markets or large supermarkets for fresh fruit and vegetables – your local corner shop may be convenient, but is often more expensive.
- ⊙ Make the most of student discounts for coach and rail travel, clubs, restaurants and hairdresser.
- ⊙ Use the library rather than buying books – has your uni got a second-hand bookshop?
- ⊙ Withdraw only the amount of cash you actually need on a weekly basis from the bank – otherwise it will disappear.

Personal loans

This is quite different from an overdraft. It is usually used when you want to borrow a much larger sum, over a longer period – say several years. It differs from an overdraft in that you borrow an agreed amount over a set period of time and the repayments are a fixed amount, generally monthly. You might take out a loan to pay for your course fees, but not for short-term credit to tide you over until your next grant cheque arrives.

How the student adviser can help

Don't be afraid to go into your bank and ask for help. Most banks have specially trained student advisers on the premises to help students like you. They will arrange bank accounts, discuss overdrafts and help with budgeting. It's what they've been trained for. Many of them have recently been students, so they know the ropes – and the difficulties.

A bank manager's view

'The problems students have are very real. As a bank manager, all too often we find we are just picking up the pieces when things have gone too far. Debt brings stress, and that will affect your ability to study. Come sooner rather than later.'

Don'ts

(Which unfortunately some students do!)

- Don't fall into the hands of a loan shark. Any loan offered to students, except from a recognised student-friendly source, eg banks, building societies, parents or the Student Loans Scheme, should be treated with the utmost caution and suspicion. It's bound to cost you an arm and a leg, and lead to trouble.
- Don't run up an overdraft with your bank without asking first – even the much-vaunted interest-free overdraft offered by most banks to students should be checked out first, otherwise you might find you are being charged. They need to know you are a student.
- Don't forget to pay your gas and electricity bills. Make them top priority. A week or two on bread and (cheap) jam is better than having to pay court costs.
- Don't pawn your guitar, only to find you can't afford to get it out to play at the next gig.
- Don't try 'kiting'. The banks have got wind of what's been going on, and you're bound to be found out and in real trouble. For the uninitiated (like this author), kiting is the dishonest practice of making the most of the time lapse between people reporting that their credit card is missing and it being recorded as stolen. Be warned: it is a criminal offence, and could end up increasing your debts – or even worse.
- Don't get blacklisted with the bank. 'Kiting' is a sure way of getting a bad record. Running up an overdraft is another.
- Don't see credit cards as another source of income.

Savings?

Most books on budgeting give lengthy advice on saving. We think it unlikely that students will do more than just make ends meet, and even that will be a struggle. However, if you do find that you have some surplus cash, or have taken out the student loan as an investment, it would be advisable to open a savings account at a bank, a building society or the Post Office. Check out the interest rates and the terms and conditions. Many high-interest accounts give limited access to your money – so, watch out.

A final word of advice from a student

'Before they start a degree, students don't realise just how tough it's going to be. You think, how on earth can anybody be so irresponsible as to get into £22,000 worth of debt? But once you are into university life, you know only too well. Despite the hardship, don't be put off; university is excellent – an incredible experience not to be missed!'

Top tips for students

Most banks close to universities have student advisers. Barclays has a national network of over 200, whose full-time job is to advise students on how best to manage their money while at university. This is their list of top tips on managing your money. Some have already been suggested by students elsewhere in this book, but repetition can't hurt if it keeps you out of debt.

⦿ Don't wait until you get to college to open an account. Open one at your local branch. You will need it in order to apply for a student loan.

⦿ Once you know how much you will have to live on per term, ask your bank for advice on budgeting. Don't be worried about going back for further guidance if you're finding it hard to cope.

⦿ Limit your borrowing to a few sources. Spreading debts around too much makes it difficult to keep track of them and can only create problems later.

⦿ Be cautious about how much money you borrow on your overdraft, even if it is interest-free.

⦿ Arrange to have your monthly statements sent to your term-time address to help you monitor your budget.

⦿ Try to limit your trips to the cash machine to once a week, otherwise you could easily lose track of how much you are spending.

⦿ Insurance is vitally important, but ask your parents first if you can be included on their house insurance.

⦿ Wait until you arrive at university before buying expensive books and equipment; then you will know what you really need. Ask around for places offering the best deals, such as your university bookshop, or buy second-hand textbooks from students in the years above.

⦿ As your loan comes termly, it is often a good idea to get your loan money paid into your savings account and then transfer money over perhaps every week or every month. This will help you budget and spend within your means.

⦿ Familiarise yourself with the student services available to you at your university. Student support centres are in place to help you with all aspects of student life, including your finances.

⦿ Keep checking your account to ensure all payments are made.

⦿ Always deal with bills and statements as they arrive – try to avoid putting them to one side or forgetting to pay bills. We recommend paying by Direct Debit if possible.

⦿ If you've got problems, remember that your bank's student adviser is there to offer advice and support. Don't ignore a problem, hoping it will go away by itself – because it won't.

Index